"This luminous and lucid ~~........ given to every bishop~~ and pastor in the world; indeed, it would be of immense benefit to every Catholic believer, if he would but read it with prayerful attentiveness. It is a banquet of sound teaching, of wisdom, of reasoned argument, and of a holy zeal for the restoration of the House of the Lord. No one who reads it will remain unchanged."

—Michael D. O'Brien
Author, *The Lighthouse*

"Until we know Jesus—and know Him on *His* terms—we will not have peace in our lives or in our society. In the Eucharist, Jesus has accommodated Himself to us with unimaginable generosity. Dr. Kwasniewski has set himself the task of understanding Our Lord's terms of engagement, so that we may know Him and know peace. This book is admirable biblical theology after the pattern of St. Thomas Aquinas."

—Scott Hahn
Professor of Biblical Theology,
Franciscan University of Steubenville

"What a beautiful book about the 'Beauty so ancient yet ever new'! It surprised me by showing me, in a way that was powerfully new by being powerfully old, the centrality of Christ's Real Presence in the Eucharist; that nothing could be a more potent hidden weapon for revitalizing the Church, the culture, and the world than revitalized Eucharistic devotion; and that nothing could weaken these mission fields of the 'new evangelization' more than its weakening. The power of the unforgettable image that begins the book also permeates it: receiving Holy Communion is like eating the sun."

— Peter Kreeft
Professor of Philosophy,
Boston College and The King's College

"No dry treatise, this invitation to Eucharistic holiness is a prayerful provocation, asking how devoutly we approach the Lord in His Holy Sacrifice. It not only aims to remedy commonplace liturgical abuses but also bids us all to unite our lives to the Sacred Host in a fruitfulness we cannot yet imagine. Dr. Kwasniewski draws upon millennia of Sacred Tradition to show that proper reverence and reception of the Lord's Eucharistic Body is the only antidote to the abuses within, and the assaults upon, Christ's Mystical Body."

— Fr. David Meconi, SJ
Director, Catholic Studies Centre, Saint Louis University;
Editor, *Homiletic & Pastoral Review*

"At a time when many consider the sacred liturgy as a means of personal expression, and the Most Blessed Sacrament is treated as something ordinary, recovering reverence and order at Holy Mass is essential. In this wonderful reflection — spiritual, informative, and scholarly — Dr. Kwasniewski provides both the rationale and a kind of roadmap for the reforms that are so necessary."

—Msgr. Charles Pope
Archdiocese of Washington, D.C.

The Holy Bread of Eternal Life

Other books by Peter Kwasniewski

On Love and Charity

Sacred Choral Works

Resurgent in the Midst of Crisis

Noble Beauty, Transcendent Holiness

Tradition and Sanity

Reclaiming Our Roman Catholic Birthright

Newman on Worship, Reverence, and Ritual

A Reader in Catholic Social Teaching

Peter A. Kwasniewski

The Holy Bread of Eternal Life

Restoring Eucharistic Reverence in an Age of Impiety

with
"The Crusade of Eucharistic Reparation"
by Bishop Athanasius Schneider

SOPHIA INSTITUTE PRESS
Manchester, New Hampshire

Sophia Institute Press
Box 5284, Manchester, NH 03108
1-800-888-9344

www.SophiaInstitute.com

Sophia Institute Press® is a registered trademark of Sophia Institute.

Paperback ISBN 978-1-64413-433-7

eBook ISBN 978-1-64413-434-4

Library of Congress Control Number: 2020946561

*With gratitude for the intercession of
Little Nellie of Holy God (1903–1908),
who helped me to see that little ones — and little things —
are precious in the sight of the Lord*

O LORD, I FIRMLY BELIEVE AND PROFESS
that you are truly the Christ,
the Son of the living God,
who came into the world to save sinners,
of whom I am the first.
Accept me as a partaker of your Mystical Supper,
O Son of God,
for I will not reveal the Mysteries to your enemies,
nor will I give you a kiss as did Judas,
but like the thief, I confess to you:
Remember me, O Lord,
when you shall come into Your kingdom.
Remember me, O Master,
when you shall come into Your kingdom.
Remember me, O Holy One,
when you shall come into your kingdom.
May the partaking of your Holy Mysteries, O Lord,
be not for my judgment or condemnation,
but for the healing of soul and body.
O God, be merciful to me, a sinner.
God, cleanse me of my sins and have mercy on me.
O Lord, forgive me, for I have sinned without number.

I believe also that this which I am about to receive
is truly your most pure Body and life-giving Blood;
wherefore, I pray, have mercy on me
and forgive my transgressions,
both voluntary and involuntary, in word and deed,
committed in knowledge or in ignorance;
and grant that I may partake of your Holy Mysteries
without condemnation
for the forgiveness of all my sins
and for life everlasting.

Prayers before Communion
Byzantine Divine Liturgy

O LORD JESUS CHRIST,
Son of the living God,
who according to the will of the Father,
through the co-operation of the Holy Ghost,
hast by Thy death given life to the world:
deliver me by this,
Thy most sacred Body and Blood,
from all my transgressions and from all evils;
make me always adhere to Thy commandments
and never suffer me to be separated from Thee,
who with the same God the Father and the Holy Ghost
livest and reignest God, for ever and ever. Amen.

Let not the partaking of Thy Body,
O Lord Jesus Christ,
which I, though unworthy, presume to receive,
turn to my judgment and condemnation,
but through Thy goodness may it be unto me
a safeguard and a healing remedy
both of soul and of body,
who livest and reignest with God the Father
in the unity of the Holy Ghost,
God, world without end. Amen.

I will take the bread of heaven,
and call upon the name of the Lord.

Lord, I am not worthy
that Thou shouldst enter under my roof;
say but the word and my soul shall be healed.

May the Body of our Lord Jesus Christ
preserve my soul to life everlasting. Amen.

Prayers before Communion
Roman Rite of Mass

Contents

Preface

Offerimus præclaræ majestati tuæ,	We offer to Thy sovereign Majesty
de tuis donis ac datis,	from among Thy gifts bestowed upon us,
hostiam puram,	a pure Victim,
hostiam sanctam,	a holy Victim,
hostiam immaculatam,	a spotless Victim,
Panem sanctum vitæ æternæ	the Holy Bread of eternal life
et calicem salutis perpetuæ.	and the Chalice of everlasting salvation.
Canon Missæ	*Canon of the Mass*

This book is the result of longstanding concerns and more recent alarms. It was about twenty-five years ago that I first realized the extent to which the Catholic Church after the Second Vatican Council has been and still is permeated with Eucharistic abuse, from systematic violations of liturgical norms and rubrics to practices that facilitate profanation and sacrilege, and how much this abuse is tied up with other forms and patterns of abuse. The Pew Research Center survey released in July 2019 offered evidence that the majority of practicing Catholics do not believe that the bread and wine are changed at Mass into the Body and Blood of Christ, which prompted many reactions of real or feigned dismay but only a few honest admissions of the train of causality behind this landslide of apostasy. The coronavirus panic of 2020 has occasioned a further wave of sacramental manipulation and desacralization that has left almost no Catholic in the world untouched. These disturbing "signs of the times" call for an unsparing reassessment of official and unofficial policy, dominant practices and customs, and widespread attitudes, together with a fresh appreciation for "creative minorities" that are taking a different, more difficult, and more successful path.

In honor of the Most Holy Trinity, to whose glorification all of the Church's life is (or surely ought to be) directed, this book has been arranged in three parts, for it treats of the Father's gift of His Son in the flesh as Savior of mankind, the Son's gift of Himself in the Eucharist as the bread of wayfarers, and the Holy Spirit's gift of unifying love, which is offered to us in the sacred liturgy.

Part I, "The Most Wondrous of God's Gifts," speaks of the glory and treasure that is ours in the awesome mystery of the Holy Eucharist. The five chapters draw on the Old Testament, the New Testament, the Fathers of the Church, and St. Thomas Aquinas to help us appreciate more deeply the ineffable blessings of Holy Communion.

Part II, "Approach with Faith and Fear of God," enters into the dispositions we should have and the conditions laid down by the Church for a fruitful sacramental reception of the Lord. The chapters delve into the all-important virtues of faith and devotion, the practice of frequent Communion, the need for fasting, the preservation of chastity, the appropriateness of outward signs of reverence, and the crucial place of Eucharistic Adoration. The practice of receiving Communion on the tongue, kneeling, is vigorously defended, while its alternative, Communion in the hand, standing, is subjected to a multifaceted critique, as are "extraordinary ministers."

Part III, "Eating and Drinking Judgment," turns to some of the evils plaguing the Church in our times: the violent alteration of the *lex orandi* (law of prayer) through the postconciliar liturgical reform's removal of Scripture's solemn warning against unworthy Communions; the many concurrent processes by which the faithful have been desensitized to the reality of the Real Presence and the demands it places on us; the link between liturgical abuse and clerical sexual abuse; the stalwart refusal of most bishops to discipline public sinners, together with episcopal measures taken against clergy and laity in good standing; the ways in which the desacralizing ideas and impulses of the liturgical reform have reached their apogee in ecclesiastical responses to the COVID-19 pandemic; and the agony of conscience in many faithful sons of the Church, torn between deep-seated convictions about Eucharistic reverence and the demands of obedience to authority—or the cost of disobedience in the name of higher principles.

Part II and Part III consist of seven chapters each, to remind us of the seven sacraments, which, when rightly used, sanctify our souls and bodies, and which, when abused, place us in the company of Judas the traitor; of the seven heavenly virtues by which we make our way to heaven, along the narrow path trodden by Our Lord and all His saints; and of the seven deadly vices that lead to perdition, all the more as they are practiced by those consecrated for a higher calling.

Since I have written other books about the liturgy in general and, more particularly, about the Mass as a true and proper sacrifice, I will touch only lightly on these subjects in the present book. Nor will I delve into the many controversies surrounding the Second Vatican Council, the liturgical reform, or the last several papacies.[1] This is a book about the Real Presence of Our Lord in the Eucharist, the fitting veneration and handling of this immense mystery of love, and the mystical banquet of Holy Communion. It is a book about the divine gift of the Most Holy Sacrament of the Altar, which can never be too much adored, too much loved, too much cared for, too much sacrificed for. Truly, how the Blessed Sacrament is treated is the "litmus test" of Catholicism, showing whether it itself is present or absent. As I hope these pages will demonstrate beyond doubt, there is far more at stake in today's debated questions concerning Holy Communion than preferences to be indulged or slip-ups to be tolerated. At stake, quite simply, is whether we *believe* in Jesus Christ, true God and true man; whether we acknowledge and accept His lordship over us, making Him King of every aspect of what we do and say,

---

[1] The select bibliography recommends further reading on these topics.

how we act and react, how we worship and pray; whether we take pains to wear the wedding garment of sanctifying grace for the nuptial feast of the Mass (Matt. 22:11–12), so that, in the words of the Divine Liturgy of St. John Chrysostom, we may appear "without shame or fear before the dread judgment seat of Christ" and be welcomed into His everlasting joy.

As we realize the sheer multitude and magnitude of sins being committed against Our Lord in the Holy Eucharist and the treachery of too many of His friends, our hearts will be pierced with repentance at our own complicity and lack of fervor, and we will long to make reparation and to give to Him the adoring love and unwavering devotion He deserves. I was deeply moved when I first saw, in July 2020, the document in which the Most Reverend Athanasius Schneider proposed "a crusade of Eucharistic reparation," accompanied by a prayer written for that purpose. His Excellency explains how Jesus, without diminution of His eternal glory and infinite bliss, mysteriously suffers from the neglect, ingratitude, lukewarmness, contempt, and malice of sinners, and how our presence, our prayer of adoration, our penances *console* His Heart—a truth no less mysterious than His suffering!—and win graces of conversion for the world. I am therefore grateful to His Excellency for giving me his permission to include the text of this document and of the "Prayer of the Crusade of Reparation to the Eucharistic Heart of Jesus" as an appendix.

The chapters of this book were developed out of articles first published online at *New Liturgical Movement*, *OnePeterFive*, *The Remnant*, *Views from the Choir Loft* (Corpus Christi Watershed), *Rorate Caeli*, and *LifeSite-News*. Chapter 5 was co-written with my dear friend Dr. Jeremy Holmes. The transcript in chapter 9 was kindly provided by Voice of the Family.

Whenever my footnotes make reference to an online article, I generally give only the name of the site and the date of publication, as I despise the clutter of hyperlinks, and an Internet search can hit the target in less than a second.

There is a method in my use of lowercase and uppercase letters. I use "Communion" when referring directly to the Blessed Sacrament, under the aspect of food to be given to us (e.g., "receiving Communion"), and "communion" for more general uses or related items (e.g., "communion with Christ," "communion rail"). Similarly, "Confession" is capitalized when referring to the sacrament of Penance, otherwise not. "Adoration" is usually capitalized in reference to the devotion popularly known as Eucharistic Adoration — technically, solemn Eucharistic exposition — when the Host is placed in a monstrance for the worship of the faithful.

Psalms are cited by their LXX/Vulgate numbering, not by the Masoretic numbering.

This book bears a dedication to Ellen Organ (1903–1908), usually known as "Little Nellie of Holy God," about whom I first learned in the children's book of the same name by M. Dominic, R.S.G., with illustrations by Sister M. John Vianney, S.S.N.D. (TAN Books, 2009), which my own children enjoyed having read aloud to them. In spite of her young age, her crippling defects, and her continual suffering, Little Nellie's faith in the Blessed Sacrament was so strong that, at the age of four, she began to ask the religious sisters who cared for her if she could make her First Communion. Prior to this, she had asked the sisters returning from Mass to kiss her so that she might be nearer to "Holy God" (as she always called the Eucharist; moreover, she called the chapel "the House of Holy God"). The sisters' chaplain, after speaking with her, concluded she was indeed ready; the local bishop gave his consent. Little Nellie received Holy God thirty-two times before she succumbed to tuberculosis on February 2, 1908. Her story became known to Pope St. Pius X, who, it is said, was moved by it to lower the age of First Communion. This tiny child, illuminated by the Holy Spirit, had a perfection of simple faith, a spiritual hunger, and a love for the Lord's sufferings that greatly exceed those of many a professional theologian and churchman today. Instead of stubbornly adhering to the failed liturgical practices of recent decades and to worse-than-useless "pastoral programs," it is high time we return to the fundamentals of the Faith.

I believe, more to the point, that Little Nellie had a hand in moving me to bring out this book at just this time. Like many families, my own family has the custom of picking out "saints for the year" on the first of

The Holy Bread of Eternal Life

January (we put our slips of paper in an old cookie tin). This past January, when we had the blessing of spending most of the Twelve Days of Christmas at Silverstream Priory in Ireland—Nellie's homeland—where the same custom obtains, we were offered the opportunity to pick out our annual patrons from the mixed slips of paper left in the hat after it had made the rounds among the monks. My slip of paper told me that Little Nellie was my patroness and that she was asking of me the practice of Eucharistic adoration.

Laudetur sacrosanctum et augustissimum Sacramentum in aeternum. May the most holy and most august Sacrament be praised for all eternity.

Peter A. Kwasniewski
September 14, 2020
Feast of the Exaltation of the Holy Cross

The Holy Bread of Eternal Life

Part 1

The Most Wondrous of God's Gifts

1

Eating Fire and Spirit

Imagine eating the sun — and imagine you could do it without perishing. What would happen? You would receive into your body the source of light and warmth. You would have within you all the light and heat that you could possibly ever need or want. No more heating bills, no more lightbulbs, no more winter trips to warmer climes.

When we receive Jesus in the Most Blessed Sacrament, we receive the source of all supernatural light and warmth, the light of truth, the heat of love, for indeed He is the "Sun of Justice." We receive God Himself, the very Son of God, Who is inseparable from the Father and the Holy Spirit. Saint Ephrem the Syrian wrote:

> He called the bread his living body and he filled it with himself and his Spirit.... He who eats it with faith, eats Fire and Spirit.... Take and eat this, all of you, and eat with it the Holy Spirit. For it is truly my body and whoever eats it will have eternal life.[2]

That we are not killed instantly by this contact with eternal and infinite Fire is, in its own way, a greater miracle than would be eating the sun without perishing. Our Lord protects us, courteously hiding His blazing glory lest we be overwhelmed, and gently radiating His peace.

---

[2] *Sermo IV in Hebdomadam Sanctam*, in *Corpus Scriptorum Christianorum Orientalium* 413/Syr. 182:55, quoted in John Paul II's Encyclical Letter *Ecclesia de Eucharistia* (April 17, 2003), §17.

The Holy Bread of Eternal Life

It is because we receive divine fire — a fire far more potent in the range and reach of its possible spiritual effects than any physical fire — that the worthy reception of the Eucharist is purifying, illuminating, and unitive. The Holy Eucharist does within and upon the soul that which fire does within and upon combustible matter, burning away contrary dispositions and transforming the matter into itself. But since the spiritual soul is incorruptible, the soul can become fire without perishing, like the miraculous burning bush. The Eucharist does for the soul what the fire of the sun does for the earth, spreading light, warming bodies, causing growth.

As we learn from the Fathers, Doctors, and mystics of the Church, the Real Presence of Jesus has a proper effect on our soul *and* our body. It acts principally on the soul, for, again like the sun, Jesus radiates grace to everything that surrounds Him, everything with which He comes into contact, according to His will, "according to the measure of the giving of Christ" (Eph. 4:7, DR).

Like the healing of the woman with the flow of blood (see Luke 8:43), the diseased blood of the old Adam cannot be healed by any human medicine, but only by the touch of the new Adam, the physician of souls. The Lord touches first the essence of the soul, increasing in it the grace that makes the soul pleasing to God, an adopted son of the Father, a sister and bride of the Son (*soror mea, sponsa mea*[3]), a temple of the Holy Spirit.[4] He touches the powers of the soul, informing them with virtues, strengthening virtuous habits. He stirs these powers into operation — He produces within us *acts* of faith, hope, charity, and all the virtues. Only in the life to come will we be given to know just how many times it was Jesus who, faced with the listless torpor of our fallen condition, animated our souls into action and prompted us to bear fruits pleasing to God and profitable to us.

Holy Communion influences the body, too. This is very important to see, even if we cannot understand it completely. Wrapped in the long

---

[3] See the Canticle of Canticles 4:9–10, 12; 5:1–2.
[4] See St. Thomas Aquinas, *Summa theologiae* I-II, qu. 110.

shadow of Descartes, modern Westerners seem afflicted with a tendency to consider "spirituality" the exclusive domain of the spirit—leaving the flesh to fend for itself like an abandoned orphan. This is not what the Lord who created heaven and earth has in mind for us material creatures. By means of the Holy Eucharist, our flesh is made more obedient and docile to the soul, rendered more receptive to the informing power of soul and virtue.

The Lord is sown into the flesh as a seed of immortality: He radiates divine life, divine existence, upon what has merely earthly life and earthly existence. His presence is like a beneficial radiation. We know that ordinary radiation causes deformity of cells. But the radiation of the Son of God is exactly the opposite; it causes a hidden perfection in cells, in all the matter of the body, so that on the last day the flesh will be recognized in the sight of God as flesh marked by and belonging to Christ, as flesh worthy and able to be resurrected in the image of the glorified King. He wants to change the flesh, day by day, into flesh that He will resurrect as if it were His very own.

Those who have eaten the Eucharist have eaten the flesh and drunk the blood of Him who is the Resurrection and the Life. Their own flesh and blood is invisibly stamped with the signature, the seal, of the eternally living flesh and blood of Jesus. To the all-seeing eyes of God the Father, the man or woman fed on the Eucharist *looks different* from the one who has not been so fed. Not only in his soul, but in his very flesh, he bears the marks of the Lord Jesus (see Gal. 6:17). As Saint Thomas says, we receive *Christus passus*, "the Christ who suffered," who is now glorified.[5] The body that is conformed to the suffering Christ is conformed to His glory, Saint Paul tells us.[6]

An inverse example may illustrate. If you sow a field with salt, as the Romans did the fields of Carthage, the soil's capacity to bear fruit

---

[5] *Summa theologiae* III, qu. 66, art. 9: "The Eucharist is a commemoration of Christ's death, in so far as the suffering Christ Himself is offered to us as the Paschal banquet."

[6] See, *inter alia*, Rom. 8:17.

is destroyed; it cannot produce crops for many generations. But if you sow the field of the human body with the salt of Jesus Christ, this makes the field fertile for all ages, for eternity; the salt of the Spirit preserves the flesh from corruption. And this is something God *finds* in the body of the communicant, shaped and affected by the presence of the Son received in Holy Communion. God does not "imagine" a difference; there *is* an ontological difference. As Réginald Garrigou-Lagrange expresses it: "The Eucharist leaves, as it were, seeds of immortality in the body, which is destined to rise again and to receive a reflection of the glory of the soul."[7]

There is a *causal* connection between eating the risen Lord and being raised up, between eating His body and being resurrected in body on the last day to a glorious eternity. Those who have not so eaten are indeed raised from the dead, but their resurrection is a punishment, not a reward; it is a resurrection to judgment and everlasting death, not to life and glory. Saint Thomas notes that the flesh of the damned is not perfect like the flesh of Christ, but rather, is kept permanently susceptible to pain, ever dying but never dead. May the Lord in His mercy spare us from such an inglorious resurrection; may He grant us a share in His glorious triumph over sin and death!

In his Encyclical *Mirae Caritatis*, Pope Leo XIII bears witness to this twofold effect of the divine Sacrament, on the soul and on the body:

> By this same Sacrament our hope of everlasting blessedness, based on our trust in the divine assistance, is wonderfully strengthened. For the edge of that longing for happiness which is so deeply rooted in the hearts of all men from their birth is whetted even more and more by the experience of the deceitfulness of earthly goods, by the unjust violence of wicked men, and by all those other afflictions to which mind and body are subject.

---

[7] *The Three Ages of the Interior Life*, trans. Sr. M. Timothea Doyle, O.P. (Rockford, IL: TAN Books, 1989), 2:112.

Now the venerable Sacrament of the Eucharist is both the source and the pledge of blessedness and of glory, and this, not for the soul alone, but for the body also. For it enriches the soul with an abundance of heavenly blessings, and fills it with a sweet joy which far surpasses man's hope and expectations; it sustains him in adversity, strengthens him in the spiritual combat, preserves him for life everlasting, and as a special provision for the journey accompanies him thither. And in the frail and perishable body, that divine Host, which is the immortal Body of Christ, implants a principle of resurrection, a seed of immortality, which one day must germinate. That to this source man's soul and body will be indebted for both these boons has been the constant teaching of the Church, which has dutifully reaffirmed the affirmation of Christ: "He that eateth my flesh and drinketh my blood hath everlasting life; and I will raise him up at the last day" (John 6:55, DR).[8]

St. John Chrysostom similarly bears witness:

Let us not, I beg you, slay ourselves by our irreverence, but with awe and purity draw near to it; and when you see it set before you, say to yourself: "Because of this Body am I no longer earth and ashes, no longer a prisoner, but free: because of this I hope for heaven, and [I hope] to receive the good things therein, immortal life, the portion of angels, to converse with Christ."[9]

Here, then, is the question we must ask ourselves: *Do* we believe that Jesus Christ, the Lord of heaven and earth, is really, truly, substantially present in the Most Holy Eucharist? If so, we can do far more than just follow Him at a distance, like the timid apostles during the Passion: we

---

[8]   Leo XIII, Encyclical Letter *Mirae Caritatis* (May 28, 1902), §9.

[9]   St. John Chrysostom, *In epistulam I ad Corinthos* 24.4 (PG 61:203), quoted in Pope Benedict XVI, *Letter on the Occasion of the Sixteenth Centenary of the Death of St. John Chrysostom* (August 10, 2007).

can *eat* the Way, the Truth, and the Life, we can become *one* with Him and allow His reality to shape our very self.

The Truth we are striving to know and to behold face to face in the beatific vision — that same Truth is our food, we can *consume* it and be one with it. The Life we long for, the blessed life, the life of heaven: this Life we can take into ourselves. That God should give us *Himself* is completely beyond our limited understanding, but not at all beyond His unlimited power. The Way we seek to follow, the Gospel way, is not a philosophy but a Person, the Word made Flesh, and this Person gives Himself to us.

Do we believe He is Emmanuel, "God with us," God dwelling in our midst? Hidden, yes, but also real — indeed, *far more real than we are*. Let us go to Him, let us run to reality! God is the source of all reality, all goodness, all holiness, all happiness.

> Every one who thirsts, come to the waters; and he who has no money, come, buy and eat! Come, buy wine and milk without money and without price. Why do you spend your money for that which is not bread, and your labor for that which does not satisfy? Hearken diligently to me, and eat what is good, and delight yourselves in fatness.[10]

What does Our Lord say in the Gospel of John? "This is eternal life, that they know thee the only true God, and Jesus Christ whom thou hast sent" (John 17:3). He also says: "I came that they may have life, and have it abundantly" (John 10:10). Holy Mass is the Sacrifice of Christ made real again in our midst; it is His self-offering and ours, too, united with His. It brings us the sacrament of His passion, death, and resurrection, and through it — or better, through communion with the Lord Himself — we suffer, die, and rise again.

It may not always *feel* like the height of one's interior life or one's Christian life, but that is beside the point. Our religion does not consist

---

[10] Isa. 55:1–2.

in feelings or even true thoughts, but communion with mysteries. It is about massive realities too big for our comprehension: God thrusts them upon us, and we respond in the darkness of faith. We have to trust not our changing feelings or our uncertain thoughts but His everlasting Word, which is the only rock we can safely build on. If we build on the rock of the Mass—the integral, authentic Mass, the unfailing garden of saints, handed down to us through the ages in Catholic tradition—our house will be stably founded forever.

Every man is either living from the Eucharist, or longing to live from it, whether he knows it or not. This is because everyone longs for the life of God, to be a god, to be immortal and perfectly happy, and the Eucharist is the food of immortality, of divinization, whereby God comes to us, and we are lifted up into Him. All this takes place in faith, in a certain darkness, but as long as we rely on the invincible and infallible promises of Jesus Christ, truly present in the Blessed Sacrament, the Eucharist becomes for us the great reassurance that we are heading toward heaven as well as the great source of power to reach this goal, which is so far beyond our power.

We must therefore cling heartily and happily to the Eucharistic Lord, and receive Him as often as we can, go before Him in Adoration, let our minds and hearts be "eucharisticized" so that our lives will be, more and more, an act of thanksgiving for His mighty work of redemption in us.

2

What Christ's Body Does for Us

Each year, as Maundy Thursday comes around, the Catholic Church celebrates three mysteries tightly bound together: the institution of the Holy Eucharist, the institution of the Christian priesthood, and the great commandment of charity. They are bound together for many reasons, but this one above all: God is asking us to love in a way that is impossible to our unaided human nature. The Word became flesh, the Word became Victim, the Word became food. He took on our humanity, that we might take on His divinity. He loved with a human heart and gave that heart to us, that we might love with God's own love.

O admirabile commercium—O wondrous exchange!

No priesthood, no Mass; no Mass, no Eucharist; no Eucharist, no life within us; no life within us, no love within us, either. The Holy Sacrament of the Altar is the concentration of all of God's saving works: they come together here like all the threads of a grand story in the final chapter. His abiding desire to save and His indescribable generosity find in this Sacrament their most outstanding—indeed, one might almost say, outlandish—expression. He is the Lover who can make reality bend to His will for the sake of reaching, touching, entering into, and taking possession of the beloved.

Do we appreciate what He has done and is doing for us, upon the altar of sacrifice, in the simple elements of bread and wine? Even when we lavish upon them all the beauty and ceremonial pomp we can muster, it is still far too little for the gift He gives us: Himself.

The Holy Bread of Eternal Life

Isn't God taking a risk that what He gives for free will be held in contempt? Don't people value things because they cost a lot? We think that a mansion or a yacht is special because so few can possess it. What about grace? In one sense, it is free; in another sense, it has a cost that cannot be counted. For its price is the soul of man. The one who opens his soul to God's invasion is the one who is visited by Him, taken possession of, and divinized. This requires the most important and most difficult act of all: surrender.

How much do we value grace, in spite of its being freely given? Or do we hold it lightly because it doesn't force its beauty upon us, it doesn't glitter like gold? Jesus is asking us to take His word for it: *"Without me you can do nothing"* (John 15:5, DR). Whatever we want to do in life, without Jesus, we cannot do it in any meaningful way. Whatever we do without Him will be lost, worthless, a cause more of disappointment or despair than of fulfillment.

All the truth we can attain, all the good we can achieve, all the beauty we can sense or dream of—all of this is already contained *there*, at the altar, in a mysterious form. In the Blessed Sacrament is the sum total of reality as it streams forth from God's hands and as it carries us back to Him. If we but eat that truth, it will nourish our souls as no amount of studying or learning or thinking can ever do. All the love we will ever find in friendship is there first in the Divine Lover—the One who makes us His friends, who makes us worthy of love and equips us to love ourselves and each other. Without Him there can be no love, no friendship. If you are one who loves or one who wants to be loved—and who does not fit this double description?—know that your love comes from Him and should return to Him, together with all that you love here below.

This is the inexhaustible mystery of the Last Supper: the final meal of the Master with His disciples, the communion of the divine Lover with His beloved friends, the anticipation of His supreme act of love on the Cross, the institution of that unbloody sacrifice that will never cease to rise up like incense until the end of time, when He brings all symbols to an end in the new Heavens and the new Earth.

Judas is the only sour note in this symphony of Maundy Thursday. He is the one disciple who knows better than the rest—who, it seems, knows better than the Master. He is impatient of all this solemnity and sublimity; he wants concrete results, here and now. He is the model and inspiration of all the pragmatists down through the ages who prefer a bit of bureaucratic philanthropy to a lofty espousal of souls. Had he lived in a different century, he might have been made the secretary of the Consilium, entrusted with the great task of making liturgy safe for democracy, more efficient, more participatory, more suited to the common man. No free grace for him, no; thirty pieces of silver. Now, *that's* something you can handle and count, as any tax collector might do. Judas is the patron non-saint of all horizontalists.

Jesus is uncompromising. Horizontalism fails every time, as Judas failed when he chucked his bag of coins away in disgust and hanged himself with a horse's headgear. Judas chose a death of despair. Christ chose a death of love, lifted up vertically on the Cross, so that He might draw all men upward to His kingdom, which is not of this earth.

It does no good to try to live a horizontal life, a life that keeps God somewhere at the margins, pursued *after* a number of other finite goods have been pursued. God is at the center of reality, and we are on the outside. We need to get inside, into the center, if we are going to become as real as we can be, rather than shadows or stick figures.

He is the magnet drawing us toward Himself; we are perverse iron filings that resist His magnetism. Don't resist; surrender and let Him draw you. His grace will not be lacking. Will your free choice be lacking? Do you want to be a stick figure or a fully fleshed-out human being? You want to be fully human. The only way to be fully human is to be divinized, to be united with the font of all life, the maker of man.

Many Catholics experience pain because they cannot make it to Mass. Perhaps their work schedule allows them no time for it, or the church is too far away, or there is no reverent priest in their area, or no traditional Latin Mass. Such people would give almost anything to have a Mass close by that they could attend for their spiritual profit. What about those of us who have a worthily celebrated Mass close by, and take little advantage of it?

We should be brutally honest with ourselves. Sometimes we feel no attraction to the Holy Mass or the Holy Eucharist; sometimes we go out of a sense of obligation or human respect. If this is how you feel, it's time to ask the Lord, beg the Lord, for a change of heart. Ask Him to soften your resistance, to give you a hunger and thirst for Him. "Lord, you know how it looks to me; I don't see in myself any real desire for holiness. Please give me that desire. Make me want to be holy. Move me to do what I should do." It is a breakthrough to be humble enough to realize that we must ask for help, even when we don't feel like being helped.

The Church mandates attendance at Mass on Sundays and Holy Days but not on weekdays. The reason is that we are required by divine law to worship God regularly, and the Church has determined that the minimum fulfillment of this law is to meet once a week, on the "little Easter" of Sunday. Yet no one has become a great saint, a great missionary, a great kindler of fires in this world, by doing the minimum. King St. Louis IX, the best ruler the world has ever seen, attended two Masses each day. Saint Thomas Aquinas, the best theologian the world has ever seen, celebrated his morning Mass and then immediately served Mass for a fellow friar.

I'm not suggesting that all of us ought to go to Mass twice a day. The point is that difficult times, like the new and darker Dark Ages we are in, require spiritually strong men and women, and that heroic deeds can only be done by heroic souls. Such souls derive their nourishment, strength, and consolation from the sacrificial banquet of the Mass. Our Lord knew what He was doing when He instituted the Mass on Maundy Thursday.

The Lord knows how much we need prompting, how much we need opportunities to be rolled out in front of us so that we can be reminded to take advantage of them. That is why he created a Church in which the sacrifice of His Son would be renewed each and every day; that is why Jesus taught us to pray for our daily bread: *panem nostrum quotidianum da nobis hodie*. We know that we are supposed to pray, to listen to God's word, and to ask for His grace; we know we need these things. By going to Mass, we do them all, and not according to our own preferences or ideas, but in the way that Jesus Himself conceived in His Heart, instituted with His own hands, and commanded us to do in remembrance of Him, before achieving the foreshadowed reality by stretching out those hands on the Cross and letting that Heart be pierced with a lance.

I am invited, you are invited, to that sacred banquet. The once-for-all sacrifice of Calvary is offered to God, for us. The fruit of the Tree of Life is ours to eat.

3

The Usefulness of Leviticus: Sacrifice for Catholics

The Church tells us we should venerate Sacred Scripture, study it, pray with it, because it is the Word of God spoken to mankind, to the Church, to the heart and mind of each believer. It is uniquely inspired by God Himself, free from error, and always beneficial to the soul.[11]

Yet this does not make it free from difficulty for us, nor is it always obviously beneficial. As St. Augustine says, the Lord mingles easier and harder passages, clearer and more obscure, consoling messages and challenging ones, to satisfy our hunger while urging us on to greater growth in the spiritual life. The Bible tests our fortitude and perseverance even while giving us radiant lights to follow.

A case in point, perhaps *the* case in point, is the Book of Leviticus, which makes for notoriously difficult reading. First, it is likely to strike readers as a dry legislative text, as it minutely specifies the dozens of sacrifices and other ritual actions instituted by God through Moses for the people of Israel. On top of this, Leviticus is a bloody book, full of animal slaughter and dismemberment. We are tempted to wonder why God instituted this kind of religion for his Chosen People. Couldn't there have been a more "spiritual" worship, a more PETA-friendly way of doing things? The early Church ecclesiastical writer Origen (c. 185–254) reports that some Christians in his day objected: "Why should these things be

[11] For more, see my article "The Inspiration and Inerrancy of Sacred Scripture," *OnePeterFive*, March 2, 2015.

read in church? Of what use are Jewish observances to us? Those things concern the Jews; let the Jews worry about them." In a recent edition of the Pentateuch we find this comment: "A superficial reading of Leviticus could give one the impression that this book is very difficult to understand and has no relevance to our own time."[12]

But since Leviticus is no less God's inspired word than the Gospels are, we know that it was He, the all-wise Father, who instituted this sacrificial system for Israel, and that He must have had good reasons for doing so. In contrast to our reaction, the Fathers of the Church read this book with considerable interest and even excitement, for what they found in it was a tightly interlocked set of symbols pointing ahead to the all-sufficient sacrifice of Jesus Christ, the unblemished Victim, on the altar of the Cross. *This* was the inner meaning of the external ceremonies covered in Leviticus.

A brief tour of the book

Leviticus is the middle book of the Torah or Pentateuch, preceded by Genesis and Exodus and followed by Numbers and Deuteronomy. Its central position is deliberate and symbolic. Since God created man to be a royal priest who offers up the universe to its Creator in praise and thanksgiving, and since Israel was created to be a royal priestly people through whom this original plan would be restored, it makes sense that the "how-to" manual of worship would be at the center of the Law. The sacrifices by which the Lord asks to be worshiped are the central act of the true religion that the true God has revealed. In Exodus, the Lord calls His people to become a holy nation, a kingdom of priests. In Leviticus, He specifies what they need to do to attain that holiness, how they are to function as a priestly kingdom.

It would be nice if the story were that simple, but there's more going on. The situation of Israel was desperately complicated by the covenant-breaking apostasy of the golden calf, "Israel's original sin," which we find

---

[12] *The Navarre Bible: Pentateuch* (New York: Scepter Publishers, 1999), 417.

narrated in Exodus 32–33. God's response to this apostasy takes the form of making several changes in the law that had been given up to that point.[13] Prior to the golden calf, it was God's intention that every firstborn son of the Israelites should be a priest. After the apostasy, God transfers the priesthood exclusively to the tribe of Levi, such that Levites substitute for the firstborn sons. Moreover, while God had earlier intended a renewed intimacy between Himself and each Israelite, He now exalts Moses as mediator between God and a sinful people, in this way foreshadowing the greater Lawgiver and Mediator who was to come.

Lastly — and this brings us right into Leviticus — God mandated that the newly ordained Levites offer regular animal sacrifices in the tabernacle on behalf of the other tribes of Israel. Why was this introduced only *after* the golden calf incident? Scott Hahn compares the Israelites' proneness to idolatry to the experience of an alcoholic attached to, and overmastered by, alcohol. The people's hearts are still stubbornly clinging to their Egyptian idols; they are addicted, as it were, to paganism. Thus, says Hahn, "it wasn't enough for them to make a one-time offering at Sinai (Exod. 24:3–11) by slaughtering the animals the Egyptians venerated as gods (Exod. 8:26)."[14] On the other hand, Israel was not yet ready for the definitive cure, the redemption that only God could bring "in the fullness of time" (see Gal. 4:4).

What was needed was a way of training the people in habits of obedience and deference to the Lord, while at the same time reminding them of their "accursed condition" and their need for "circumcision of the heart."

The Israelites had to fight a protracted war against idolatry, which they were commanded now to wage by daily animal sacrifice,

---

13 As Scott Hahn observes, "the legal procedure for renewing Israel's broken covenant — while temporarily suspending their sentence — takes up the rest of Exodus, all of Leviticus, and the first ten chapters of Numbers" (*A Father Who Keeps His Promises: God's Covenant Love in Scripture* [Ann Arbor, MI: Servant Publications, 1998], 155).

14 Ibid., 165.

among other things. Within the Father's remedial program lay a subtle strategy. On the one hand, Israel couldn't slaughter — or eat — the animals that the Egyptians sacrificed to their gods; they were declared unclean. On the other hand, Israel had to slaughter and eat the animals that the Egyptians venerated but never sacrificed; they were clean.[15]

The idea is: sacrifice and consume the things venerated by the pagans. Animals worshiped in the Egyptian cult as gods — Hathor in the form of a cow, Ares in the form of a sheep — have to be ritually slaughtered. Since all the pagan nations in the territory of Canaan round about the Israelites had similar idols, the Levitical code was a constant reminder to the Israelites that the Lord is the true God to be loved and followed, and the rest are false gods to be rejected. This lesson remains true for us.[16]

A code of holiness

A first-time reader of Leviticus may come away with an impression of randomness in the material. Yet as with all biblical texts, further probing and reflecting disclose a definite ascending pattern to the four parts of the book. As one commentary elucidates:

> Around his central theme, the worship of the thrice-holy God (cf. Isa. 6:3), the hagiographer built up a series of steps of legislative material. First came the *rites* to be followed when offering sacrifices; then, on a higher level, those to do with the ordination of the men whose task it would be to *offer* these sacrifices, the priests; higher still, the rules which show priests and people how to be "pure," that is, to be worthy to *take part* in worship; finally, at the very top,

---

[15] Ibid., 166.
[16] See my lecture "A Theological Review of the Amazon Synod," *OnePeterFive*, December 4, 2019.

the rules about divine worship itself, the rules about "holiness," which is what this Law covers.[17]

This structure already contains lessons of universal importance in the Catholic Faith. First, there is a definite way of worshiping God that *He* introduces as pleasing to Him. Second, there are definite ministers who must be qualified for, consecrated for, and involved in such worship. Third, those who are to take part in worship, whether as offering or as receiving, must be pure. Fourth, the ultimate goal is to become holy as God is holy.

If we look at these negatively, we can see no less crucial lessons. First, God is not to be worshiped haphazardly, according to our whims, feelings, and preferences; the Church's liturgical law must be respected.[18] Second, not just anyone can take it upon himself to stride up to the altar and act as a priest, but a divine mandate is required, and an ordination of the priest. Third, there is such a thing as being spiritually unprepared for worship, and we have to make a conscious effort to prepare ourselves so that our participation will not be in vain. Lastly, the *worst* condition of man is to be unholy — that is, lacking in grace, lacking in righteousness. This, above all, is what we want to avoid.

The sacrificial law placed upon the guilty nation of Israel an abiding need for symbolic atonement by burnt offerings.[19] These offerings in and of themselves cannot "justify" or make holy, but they do symbolize the repentance and reconciliation that God's gift of grace effects in the heart. Man is not sanctified by the blood of bulls or rams, but by means of such offerings he can manifest contrition, thanksgiving, or a desire for holiness. Taken as the exterior sign of an interior sacrifice, they do have

---

[17] *Navarre Bible: Pentateuch*, 416. It should be noted that the "codes" are indeed distinct (the prevailing content makes this clear), but some of the same sayings and particular rules are repeated in different codes, as refrains (e.g., 11:44 and 20:7) or to accentuate their importance.

[18] See my article "Fidelity to Liturgical Law and the Rights of the Faithful," *OnePeterFive*, July 3, 2017.

[19] The "burnt offering" is also sometimes translated "holocaust," a Greek word meaning "burnt in its entirety."

value; taken in a purely ritualistic or formalistic way, they are empty of value. This explains the constant polemic of the Old Testament prophets against sacrifices done mechanically, without interior piety and without a genuine love for one's neighbor, especially the poor.[20] Here, too, we have a warning that remains relevant: our liturgy is to be done with sincere faith, great care, reverence, and beauty, not in a slipshod or rushed manner,[21] cutting corners to save time or money, and it must be at once the vanguard and rearguard of our spiritual and corporal works of mercy.

The five different kinds of sacrifice spoken of in Leviticus—the burnt offering, the grain offering, the fellowship offering, the sin offering, and the guilt offering—illustrate different facets of man's relationship with God. This relationship involves, first and foremost, a total surrender to God's providential love, giving everything back to Him from whom it came. It involves giving of the substance of our labor, as we do with tithing. It involves seeking peace and unity with God by seeking them with our neighbors. It involves expressing sorrow for sins and repairing the wrong done. The Levitical rituals are, one might say, the virtue of "religion" writ large, made evident and graphic.[22]

A good example of the language of symbols would be the triple consecration of ears, hands, and feet often mentioned in Leviticus—"smear some blood on the right ear, then on the thumb of the right hand, then on the great toe of the right foot." This symbolizes that the priest, or servant of God, should listen to the voice of God, turn his hands to the work of worship, and walk in holiness.

---

[20] See Isaiah 1, Jeremiah 6, Amos 5:21, Hosea 6:6, Mark 12:33, etc.

[21] See my article "Two Modest Proposals for Improving the Prayerfulness of Low Mass," *New Liturgical Movement*, November 12, 2018.

[22] On the virtue of religion, see the entry under that phrase in *The Catholic Encyclopedia*, vol. 12 (New York: Robert Appleton Company, 1911), online at New Advent; also Peter Kwasniewski, *Reclaiming Our Roman Catholic Birthright: The Genius and Timeliness of the Traditional Latin Mass* (Brooklyn, NY: Angelico Press, 2020), 332–33.

The true and perfect sacrifice

After Israel's "original sin," God institutes a remedial-pedagogical sacrificial religion for the nation. Initially, at least, the people are probably not much aware of its pedagogical value; they see it as a bunch of prescriptions handed down from the Lord through their leader Moses. However, on a basic level, this system is "weaning" Israel from its attachment to regional idols, which usually took an animal form.

On top of this, and more valuable, is the spiritual discipline of obeying prescriptions simply because God asks you to do so. In the Garden of Eden, the one and only requirement laid on our first parents was the requirement of not eating the fruit God asked them not to eat. God did not have to explain to them the whys and wherefores of this prohibition. He was asking the creature to trust in the Creator's wisdom — to obey without seeing why. Unlike Adam, Abraham demonstrates this trust or faith in God's Providence, for he does not quarrel with God or second-guess him. Abraham simply does as he is told. And given the fairly primitive mentality that appears to be operative in Israel at this early stage, a large part of the sacrificial system's value is that it keeps the people really busy fulfilling their obligations. If the old saying is true, "idle hands are the devil's tools," then the devil won't be able to find many tools among the busy hands of observant Israelites as they strive to put into practice the hundreds of commandments of the Mosaic law.

Then we may ask: What is the meaning of sacrifice in general? It is an offering of something valuable, as a sign of an interior offering of self. An expiatory offering is a sign that one's own sins are placed humbly into the fire of God, and then annihilated by His mercy. Jews over the centuries came to understand that the actions they performed were really about *themselves in relation to God*, not about something external to themselves; it was not that God needed animal victims, but rather that *we* needed to express our praise, thanksgiving, penance, etc., by means of visible signs, for we are creatures of sensation and imagination. We know from the Gospels that this legislation runs the danger of hardening into legalism, but without the law of Moses there would never have been a receptive dwelling for Jesus Christ in the bosom of the human race.

Beyond the remedial, pedagogical, and moral benefits of the sacrificial system stands a more profound purpose: to prepare Israel for the One who redeems and saves mankind—namely, the one in whom all that Israel was supposed to be, all that man is supposed to be, is found: Jesus Christ, the firstborn son of God.

Enter the "Dumb Ox"

One of the most profound commentaries written on the ceremonial precepts of the Old Law is that of St. Thomas Aquinas in his *Summa theologiae*. Building on the work of the Church Fathers, St. Thomas brilliantly unfolds the allegorical meaning of the Old Testament sacrifices. The value of his analysis is such that it merits being quoted in full:

> The ceremonies of the Old Law had a twofold cause, namely, a *literal* cause, according as they were intended for divine worship; and a *figurative* or *mystical* cause, according as they were intended to foreshadow Christ; and in either way the ceremonies pertaining to the sacrifices can be assigned to a fitting cause.
>
> For, according as the ceremonies of the sacrifices were intended for divine worship, the causes of the sacrifices can be taken in two ways. First, in so far as the sacrifice represented the directing of the mind to God, to which the offerer of the sacrifice was stimulated. Now in order rightly to direct his mind to God, man must recognize that whatever he has is from God as from its first principle, and direct it to God as its last end. This was denoted in the offerings and sacrifices, by the fact that man offered some of his own belongings in honor of God, as though in recognition of his having received them from God, according to the saying

of [King] David: "All things are Thine: and we have given Thee what we received of Thy hand" (1 Chron. 29:14). Hence in offering up sacrifices man made protestation that God is the first principle of the creation of all things, and their last end, to which all things must be directed. And since, for the human mind to be rightly directed to God, it must recognize no first author of things *other* than God, nor place its end in any other [thing], for this reason it was forbidden in the Law to offer sacrifice to any other but God, according to Exodus 22:20: "He that sacrificeth to any gods other than to the Lord shall be put to death." So another reasonable cause may be assigned to the ceremonies of the sacrifices, from the fact that men were thereby withdrawn from offering sacrifices to idols. Hence too it is that the precepts about the sacrifices were not given to the Jewish people until after they had fallen into idolatry, by worshipping the golden calf: as though those sacrifices were instituted so that the people, being ready to offer sacrifices, might offer those sacrifices to God rather than to idols....

Now of *all* the gifts which God vouchsafed to mankind after they had fallen away by sin, the chief is that He gave His Son; thus it is written (John 3:16): "God so loved the world that He gave His only-begotten Son, that whosoever believes in Him may not perish, but have eternal life." Consequently the chief sacrifice is that whereby Christ Himself "delivered Himself...to God for an odor of sweetness" (Eph. 5:2). And for this reason all the other sacrifices of the Old Law were offered up in order to foreshadow this one individual and paramount sacrifice—the imperfect forecasting the perfect. Hence the Apostle says (Heb. 10:11–12) that the priest of the Old Law "often" offered "the same sacrifices, which can never take away sins, whereas" Christ offered "one sacrifice for sins, for ever." And since the reason of the figure is taken from that which the figure represents, therefore the reasons of the figurative sacrifices of the Old Law should be taken from the true sacrifice of Christ.[23]

In other words, God, Creator of the universe and Governor of history, appointed certain sacrifices for the Jews precisely with a view to the one all-sufficient sacrifice of Christ.

In the same question of the *Summa*, St. Thomas shows how each major element of the Levitical code has both a valid historical reason and a figurative or mystical meaning. The text is too lengthy to reproduce here, but I will share a couple of highlights.

Why, according to Leviticus, do the animals have to be *killed* rather than, say, brought in for a moment, and after a quick prayer, taken away and put back in the flock? St. Thomas explains:

> The animals which were offered in sacrifice were slain, because it is by being killed that they become useful to man, forasmuch as God gave them to man for food. Hence, too, they were burnt with fire: because it is by being cooked that they are made fit for human consumption. Moreover, the slaying of the animals signified the destruction of sins: and also that man deserved death on account of his sins; as though those animals were slain in man's stead, in order to betoken the expiation of sins. Again, the slaying of these animals signified the slaying of Christ.

Elsewhere St. Thomas tells us why the non-animal items specified for worship — bread, wine, oil, incense, and salt — are not arbitrary:

> The products of the soil are useful to man, either as food, and of these bread was offered; or as drink, and of these wine was offered; or as seasoning, and of these oil and salt were offered; or as healing, and of these they offered incense, which both smells sweetly and binds easily together. Now the bread foreshadowed the flesh of Christ; and the wine, His blood, whereby we were

---

[23] *Summa theologiae* I-II, qu. 102, art. 3.

redeemed; oil betokens the grace of Christ; salt, His knowledge; incense, His prayer.

Through Him, with Him, in Him

The Angelic Doctor helps us to appreciate why the activity of offering sacrifice to God is something that should be natural to us, if we are thinking rightly about ourselves and God. Aversion to the very idea of sacrifice, which is common in our day and age, finally comes back to a too limited notion of God. If we think of God as a fellow player on the field of the universe, a kind of superhuman force, then we might feel comfortable letting God have *some* dealings with mankind, but there could be no question of yielding ourselves up to Him as a burnt offering. To deserve *this* kind of action — nothing less than the offering up of one's entire self — God must be wholly beyond us, infinitely great and worthy of all our love, indeed worthy of all the love we could never even give because we are finite. God, to be God, must be "higher than the highest in me yet more intimate than the innermost in me,"[24] the absolute origin of all that I am, and the single goal of all that I will be. If this is what we mean by "God," then yes, the most natural and spontaneous and joyful thing I could do is to give myself up to Him entirely, seeking out symbolic ways in which to make visible and tangible this inner desire to give myself to Him.

But then we find, to our dismay, that we cannot fulfill this desire on our own. All men are born, so to speak, in the Old Testament; we have to be lifted up out of our proneness to idolatry in all its different forms. We are born in the shadow of the golden calf and have to be weaned from the temptation to pull God down to our level and make of Him a rival in the contest for self-determination. We need a savior, a rescuer, who has stooped to our condition, has entered into it so fully that He can lift us up on His shoulders and bring us to where we are supposed to be.

---

[24] St. Augustine, *Confessions* III.6.11.

The Holy Bread of Eternal Life

The New Testament gives us the key that interprets the whole of the Old Testament, and with it, the whole of human history. It is Our Lord Jesus Christ who offers the perfect sacrifice, the perfect worship, that fulfills the original plan of creation and makes it possible for the rest of us to enter that fulfillment. He accomplishes this end not by observing Levitical sacrifices with fastidious correctness,[25] but by substituting Himself as the sinless victim, the Paschal Lamb. As Joseph Ratzinger beautifully says:

> The Shepherd [of Israel] has become a Lamb. The vision of the lamb that appears in the story of Isaac, the lamb that gets entangled in the undergrowth and ransoms the son, has become a reality; the Lord became a Lamb; He allows Himself to be bound and sacrificed, to deliver us.[26]

In so doing He brings to an end the sacrificial system contained in Leviticus. He is the reality that the symbols of the Jewish religion point to. He is the agent in whose person and by whose action fallen human beings can resume their rightful place as royal priests who bring the world back to its original purpose, who help the universe achieve its destiny. That is what is at stake!

God gives Himself to us

But how do we make His perfect sacrifice of love our own? Or better, how does He share this sacrifice with us? Jesus makes Himself our food and drink so that we may share His life and the reality of His immolation on the Cross.

If we turn to the Gospel of John, we can see this more clearly. By the time St. John is writing his Gospel, his Christian readers or listeners

---

[25] And in any case, He Himself is from the tribe of Judah, not that of Levi.

[26] "The Theology of the Liturgy," in *Looking Again at the Question of the Liturgy with Cardinal Ratzinger*, ed. Alcuin Reid (Farnborough: Saint Michael's Abbey Press, 2003), 24.

already know the "institution narrative" from the liturgy. They know that the Eucharist has fulfilled and replaced the Passover meal. John plays on this in a remarkable way. Just when readers accustomed to the Synoptic Gospels expect the account of Jesus lifting up bread at the Last Supper, they get instead the body of Jesus being lifted up on the Cross as the Passover Lamb.

John has the Jewish Passover being prepared on Good Friday—and he adds this poignant detail in John 19:14: "Now it was the day of Preparation of the Passover; it was about the sixth hour" [i.e., noon]. This is the hour, according to ancient Jewish sources, when all the lambs were ritually slaughtered in the court of the Temple, in order to be brought to the homes where the meal would be celebrated. Jesus, the true Lamb of God, is handed over at this very moment to be sacrificed on the Cross.

Now, since (as John is dramatically showing) the body of Jesus on the Cross *is* the Passover Lamb, and since (as the Christians already know) the Eucharist is the new Passover meal, therefore *the Eucharist is the very same body of Jesus that hung on the Cross for our salvation—the same Jesus who is our salvation*. To eat this Passover meal, therefore, means that we are incorporated into the Son of God: we become living members of His body, and we are spared the destroying angel.

Living from and for the Mass

With these marvelous truths in mind, what are some concrete applications to our life as Catholics, our way of thinking and acting?

From the time of the Apostolic Fathers to the present, the Church has understood the Mass to be nothing other than the redemptive sacrifice of Jesus Christ on Calvary, made present to us under the appearances of bread and wine—the forms Jesus chose at the Last Supper, the Passover meal He transformed into the first Mass. The Mass is the true and perfect sacrifice that makes possible, fulfills, and inspires all sacrifices of love. There is no unselfish love in this world that does not derive from the Cross, which translates into: from the Holy Mass offered day after day, year after year, century after century, until Christ returns in glory. As St. Pio of Pietrelcina once said: "It would be easier for the world to exist without the sun than without the Holy Sacrifice of the Mass."

The offering of the sacrifice of the Cross, made present by the double consecration that symbolically separates body from blood, is therefore the central action of the Mass, the main reason it exists, the main reason we are there, and—here we have to think big—the main cause of the universe attaining its destiny. Without the continual celebration of the Mass, the world would literally fail to achieve the purpose for which God created it. The Mass is the most vital, most urgently needed, most solemn event that could ever and does ever take place. This means that the way it is celebrated, as well as our own interior attitude when we attend, should be a faithful reflection of its cosmic magnitude and mystical density. We are assisting at the world-redeeming sacrifice of Calvary, and thus we should conform ourselves spiritually to this sacrifice as Mary did at the foot of the Cross, so that we may "complete what is lacking in Christ's afflictions for the sake of His Body, that is, the Church" (Col. 1:24).[27] We are being asked to throw ourselves into the life-giving mystery of the Cross, which will make us worthy of tasting the fruit that grows from this Tree of Life. We are praying that we shall become fruitful branches of the true vine, Jesus Christ, who desires to see us grow strong and spread into the world that He created, then entered into as a man, and on the last day will judge in the sight of the angels. When we assist at Mass and join ourselves spiritually to the sacrifice of the Lamb of God, we are helping to lead the world back to its original purpose and hastening the glorious coming of Our Lord Jesus Christ.

These things being so, let us examine ourselves as God's priestly people. Am I fully "on board" with God's plan for creation—starting

---

[27] See Peter Kwasniewski, *Noble Beauty, Transcendent Holiness: Why the Modern Age Needs the Mass of Ages* (Kettering, OH: Angelico Press, 2017), ch. 3: "The Spirit of the Liturgy in the Words and Actions of Our Lady," 53–87.

with the purpose of my own existence? Do I desire to hasten the coming of Him who is the Judge of the Living and the Dead, who will purify the world with fire and carry into His kingdom all that is pure? We are being asked to adopt a radically heaven-centered perspective; we are being asked to adopt eternity, not time, as our basic frame of reference. Through Leviticus, the Cross, and the Mass, Our Lord is beckoning us to think of *sacrifice*, meaning *the gift of self*, as our fundamental cast of mind and way of life, rather than acquisition, mastery over others, or autonomous self-determination — all the idols that dominate the minds of modern Americans and Europeans. Our way of life is to be Eucharistic, which means, having given thanks to God and partaken of His strength even unto death, we then allow ourselves, our time, our energy, our gifts, to be blessed, broken, and distributed to others, to bring them His life.

4

St. Paul Tells Us How to Fix Our Liturgical Problems

The Good Book was never meant to give us a detailed program for every aspect of ecclesiastical and individual life. For example, nowhere are we told, in so many words, what to think about nuclear weapons, *in vitro* fertilization, or plasma TVs. Instead, it gives us luminous first principles; methods to follow; many models to imitate — or to avoid imitating; archetypal scenarios that play themselves out again and again; and judgments concerning a broad range of goods and evils, to which the rise of new goods and evils can be compared.[28]

An elegant example is the First Epistle of St. Paul to the Corinthians. At the time the Apostle was writing (ca. AD 57), the Church's liturgy was still fairly simple, consisting of elements borrowed from temple and synagogue worship enriched with distinctively Christian prayers and

---

[28] Recognizing this simple fact is the first step to recognizing why Christ instituted a Church and why, indeed, if He chose not to remain with us on earth in His visible presence as the King of the new Israel, He *had* to institute a visible Church with the authority to teach in His Name. It is impossible for any single book, even an inspired one, to address every single question that will arise in however many thousands of years the human race will endure. Someone must be able to say, definitively, how the truth revealed to us applies to new issues. However, the same argument shows why the Magisterium cannot contradict itself, otherwise, it would be useless as a guide. Hence, the very God-givenness of the Magisterium is the reason why Modernist simulations of it must be refused and resisted by Catholics.

hymns; indeed, the Temple in Jerusalem was still some thirteen years away from its prophesied destruction by the Romans. Yet St. Paul already has clear ideas about how Catholic worship ought to be done and how it should *not* be done, and he tells them to the community at Corinth in no uncertain terms.

Minding Christ crucified

In chapter 1,[29] Paul appeals to the Corinthians to set aside their dissensions and to be of one mind. This sets the stage for his complaints later on that their liturgy plays favorites with different parties and fails to reflect the unity of the Church. Paul also insists front and center that the Cross is the central mystery of the Faith: "we preach Christ crucified" (1 Cor. 1:23). The Mass is indeed the unbloody making-present of the sacrifice of the Cross in our midst, and that is why sinning against the Eucharist is so serious.

In chapter 2, Paul notes that only the spiritual man can discern spiritual things, a foreshadowing of what he will say in chapter 11 about discerning the Body and Blood of the Lord under the appearances of the consecrated bread and wine.

In chapter 3, the Christian's body is said to be a temple of the Holy Spirit. The spiritual man is precisely the one in whom the Holy Spirit dwells; it is only such a one who can receive worthily the spiritual food that unites us to God in love (see 1 Cor. 6:19; 8:3). The apostles must be respected, since they are "the servants of Christ and stewards of the mysteries of God" (4:1; see chapter 9) — that is, of the sacraments, which the Church has received and which she must pass on faithfully (see 4:7).

---

[29] The division of the Bible's books into chapter and verse was a medieval invention to facilitate theological discourse. The divisions do not always correspond to the articulation of the argument or narrative in the original author, so we should be careful about placing too much emphasis on them; they are merely for convenience.

Making our bodies holy for the Body of Christ

In chapters 5 through 8, St. Paul turns to various ways in which Christians can sin by making an improper use of their bodies, thereby sinning against the Body of Christ (both Eucharistic and ecclesial). Those who sin in the flesh include "fornicators, idolaters, adulterers, effeminates and sodomites, thieves, the greedy, drunkards, revilers, robbers" (see 6:9–10), the litigious, and those who scandalize weaker brethren. It is as if Paul is providing, ahead of time, a list of the sort of people who must *not* receive Holy Communion until they repent—or who, if they dare to receive it, will be made worse by it, not better.

Notably, in chapter 7, St. Paul provides the lengthiest defense of celibacy in the New Testament, explaining how perpetual continence, the way of life he himself has chosen, frees a person up for complete dedication to the Lord's service. It is the gift of one's life in the body to Christ who is the Life in His Body. Although the reasoning here can certainly be applied to the clergy, it applies more obviously to missionaries like Paul and to those who withdraw from the world to give themselves wholly to God, who would later be called "religious." Certainly, this chapter was an inspiration for the first monks and nuns in the Church.

Especially from chapter 10 onward, St. Paul's whole thrust is to move the Corinthians to a deeper appreciation of the sacramental life and a more reverent and strict liturgy. In other words, some parts of the first-century Church had it wrong and needed reform. In that way, the first century and the twenty-first share much in common.

In chapter 10, Paul refers obliquely to baptism and warns the Corinthians not to "put the Lord to the test" (10:9) by falling into immorality,[30] as the Israelites did again and again. What happened to Israel happened

---

[30] The Greek word for "immorality," *porneia*, carries the sense of sexual immorality; it is sometimes translated "fornication." See, for further implications, Jonas Alšėnas, "Porneia and Communion in the Hand," *OnePeterFive*, March 3, 2020, and "Spiritual Porneia and the 'Lump' Destroyed," *OnePeterFive*, March 26, 2020.

"for our instruction" (10:11). Christians must shun idol worship—a convenient way of summing up all the immorality Paul has already discussed—because "the cup of blessing which we bless, is it not a participation in the blood of Christ? The bread which we break, is it not a participation in the body of Christ?" (10:16). If eating food offered to idols makes us partners with demons (10:20), eating the food of Christ makes us partners with Him. Those who "provoke the Lord to jealousy" will be defeated (10:22).

Chapter 15 speaks of the literal truth of the resurrection of the dead as the foundation of the Christian faith: we are looking ahead to eternal life in the flesh with the Son of God, who shares His glorified, immortal flesh with us in the Eucharistic sacrifice (see John 6:53–54). The uncompromising bodily realism of this epistle makes it astonishingly relevant in the context of today's neo-gnostic denial of the body-soul integrity of the human person.

Mandating reverence and discernment

Chapter 11 brings up three important issues connected with the Mass. First, St. Paul advises women to cover their heads with veils in church, a rule that was observed by Catholics from ancient times until the 1960s, when it was suddenly dropped as outdated.[31]

Second, St. Paul speaks of abuses at the Mass. The custom of having a "common meal" prior to the breaking of the Eucharistic bread was leading to divisions within the community: some people got too much food and drink, others not enough, and the poor, in particular, were excluded. The Apostle then recounts the institution and meaning of the Eucharist (11:23–26), focusing it on the Lord's death on the Cross (11:26), which represents to us and demands of us the love that He showed.

This transitions seamlessly into his third main point: the warning against the unworthy reception of Holy Communion (11:27–30), because

---

[31] See my article "The Theology behind Women Wearing Veils in Church," *OnePeterFive*, November 13, 2019.

the Eucharist is Jesus Himself: "Whoever eats the bread or drinks the cup of the Lord in an unworthy manner will be guilty of profaning the body and blood of the Lord.... For anyone who eats and drinks without discerning the body eats and drinks condemnation upon himself" (see 11:27, 29). Paul says that we must examine ourselves before we receive (11:28). These three verses (11:27–29)—which concern a matter so important that salvation or damnation hinges on it!—are read at least three times each year in the traditional Latin Mass. They were, however, systematically excluded from the Novus Ordo, where they are never read.[32]

The Apostle also points out that unworthy reception of Communion can lead to physical sickness and death (11:30). St. Paul's advice that Christians should first eat at home and then come later on to the Mass (11:34), emphasizing its proper dignity as a heavenly banquet, shows the remote origins of the discipline of the Eucharistic fast.[33]

Moderating our appearance and actions

In chapter 12, St. Paul speaks about the proper division of duties within the Church and the importance of modesty—two themes of capital importance to Mass-goers in the twenty-first century, living in the ruins of democratic (or pseudo-democratic) political revolutions and surrounded by the fallout of the Sexual Revolution.

In the justly famous chapter 13, he addresses the primacy of charity and mentions the need to give up childish ways of behavior—too many of which reappeared in the 1960s and '70s. The Eucharist is indeed the sacrament of charity, having as its inmost reality the unity of the Mystical

---

[32] See chapter 13. A note on terminology: some people are under the mistaken impression that the phrase "Novus Ordo [Missae]" is a disrespectful label invented by traditionalists. In fact, it was used first by Pope Paul VI, who was extremely fond of using words like "new, novel, innovation," and so forth when discussing his liturgical project, as documented in my book *Reclaiming Our Roman Catholic Birthright*, 328–29.

[33] See chapter 6.

Body of Christ, so it is highly fitting that this chapter should appear in a heavily liturgical epistle, from which, alas, it is often taken out of context and read as a sentimental "Hymn to Luv."

In chapter 14, he warns against seeking charismatic gifts for their own sake and advises seeking the greater gifts, which redound to the unity of the Church. Notably, the Apostle urges that liturgical worship be orderly and edifying, without excessive talking in church (14:26–33), "for God is not a God of confusion but of peace"—a striking observation, given that the most chaotic moment in the Novus Ordo is usually the so-called "sign of peace," thankfully under an indefinite ban at the present moment. (His advice at the end—"Greet one another with a holy kiss" [16:20]—stands at the basis of the formalized "kiss of peace" found in the traditional Latin Mass.)

Paul reinforces the apostolic custom that only men should speak aloud: "As in all the churches of the saints, the women should keep silence in the churches.... For it is shameful for a woman to speak in church" (14:33b–35b).[34] He concludes this section: "All things should be done decently and in order" (14:40)—a perfect description of how every traditional liturgical rite, Eastern or Western, operates, perhaps most especially the classical Roman Rite.

Growing up at St. Suburbia's Catholic Community, I remember seeing so many laity, especially eagerly volunteering women, flowing freely up and down the sanctuary without the slightest sense of the reality of the Blessed Sacrament, without so much as a bow, let alone a genuflection, rummaging through the tabernacle as though they were cleaning out a cupboard, all the while presenting (I speak of the ladies) a self-confident, competent, and non-subservient look—which came across as ironic when the priest, with subtle clericalism, was watching them serve him.

When we look again at St. Paul speaking of the Body of Christ and its appointed hierarchical ministers, when we hear him promoting charity

---

[34] On this question, see my article "Should Women Be Lectors at Mass?," *OnePeterFive*, March 4, 2020.

above charisms, and when we realize he is saying the Eucharistic liturgy and especially Communion can be done *unworthily*, it is overwhelmingly clear that his message to the Corinthians is this: "Laity, it's time to back off: let those be in charge who are supposed to be in charge. Let the women cover their heads and be silent. Let everyone examine his conscience. Do everything in an orderly and edifying manner."

Paul warns the Corinthians to avoid bad company because it will ruin their morals (15:33), which is reminiscent of his earlier command that they must avoid the man he has excommunicated (5:1–8). Unlike many of his latter-day successors, this prince of the apostles does not hesitate to use his authority to crack down on the disorderly, the immoral, and the heretical.

Lastly, in chapter 16, Paul speaks of the collection to be taken up for the poor in Jerusalem. Passing the collection basket around at Mass really goes back that far!

Maintaining the apostolic requirements

Looking back over this wonderful epistle, we can see that the Apostle's insistence on orthodoxy and encouragement of unity goes hand in hand with his careful liturgical directives — a mini-treatise on how to make the community's liturgy more reverent, more true to its nature, more demanding and sanctifying for the participants. Although the liturgy in its prayers, music, and ceremonies developed greatly from century to century after Paul's time, the universal "dos and don'ts" in his epistle always remained true and applicable.

The traditional Latin Mass fulfills each of St. Paul's desiderata, while the Novus Ordo frequently fails to do so and exhibits just the problems he criticizes. Note that Paul never advocates more laxity, a more casual style of worship, more options, or a more horizontal "Vatican II"–style Church where boundaries between offices are blurred. In every instance, he calls for tightening up the discipline. As Martin Mosebach says, genuine reform always means "return to form," that is, *more* definition and discipline, not less.

The Holy Bread of Eternal Life

It seems to me that the teaching of 1 Corinthians will especially resonate with those who have attended (or still attend) both the old and the new Mass, since these two contrasting forms furnish numerous illustrations of the kinds of things St. Paul is talking about, both positively and negatively. In any case, it might be a way of consoling yourself in retrospect: God was allowing you to do "field research" in order to open up to you the meaning of His inspired word.

The rulers of the Catholic Church have never allowed liturgical practice to degrade to the extent that it has done in the past half-century. True, there were sketchy periods in the Dark Ages and the Middle Ages, but the means of instant communication that could have identified egregious problems quickly and addressed them effectively were lacking. The modern hierarchy's indifference to, or positive encouragement of, the liturgical abuse of which St. Paul speaks—symbolic dissonance, irreverence, profanation, idolatry, sexual immorality, inversion of charity and charisms, and usurpation of ministries—makes the evil qualitatively different.

In addition, therefore, to its value for individual Christians who wish to assess their beliefs and behavior, the First Epistle to the Corinthians constitutes a guide to the universal principles of true liturgy and therefore of correct reform, and, accordingly, functions as a liturgical "examination of conscience." Thanks be to God, and surely thanks to the intercession of the great martyrs of Rome, Peter and Paul, the traditional Roman Rite—the ultimate standard in the Latin Church for the worthy worship of Almighty God—remains alive today and keeps alive our glorious apostolic heritage.

5

The Angelic Doctor and the Glory
of Eucharistic Theology

Saint Thomas Aquinas (1225–1274) has sometimes been portrayed as a hidebound medieval scholastic trapped in a rationalistic methodology, whose works lack a spirituality that resonates in the hearts of modern people. As a lifelong student and teacher of Aquinas's works, I have two reactions: first, this stance betrays a poor understanding of the enterprise of theology itself; and second, it is simply not true on the ground, if I may judge from countless experiences over the past twenty-five years with students from many countries, whom I have had the privilege to see coming alive in the joy of intellectual discovery and in a growing love for the Catholic Faith, as they go more and more deeply into the wisdom found in Aquinas's works.

With St. Thomas, we learn that the essential purpose of investigating a divinely revealed truth that is inaccessible to natural reason is to raise our minds to a more intense appreciation of the very *mysteriousness* of the mystery. In other words, we are helped to see it in all its "dark luminosity," a *mysterium tremendum et fascinans*, opaque to our intellects but full of wonder and fascination. We see the mystery *as* mystery only when we apply our reason to the fullest extent; we see the marvelousness of the supernatural, the super-rational in its very beyondness. This is true of the Blessed Trinity above all, and of the Incarnation, and therefore of the Eucharist, which is a kind of replication or representation of the

The Holy Bread of Eternal Life

Incarnation and the primary means by which the life of the Trinity, the life of grace in the soul of Christ, is poured into the Christian soul.

A secondary purpose is to defend the Faith against the objections of unbelievers, and to defend our own faith against the kind of doubts that our fallen, sense-bound, rationalistic nature will suggest to us, if we are thoughtful people. God wants us to be thoughtful people, otherwise He would not have created us as intellectual beings; but He wants us to be thoughtfully *faithful*, rather than superficially skeptical, which is generally the alternative. The most thoughtful people are either already believers or on their way to becoming believers.

There is a danger in intellectual study of the highest truths, and that is that we will forget that their opacity is due to our feebleness of intellect, our lack of profound meditation, and our distractedness, and we might begin to attribute the lack of light to a lack of intelligibility in the *object,* the thing known, rather than in the *subject,* the one knowing. We may also find a stumbling block in the relative dryness of the intellectual approach itself, which is like dry seed that must be watered by the dew of devotion — that is, personal prayer and a sacramental life — in order to grow into healthy vegetation. The fault, again, is not in the scholastic style, which has a kind of intense purity to it, but in the carnal weakness of our mind, which is usually not equipped to sustain such exercises. It's like being in poor physical shape. A race that would exhilarate another person may leave us feeling half dead.

Study must be surrounded by prayer the way the earth is surrounded by a life-giving moist and oxygen-rich atmosphere. Without this atmosphere, the earth could not sustain life, but would be a frigid desert like Mars or a furnace like Venus.

There have been thousands of documented miracles in the history of the Church. Every beatification or canonization requires miracles, with testimony taken by preference from non-Catholic witnesses. We are inclined to think of the more dramatic miracles as most deserving of our admiration: the miracle of the dancing sun at Fatima, for example. But more wondrous than any miracle that has been or could be performed is the quiet daily miracle of transubstantiation, by which the Creator effects in a hidden way a suspension of the most fundamental metaphysical relationships in order to feed our bodies and souls. He stops at nothing to ensure that we may come into direct contact with the only Reality that can save us from our unreality.

This is why, in his final Encyclical, *Ecclesia de Eucharistia*, Pope John Paul II exhorted the Church to rekindle "Eucharistic amazement" at the Sacrament of Divine Love. We easily underestimate its value, as we tend to do with anything that is readily available and often repeated. I am reminded of a passage from G.K. Chesterton:

> A child kicks its legs rhythmically through excess, not absence, of life. Because children have abounding vitality, because they are in spirit fierce and free, therefore they want things repeated and unchanged. They always say, "Do it again"; and the grown-up person does it again until he is nearly dead. For grown-up people are not strong enough to exult in monotony. But perhaps God is strong enough.... It is possible that God says every morning, "Do it again," to the sun; and every evening, "Do it again," to the moon. It may not be automatic necessity that makes all daisies alike: it may be that God makes every daisy separately, but has never got tired of making them. It may be that He has the eternal appetite of infancy; for we have sinned and grown old, and our Father is younger than we.[35]

God is the most childlike of all, because every day, like an infant, He rejoices anew at the rising of the sun, whose being and action He causes. We should ask for the grace to rejoice anew every day at the raising of the sacred Host, which is the sun of the spiritual life, the cause of our Christian being and action—and rejoice even more at the thought that

---

[35] *Orthodoxy*, ch. 4, "The Ethics of Elfland," in *The Collected Works of G.K. Chesterton*, vol. 1, ed. David Dooley (San Francisco: Ignatius Press, 1986), 263–64.

we can consume this sun, making its light and heat our own, making ourselves belong to Him, the Sun of Righteousness.

This Eucharistic theology is what I have learned from St. Thomas and from the traditional form of liturgy that he himself would have known. I pray that he continue to intercede for all of us who embark on the fearful and wonderful adventure of *fides quaerens intellectum*, faith seeking understanding; I pray that we will imitate him in his unwavering devotion to the prayer and sacraments of the Church.

✠

The mystery of the Eucharist is so unlike anything else we experience that we struggle to find language to describe it. A venerable tradition speaks of Jesus descending to the altar at the consecration to become present among us. But even so pious a way of speaking has sometimes caused trouble. The Benedictine monk Guitmund, a classmate of St. Anselm's writing in the eleventh century, reports that the heretic Berengar of Tours took it as an occasion to attack the doctrine of the Real Presence:

> To this day St. Peter is a stumbling block to Berengar, saying of the Lord, "whom heaven must receive until the time of the restoration of all things" (Acts 3:21). If he must be received by heaven until the end, Berengar says, then he never leaves heaven such that he could be detained on earth at some time.[36]

Although Guitmund points out that Jesus reigns in heaven rather than being incarcerated there as prisoner, he doesn't conclude that Jesus in fact leaves heaven:

> But far be it from the prudence of Christians to say that Christ is sacrificed on earth, or eaten, in such a way that in the meantime

[36] Guitmund, *De corporis et sanguinis Jesu Christi veritate in Eucharistia*, PL 149:1466.

he necessarily abandons heaven. For he is entire in heaven, while his entire body is truly eaten on earth.[37]

Guitmund's instinct is surely correct: Christ does not depart from heaven to descend to the altar every time a Mass is said anywhere on earth. But how, then, are we to describe his truly coming to be among us? The honor of advancing our Eucharistic language remained for the scholastic theologians, using Aristotelian texts that came to Europe after Guitmond's time. And the pinnacle of the scholastic effort came in the theology of St. Thomas Aquinas.

St. Thomas's work was technical but ultimately fruitful for piety. He frequently made use of a distinction between a "real" relation and a "logical" relation (also known as a relation of reason). A real relation is one in which two realities stand to each other in such a way that when one changes, the other also changes. For example, if I press on an apple, the apple returns the favor by resisting my pressure; if I eat the apple, not only is the apple changed, but I, too, am changed by adding the apple to my substance. But things are different when we speak of God's relation to the world. Being absolutely unchanging and unchangeable, God is not metaphysically bound to any creature in such a way that a change in the creature causes a change in Him.

Thus St. Thomas would say God has a "logical" relation to the creature, namely, the relation of a perfect cause (altogether in actuality) to an imperfect effect (in potency to His causality). All the change that God causes is therefore located *in the creature*, not in the Creator. In fact, God is called "Creator" because of a dependency that creatures have on Him, not because He changed when He created. On the other hand, the creature, which depends entirely on God for anything it is or does, is really (i.e., in its very being) related to Him. Thus we have a lopsided relationship: the creature could not exist for a moment without God causing it to do so, whereas God depends in no way on the existence of any creature.

[37] Ibid.

The Holy Bread of Eternal Life

St. Thomas sometimes expresses the doctrine of transubstantiation in terms of the relation that the Eucharistic species[38] acquire to the body of Christ. On the one hand, something happens to the being of the bread and wine at the consecration: the species acquire some real relation to Christ's body, such that Christ is substantially present under them, although we do not know what exactly that relation is because there is nothing else like it in the created universe. On the other hand, since acquiring a real relation requires a change in the thing related, it would seem that Christ's glorified body does not acquire a real relation to the species, despite the fact that the species acquire a real relation to it. If his glorified body acquired a real relation to the Eucharistic species, we would have to say that Christ's body is somehow impinged upon and affected by all the innumerable consecrations that occur every day. The relation between Christ and the Eucharistic species is real only in one direction.

---

[38] As defined in Louis Bouyer's *Dictionary of Theology*, trans. Rev. Charles Underhill Quinn (n.p.: Desclée & Co., 1965), s.v. 'species': "In theology this word (in the Latin sense of appearances) designates the *accidents* of the elements consecrated in the Eucharist, which subsist absolutely unchanged for the senses after the consecration and the transubstantiation that results from it. These species do not correspond to a proper substance, but since they are no longer anything but the sign and presence of the body and blood, the reverence given to them is given directly to Christ himself. Since the sacramental presence is bound up with them, it ceases with their adulteration. On the other hand, since the eucharistic species are not the accidents proper to the substance of the body and blood of the Savior, nothing that affects them affects Him. See St. Thomas Aquinas, *Sum. Theol.*, IIIa, q. 75–77" (p. 427). The last point means that, e.g., if the host is moved, broken, or digested, Christ's glorified Body itself in heaven is not moved, broken, or digested. Yet because of the Real Presence, how we act toward or around or with the host *is* how we act toward, around, or with Christ; for if it is true that "as you did it to one of the least of these my brethren, you did it to me" (Matt. 25:40), *a fortiori* it is true that what we do to the Eucharistic species, we do to Christ. Thus, if we ignore the Eucharist where it is present, treat it disrespectfully, approach it with unrepented sin, we are ignoring *Christ*, treating *Him* disrespectfully, insulting *Him*.

Nevertheless, as St. Thomas shows in the case of the word *Creator*, to say that a relation is real only in one direction does not make the relation in any way "fake" or unimportant. The "logical" relation between the glorified Body of Christ in heaven and the sacramental species parallels exactly the logical relation of God vis-à-vis creation and re-creation or the justification of sinners, as well as the relation between the divine and human natures in Christ. God is in no way changed when He creates, and yet nothing could be more real or important than our dependence on Him as creatures. At the moment of the Incarnation, it is not the Eternal Word who acquires something new but a human nature that changes, being assumed to the Person of the Son to subsist in Him; and yet nothing could be more real or important than the fact that the man Jesus Christ truly is the Son of God. The point can be illustrated at a lower level by a physical analogy: the sun does not become less bright or warm when another flower comes under its light, and yet the flower's entire dependence on the sun is the chief fact of its life. In a parallel way, the glorified body of Christ is not moved or changed at the consecration, and yet the species of bread and wine are really and truly changed such that when we come into contact with the species of bread or wine, we come into contact with the body of God.

Now if our speculation is right on this matter, it seems less true to speak of Christ descending to the altar than to speak of us — via the species — ascending to the heavenly temple. The metaphysical movement is upward. This should be taken not as a disparagement of the age-old way of speaking about Christ coming into our midst, but rather, as an emphasis on another part of the tradition, which sees the Mass as a joining-in with the perpetual heavenly Mass, from the Sanctus when we lift up our hearts and sing with the angels, to the mysterious *Supplices te rogamus* ("We humbly beseech Thee, almighty God, bid these offerings be carried by the hands of Thy holy angel to Thine altar on high in the sight of Thy divine majesty..."), to the *Ecce Agnus Dei* when we are invited to partake of the Lamb who reigns in the City of God, our faint participation in what the angels enjoy in heaven. The sacramental species become, so to speak, a miraculous portal that pulls us upward and inward—a small rent in the veil, through which we can peer into glory.

Both St. Thomas and the Roman Canon itself seem to bear out the claim that the Eucharist is more our being brought to God than God being brought to us. Fr. Jean-Pierre Torrell notes that the Office St. Thomas authored for the newly instituted feast of Corpus Christi conspicuously lacks the vocabulary of *praesentia corporalis*, which is strong in Bonaventure, Peter of Tarentaise, and the Bull *Transiturus* of Pope Urban IV. Rather, he speaks of "the ineffable mode of the divine presence in the visible sacrament" (Matins).

To go a step further, let us consider the arc of Thomas's own thinking on the matter. Fr. Jean-Pierre Torrell remarks:

In the earlier phase of his thought, Thomas preferred to avoid speaking about a "corporal" presence of Christ in the sacrament, for it appeared to him linked with a "localization," while the presence *in loco* pertained only to the accidents. It is only in the Tertia Pars, several years later, that he will accept speaking of corporal presence, but, as we will see later, in an entirely different sense.[39]

Some pages later, Torrell addresses this "different sense." In the Office of Corpus Christi, St. Thomas

centered the celebration on the mystery of Christ, God and perfect man, entirely contained in the sacrament, to such a point that he does not say: receive the body or the blood of Christ, but indeed: receive Christ (*Christus sumitur*, or even: *Deus sumitur*). The notion of presence also begins to be refined, and we intuit what will

[39] Jean-Pierre Torrell, O.P., *Saint Thomas Aquinas*, vol. I: *The Person and His Work*, trans. Robert Royal (Washington, DC: Catholic University of America Press, 1996), 131. Torrell refers us to *In IV Sent.*, dist. 10, art. 1, ad 4, and *Resp. de 36 art.*, prop. 33: "corpus Christi non est in sacramento ut in loco" (the body of Christ is not in this sacrament as in a place—i.e., as a body is situated in the place that belongs to it).

become the definitive formulation in the *Summa:* Christ does not become present to us (a "localizing" conception that Thomas continued to discard), it is we whom He renders present to Himself.[40]

Then Torrell cites the corpus of *Summa theologiae* III, q. 75, a. 1, where St. Thomas gives as the second reason for Christ's true presence in the sacrament:

> This befits the charity of Christ, out of which he assumed, for our salvation, a true body of our nature. And since what belongs to friendship most of all is dwelling together in a common life, as the Philosopher says (*Ethics* IX), He promises us His bodily presence as our reward (Matthew 24: "Where the body shall be, there the eagles will be gathered"). Yet meanwhile he has not left us destitute of His bodily presence in this pilgrimage, but by the truth of His body and blood He has joined us to Himself in this sacrament. Hence He says in John 6: "Whosoever eats my flesh and drinks my blood abides in me and I in him." Hence this sacrament is the sign of the very greatest charity and a support of our hope, from such an intimate association of Christ with us.

On this magnificent passage, Torrell comments:

> This evocation of hope in connection with the Eucharist does not occur by chance: full of the memory of the Passion, the celebration is entirely turned toward the eschatological achievement, since it is the pledge, the *pignus*, of future glory. According to Father Gy, who is quite convincing, this displacement of Thomas's eucharistic theology toward eschatology ... is entirely in line with his theological and spiritual personality, so deeply marked by a straining toward the vision of God.[41]

---

[40] Ibid., 135.
[41] Ibid., 135–36. See also Marie-Joseph Nicolas, O.P., *What Is the Eucharist?*, trans. R.F. Trevett (New York: Hawthorn Books, 1960), 53–55.

The Holy Bread of Eternal Life

The Eucharist is closely connected with the vision of God because in it, in a mystical way, we are already brought into God's presence, brought before His throne, carried to Him, and we embrace Him in the darkness of faith, not yet seeing the Beloved, but full of confidence and trust that He will reveal Himself to us when the fullness of time has come, when the period of trial is over: "Arise, my love, my fair one, and come away; for lo, the winter is past, the rain is over and gone.... Let me see your face, let me hear your voice, for your voice is sweet, and your face is comely" (Song of Sol. 2:10–11, 14).

The Mass of the Roman Rite confirms this Thomistic teaching in the *Supplices te rogamus* of the Roman Canon, quoted in part above:

> Most humbly we implore Thee, Almighty God, bid these offerings to be brought by the hands of Thy Holy Angel to Thine altar on high, before the face of Thy Divine Majesty; that as many of us as shall receive the Most Sacred Body and Blood of Thy Son by partaking thereof from this altar, may be filled with every heavenly blessing and grace. Through the same Christ our Lord. Amen.

This prayer, so beautiful and rich, seems to be woven of paradoxes. It asks God to command that the offerings (which are already divine) be brought by the hands of an Angel to the altar in heaven — the throne where the Lamb reigns, as in the Apocalypse — so that those who receive the Lord's Body and Blood from this earthly altar will be filled with the blessings of that heavenly altar.[42] Those who participate in the earthly offering, as represented by the species, will participate in the heavenly offering of the *ipse Christus passus* — Christ Himself, as having suffered for our sakes — to the Most Holy Trinity. By participating in the Eucharist, the

---

[42] On this prayer as a whole, and more specifically on who, or what, the "Angel" is or represents, see Josef Jungmann, S.J., *The Mass of the Roman Rite: Its Origins and Development (Missarum Sollemnia)*, trans. Francis A. Brunner, C.S.S.R. (Notre Dame, IN: Christian Classics, 2012), 2:231–37; Nicholas Gihr, *The Holy Sacrifice of the Mass, Dogmatically, Liturgically, and Ascetically Explained* (St. Louis/London: B. Herder, 1949), 696–703.

communicant is, like the Victim Himself, brought up to heaven, to the face of the Divine Majesty, by the Angel. Communion is to be re-located at the throne of the Lamb; it is divinization. This is why the sacrament is *pignus futurae gloriae*, the pledge or earnest of future glory, for that glory is nothing other than to be divinized by the face-to-face vision of God.

✠

I once had an amicable disagreement with a priest, who claimed that people who think there is a definite moment of consecration, when the substance of bread ceases to exist and Christ comes to be really present, have gotten caught up in trivial details and are missing the point—which, according to him, could be summarized: "the Eucharist is about *our* transformation." He expressed a concern that any claim about a "moment" of consecration subjects mystery to rational dissection and that it's more honest to say "we don't know." I sent him a letter with the following response.

Dear Father,

I'm glad you felt comfortable sharing your views with me. It's my turn to share with you the reasons why I disagree with them.

People are concerned to know about the moment of consecration for quite legitimate reasons, and certainly not because they have no sense of mystery. After all, some of the most poignant expressions of the conviction that consecration occurs through the "words of institution" are to be found in St. John Chrysostom, St. Cyril of Jerusalem, and St. Ambrose, none of whom could even remotely be considered rationalistic. On the contrary, they, with St. Thomas Aquinas, were well-known mystics of the Holy Eucharist.

They were also practical and pastoral men. They knew that the Lord truly present in His Body and Blood deserves our inward and outward adoration (*latria*). Therefore they quite reasonably wondered when they should *show* such adoration to the gifts on the altar. To do so towards ordinary bread would be idolatry. But to *fail* to do so when the Lord is truly present would be irreverence. As parents know, little children will ask questions like: "Daddy, when does Jesus come to the altar?" "Mommy, why is the priest kneeling now?" "Is the host Jesus yet?" Such humble, unpretentious questions are not at all displeasing to Our Lord; they are "faith seeking understanding." I believe that Jesus is more pleased by a child's naïve realism than by sophisticated postconciliar theories that leave us devotionally dry.

In his final Encyclical *Ecclesia de Eucharistia*, John Paul II called St. Thomas Aquinas "the supreme theologian and impassioned singer of the eucharistic Christ."[43] We know the beauty of Aquinas's Corpus Christi hymns and prayers. In his case, it was the very depth of his faith and the intensity of his desire to surrender himself to the mystery with all the force of his powerful intellect that propelled him to formulate such a "scholastic" question as "When does consecration take place? When is it completed or perfected?" And his answer is as serene as it is inherently plausible: when the priest finishes saying the entire formula "This is my body" or "This is my blood." The reason is that only the entire statement has the meaning that sufficiently signifies what is taking place by divine power. "This is my..." without completion, or merely the words "my body," would not signify that, but "This is my body" does.[44] By Christ's institution, these words have power to bring about what they mean to say (or, in the older language, they effect what they signify).

As an aside, it is clear that if a priest were to die after consecrating the bread alone, the Body of Jesus—and concomitantly His Blood, Soul, and Divinity—would be fully present, but the representation of the sacrifice would be imperfect and therefore another priest would have to be called in to consecrate the wine. After all, as Pius XII teaches in *Mediator Dei*,

---

[43] The phrase appears right at the end, in §62. I have supplied a literal translation of the Latin: *summus theologus simulque Christi eucharistici fervidus cantor.* The official English version translates this loosely as "an eminent theologian and an impassioned poet of Christ in the Eucharist."

[44] See St. Thomas, *Summa theologiae* III, qu. 75, art. 7, ad 1 and ad 3.

the fundamental reason for the separate consecrations is to re-present, in a sacramental fashion, the bloody immolation of the Victim on Calvary.[45]

You were concerned that my interest in "explaining" the Anaphora of Addai and Mari in terms of Thomistic sacramental theology might have been motivated by a reductionism or rationalism that sees itself as capable of "proving" what is and will always remain mysterious. This was never my intention! Rather, I sought to interpret an unusual anaphora in light of a familiar theological account that is reasonable and hallowed by tradition. My conclusion was that this familiar account did not have to be abandoned, because it has a more profound meaning than most people realize.[46]

I do not believe that speaking of a "moment of consecration" in any way lessens the mysteriousness of the event; on the contrary, for me at least, it heightens that mysteriousness by dramatically underlining the infinite divine power required to accomplish such a miraculous change, and the quasi-infinite faith it takes to accept it as fact. For me, the Mass has the shape of a mountain in which we climb to the summit and join our Savior on the Cross, to share His life; then we climb down, as it were, to our everyday life in the valley, carrying something of that immense love to everyone we meet. In that sense, the special sacramental presence of Jesus at the heart of the Eucharistic liturgy gives shape and order to the whole. He is *not* present in just that way on the credence table or on the altar during the Sanctus; He *becomes* present, and in a definite, priestly, liturgical, ecclesial way, when the gifts are transformed. To me, this speaks volumes about the drama of the divine; there is a narrative, a movement, a climax, and we are then allowed to share in that victorious redemption. God seems to like to paint in bright colors and bold strokes, rather than in muddled grays and browns.

---

[45] See Encyclical Letter *Mediator Dei* (November 20, 1947), §70; §92; §115.

[46] Peter Kwasniewski, "Doing and Speaking in the Person of Christ: Eucharistic Form in the Anaphora of Addai and Mari," *Nova et Vetera* 4 (2006): 313–79. The anaphora (or Eucharistic prayer) of Addai and Mari—at least as it has come down to us—lacks of the words of institution, familiarly known in the West as the "words of consecration."

The Holy Bread of Eternal Life

I hope you will not mind a final comment about the example you used, namely, of Communion in the hand. You say it makes little difference whether the Host touches my hands first or my tongue, because the hands and tongue of a sinner are sinful, while a man with a pure heart has pure hands. But as you well know, there is a phenomenological question here, too: what if kneeling to receive the Host on the tongue were, for most people, more conducive to devotion and helped to accentuate the seriousness of what they are doing, and what if standing in line to receive on the hand encouraged a more casual, relaxed, and unreflective attitude? Would this not be spiritually and pastorally relevant? Moreover, what if a certain posture had centuries of practice and symbolism behind it, while another was self-consciously new and lacked that benefit? Only a rationalist could ignore such immense aspects of the question.

I believe that St. Thomas, like his patristic predecessors, was not preoccupied with "pinpointing" a miracle, but rather with submitting mind and heart to the mighty mystery that descends, like the flames of Pentecost, upon the altar of sacrifice. Their concern was the concern of the lover who wishes to be maximally attentive to the beloved, the mother who wants to be right there when her baby walks for the first time, the poet who does not wish to miss the sunrise or the sunset. I don't see it as trivial at all; it shows a sensitivity to what is at stake in the act of adoration. I know that when Jesus comes, I want to be awake and ready to meet him. This is as true for his sacramental advent as for his Second Coming.

I appreciate your taking the time to consider these ideas. I hope the foregoing clarifies what moves me to follow in the footsteps of St. Thomas in regard to Eucharistic consecration.

✠

For St. Thomas Aquinas, the Lord of glory present under the consecrated species of bread and wine is the Christ-who-suffered, *Christus passus*. In the *Commentary on John*, he writes:

Since this sacrament is of the Lord's Passion, it contains within itself Christ who suffered. Hence whatever is an effect of the Lord's Passion is wholly contained in this sacrament, for it is nothing else than the application of the Lord's Passion to us.... Hence it is clear that the destruction of death, which Christ accomplished by His death, and the restoration of life, which He accomplished by His resurrection, are effects of this sacrament.[47]

This is significant for many reasons. One reason that might be overlooked is psychological. In being made to confront symbols of the death we in-flicted on Christ — the crucifix, perhaps marked with the crimson channels of blood; the sculpted corpus with five open wounds; the Host lying on the grave cloth of the corporal; the chalice filled with the "blood of the grape" — we are brought face to face with the reality of our own malice, our moral weariness, our failure to solve the problems of human existence.

Christianity does not automatically rid people of sin and every stain of sin; sincere Christians are not necessarily better than their unbelieving neighbors, and they can at times be worse.[48] But, if they are truly practicing

---

[47] *Super Ioannem*, cap. 6, lect. 6.

[48] All the same, the truth and effectiveness of the Christian faith must, in fairness, be judged not by its lukewarm half-practitioners or its apostates (should one blame a medicine that was never taken for a sickness that was not thereby ameliorated?), but by its vast company of saints who have washed their robes white in the Blood of the Lamb. Moreover, it is all too easy to take for granted how Christianized our assumptions, mores, and institutions have become due to centuries of ecclesial presence. What is routinely attributed to secular reason, to an ethic of fairness or a noble humanism, is often enough the last sputter of Gospel influence. The popes of modern times, from Leo XIII onward, have warned that if the Gospel is not welcomed as the animating principle of individuals and societies, the West will degenerate ever more rapidly into a kind of high-tech barbarism at the service of pride, greed, and lust, contemptuous of human dignity and rights. The papal prognosis has been correct, above all for the Western Europe of today — spiritually bankrupt, culturally exhausted, demographically dried up.

their faith, they are *aware* of two things: how wicked they are in turning away from the Lord, "every one to his own way" (Isa. 53:6); how blessed they are in being His creatures, sprinkled in the Blood of the immolated Lamb. They seek forgiveness and healing, ultimately resurrection, from the very One they have killed, who has already died *for them* and only awaits their turning around to Him; one might say, they merely need to "turn themselves in." It is this prevenient offering of the sinless for the sinner and, as its counterpart, the surrendering of guilty assailant to holy Victim, that the Cross symbolizes and the Mass makes present in a mirror and in an enigma.[49]

Sor Juana Inés de la Cruz (1648–1695) in her breathtaking play *El Divino Narciso* writes:

> See, at the crystal rim
> of the clear, bright fountain
> the beautiful white flower
> of which the lover said:
> This is My Body and My Blood,
> which I sacrificed for you
> through many martyrdoms.
> Do this in remembrance of my death.

St. Thomas is ever at pains to link the Eucharist with Christ's Passion, His presence, and His charity. The cumulative message is this: the love of God is made manifest and communicated in the broken Body of Jesus, who gave His life on the Cross in order to give it ever anew in the sacrament of His love. For all ages, this sacrament—whether dimly and imperfectly anticipated in pre-Christian cults or realized completely in the Mass—is the pulsing heart of the world, the center of gravity toward which everybody is attracted.[50] J.R.R. Tolkien wrote to his son Michael in March of 1941:

---

[49] See *Summa theologiae* III, qu. 83, art. 1.

[50] See Charles Journet, *Theology of the Church*, trans. Victor Szczurek, O.Praem. (San Francisco: Ignatius Press, 2004), 181–84.

Out of the darkness of my life, so much frustrated, I put before you the one great thing to love on earth: the Blessed Sacrament.... There you will find romance, glory, honour, fidelity, and the true way of all your loves upon earth, and more than that: Death: by the divine paradox, that which ends life, and demands the sur-render of all, and yet by the taste (or foretaste) of which alone can what you seek in your earthly relationships (love, faithfulness, joy) be maintained, or take on that complexion of reality, of eternal endurance, which every man's heart desires.[51]

Borrowing the Apostle's words, St. Thomas describes the highest of the three degrees of charity as a "longing to be dissolved and to be with Christ."[52] What the Lord seeks is the total gift of oneself. If noth-ing less will do for human lovers in their frenzied possessiveness, will Christ settle for a lukewarm exchange of goods and services? "I came to cast fire on the earth; and would that it were already kindled!" (Luke 12:49); "I have ardently longed to eat this Passover with you before I suffer" (Luke 22:15, NJB). Unlike earthly spouses, Christ is able to ef-fect a union of pure, total, permanent possession, in no way limited in its fullness, going to the abyss of one's being, there where "the depths of God" (1 Cor. 2:10) are darkly known and sweetly loved, are touched and savored.

No wonder we are bewildered. We are torn apart by a love that defies our logic, that multiplies our longings and frustrates our desires, which are always too few and too small. God would have it this way, for unless He rends us and remakes us, we cannot enter into His rest, be one with Him, be the temple of His glory, bear Him in our bodies, become His sons in our souls. This is the merciful cruelty of God, the blessed wounding spoken of by the mystics, and like its exemplar, the wise folly of the Cross, it belongs to the heart of the Christian experience. In essence, to be a mystic is to

---

[51] *The Letters of J.R.R. Tolkien*, ed. Humphrey Carpenter with Christopher Tolkien (Boston: Houghton Mifflin Company, 1981), 53–54.

[52] *Summa theologiae* II-II, qu. 24, art. 9.

believe in the mystery Paul announces in Galatians 2:20—"I live, now not I, but Christ lives in me"—and to strive to live this holy communion day after day with the help of God's grace.[53] This "desire to be dissolved and to be with Christ" (Phil. 1:23, DR) is why Aquinas wept so often when celebrating Mass, and why he is a master and model for all of us.[54]

In his person no less than in his pages, the Angelic Doctor brings into sharp relief the primacy of contemplation, receptivity, timeless truth, over activism, performance, timely relevance. He demonstrates that no activity is more perfect than waiting on God, listening to Him, seeking His face; that no doing of mine is better than dying to my will, clinging to the Cross; that nothing can be more pertinent to man here and now, nothing more liberating for the world, than yielding in silent faith to the hidden God, the righteous God, who "came by water and blood, Jesus Christ: not by water only, but by water and blood" (1 John 5:6, DR).

To the cynical children of Adam, all this is completely counter-intuitive, if not downright absurd. And yet, for all that, it is right; it *has* to look that way to fallen man (see 1 Cor. 1:18–31), for his eye is bleary, his ear blocked, his desire narrow. "He who would search into the mysteries of Christ must go out, in a way, from himself and from fleshly ways," states Thomas soberly.[55] Jesus knew what was in the heart of man, and He came not only preaching, but healing infirmities; not only healing bodies, but divinizing souls. It was to make us His intimates that He instituted the sacraments of the new law, chief among them the sacrament of His own flesh-and-blood love, the feast of the New Covenant that is simply—and incomprehensibly—the gift of Himself.

---

[53] See Louis Bouyer's beautiful work *The Christian Mystery: From Pagan Myth to Christian Mysticism*, trans. Illtyd Trethowan, O.S.B. (Edinburgh: T&T Clark, 1990; repr. St. Bede's Press, 2002).

[54] See Martin Grabmann, *The Interior Life of Thomas Aquinas*, trans. Nicholas Ashenbrener, O.P. (Milwaukee: Bruce, 1951).

[55] *Super Ioannem*, cap. 20, lect. 1.

✠

I don't know what it is about November, but it always makes me think more about food. It could be that the weather is getting noticeably colder (at least in the northern hemisphere) and one seems to need more sustenance, not to mention hot beverages. It could be St. Martin's day, which brings to mind the roast goose my family ate on November 11 in Austria during the years we spent there. It could, naturally, be the anticipated aroma of Thanksgiving dinner. Whatever the cause, I have tried to turn the inner rumblings to advantage by asking myself what God intended to teach us when He made us the sort of beings who have mouths and stomachs, who need to keep taking in substance from the outside in order to live, and who in this way are both dependent on the cosmos and superior to it, because we can transform some small portion of it into ourselves.

St. Thomas Aquinas, a reliable and profound guide to the seven sacraments of the Church, tells us that we can learn about the effects of each sacrament by looking to the typical effects of the material things and actions it makes use of. For example, water washes off dirt from the skin and refreshes when ingested; thus, in baptism guilt and sin are washed away and the soul is refreshed with the grace of adoption.

In the case of the Eucharist, the matter employed (by Christ's institution) is wheaten bread and wine made from grapes, which are food and drink for man — the most basic food, one might say, and the best beverage nature and human art produce for our enjoyment. Thus, the proper effect of the Eucharist can be discerned from the effects of the consumption of food and drink in the one who receives them: the restoration of lost bodily matter and, should there be surplus, an increase of bodily substance, together with a gladdening of heart. To these physical effects, St. Thomas likens the sacramental effects of an increase in "spiritual quantity" (where "quantity" means the extent of active power) by the strengthening of the virtues, a restoration of wholeness through the forgiveness of venial sin or the repairing of defects, and elation of mind.

But if we left off our account there, we would miss the most important point.

Following St. Augustine, St. Thomas says there is a crucial difference between the *bodily* food of any ordinary human meal and the *spiritual* food of Holy Communion. Bodily food achieves its effect, to restore lost flesh and increase its quantity, by being converted or turned into the one fed. Spiritual food, on the contrary — or to be more precise, Our Lord Himself, who is really, truly, substantially present in the Most Holy Eucharist — is *not* converted into the one eating; the one eating is rather converted into (i.e., turned ever more toward and likened unto) Christ, for He acts upon the communicant to turn him into Himself.

The notion of being changed into the food we eat might seem very odd, since that would be exactly the contrary of what happens with all other food and drink. Were the food in question *mere* food, it would be impossible to speak this way, as Jesus recognizes when he says: "the flesh profiteth nothing" (John 6:64, DR) — that is, as the Church Fathers interpret the saying, *mere* flesh is lifeless, in that it cannot bring the life of holiness to the spirit. But if the food is the flesh of the living Son of God, a believer's contact with it leads to life, renewal, deification, provided he is in a state to profit from it.[56]

This truth is central to the theology of St. Cyril of Alexandria (378–444),[57] the first patristic authority St. Thomas cites in the important question in the *Summa theologiae* on the effects of the Eucharist:

> The life-giving Word of God, uniting himself to his own flesh, made it life-giving. It was becoming, therefore, that he be in a certain way united to *our* bodies through his sacred flesh and precious

---

[56] See chapter 13.

[57] See Emile Mersch, S.J., *The Whole Christ: The Historical Development of the Doctrine of the Mystical Body in Scripture and Tradition*, trans. John R. Kelly, S.J. (Milwaukee: Bruce, 1938; repr. n.p.: Ex Fontibus, 2018), 337–58.

blood, which we receive in a life-giving blessing in bread and wine.[58]

As Fr. Emile Mersch explains:

> Union with food is effected in a mysterious exchange of life, in an assimilation by which one becomes the other. But in the Eucharist, the more vital of the two is the bread we receive, the "bread of life." This bread consumes and changes into itself the one who eats it.[59]

This it can do because it is none other than the Lord in person, under the appearances of bread and wine. United to Jesus through faith and love, the communicant "is transformed into Him and becomes His member," says Thomas, "for this food is not changed into the one who eats it, but turns into itself the one who takes it.... This is a food capable of making man divine and inebriating him with divinity."[60] In the *Sentences*, Thomas simply says: "The proper effect of this sacrament is the conversion of man into Christ, that it might be said with the Apostle, 'I live, now not I, but Christ lives in me.'"[61]

In addition to St. Augustine and St. Cyril, St. Thomas, devoted to the Church Fathers as he is, cites the potent words of St. John Damascene (676–749): "The fire of that desire which is in us, taking ignition from the burning coal (that is, from this sacrament), will burn up our sins and illuminate our hearts, so that by partaking of the divine fire we may be set on fire and deified."[62] When we receive the Eucharist in a state of grace, we are feasting upon this fire of love, letting it permeate and burn into all the powers and passivities of soul and body.

---

[58] *On Luke* 22:19 (PG 72:92), cited in *Summa theologiae* III, qu. 79, art. 1.

[59] Emile Mersch, S.J., *The Theology of the Mystical Body*, trans. Cyril Vollert, S.J. (St. Louis/London: B. Herder, 1951), 590–91.

[60] *Super Ioannem*, cap. 6, lect. 7, §969.

[61] *In IV Sent.*, dist. 12, qu. 2, art. 1, qa. 1.

[62] *On the Orthodox Faith*, IV.13 (PG 94:1149), cited in *Summa theologiae* III, qu. 79, art. 8, sed contra.

The Holy Bread of Eternal Life

St. Thomas gave himself body and soul to the Holy Mysteries because in them he found his beloved Lord, and through them feasted upon His love. He was convinced that of all the good things Jesus wants for us, the foremost is an intimate friendship with each person who believes in Him.[63]

All of this takes place in the dark, the darkness of faith. As Charles De Koninck writes:

> It is, then, by a truly unparalleled mercy that God has deigned to meet us in perfect night and that, in order to elevate us to his own heights, he has satisfied for all our insufficiencies, and has asked of us, in our act of faith, an abnegation analogous to that of his Son.... Is it not a mercy admirable above all that, abandoned by all, we can go nowhere else except to Him, in surrender to this mystery of Faith where hides, in a perfectly adapted silence, the one whose name is Word?[64]

This Word-made-flesh, who delivered Himself to death for me, now plants within me the seed of His glorified humanity and invincible divinity. If we have this gift, what can we be said to lack? Truly, in "the divine, holy, most pure, immortal, heavenly, life-creating, and awesome mysteries of Christ" (Liturgy of St. John Chrysostom), all has been prepared, provided, delivered. Alleluia.

✠

In a biographical sketch of St. Thomas, Fr. Simon Tugwell notes the following:

> Thomas' deep devotion to the Mass emerges clearly from all our sources. Sometimes he evidently became deeply absorbed in it and was profoundly moved by it. Toward the end of his life he

---

[63] See the passage quoted above (p. 51) from *Summa theologiae* III, qu. 75, art. 1; cf. John 15:13–15.

[64] Charles De Koninck, "This Is a Hard Saying," trans. Ronald P. McArthur, *The Aquinas Review* 1 (1994): 105–11; 111.

sometimes became so absorbed that he just stopped and had to be roused by the brethren to continue with the celebration.[65]

The contemporaries of this often silent Dominican friar testified far more often about his tears at Mass, his vigilant prayer, and his virginal purity than about his disputations and publications. As one of his early biographers, William of Tocco, writes:

> He was especially devoted to the most holy Sacrament of the Altar; since it had been granted him to write so profoundly of this, he was likewise given grace to celebrate it all the more devoutly.... During Mass he often would be seized by such strong feelings of devotion that he dissolved in tears, because he was absorbed in the holy mysteries of the great sacrament and invigorated by its offering.[66]

The narrative related by Tugwell gains all the more plausibility when we consider the well-documented lives of more recent saints—Philip Neri, Ignatius of Loyola, Padre Pio—for whom the action of offering the Mass was such an overwhelming experience that a server or assistant had to nudge them back on track, otherwise the Mass would never end.

Throughout his life, which ended on March 7, 1274, before he was fifty years of age, St. Thomas was given to taste by experience the mysteries of God, of Christ and the Church, that he pondered and wrote about with such astonishing energy and penetration. Contrary to the popular picture of Aquinas as an abstract professor, the actual hagiographical accounts left by people who knew him or could report stories from those who knew him tell us about a man who always made time to help others with their questions, who always put himself at the disposal of the Church and of his own Order of Preachers, who dealt swiftly and capably with family

---

[65] Simon Tugwell, O.P., in *Albert and Thomas: Selected Writings* (Mahwah, NJ: Paulist, 1988), 264.

[66] See *Thomæ Aquinatis vitæ fontes præcipue*, ed. Angelico Ferrua, O.P. (Alba: Edizioni Domenicane, 1968), n. 30, p. 73.

difficulties. Even his university teaching constantly involved an *extasis caritatis*, a going out of himself in charity, as he unstintingly handed over to others the fruits of his own contemplation, and as he composed apologetic and pedagogical works with a vigorous competence seldom seen in the human race. We know for a fact that he would compose multiple works at once, dictating to several secretaries in sequence. His was a soul on fire, never resting so long as the Word was to be pondered, preached, taught.

St. Thomas is temperamentally scientific but his doctrine and life are purely mystical.[67] It is fitting to recall a curious "contradiction" that has drawn the attention of all of his biographers. There is perhaps no theologian as famed for sobriety and dispassionate reasoning as Thomas, whom one finds throughout his life, at Paris, Orvieto, Rome, or Naples, busy lecturing, disputing, preaching, dictating. At the height of his work on the *Summa theologiae*, in the midst of a swirl of events in the Church and in the world, he is calmly commenting line by line on the Philosopher's *De generatione et corruptione*, a treatise on different kinds of natural change, primarily changes in substance. Yet in response to the anxious questioning of Countess Theodora near the end of her brother's life, his secretary Reginald could only say: "The Master is often borne away in spirit when absorbed in contemplation, but never have I seen him estranged from his senses for as long as today."[68]

----

[67] It is necessary to recover an authentic and profound understanding of "mysticism" and "mystical theology," in view of their distortion by conventional "spiritual theology" and, more recently, their dismantling by arrogant reductionisms (psychoanalysis, cultural history, feminism, etc.). For two brilliant contributions toward this recovery, see the aforementioned Louis Bouyer's *The Christian Mystery: From Pagan Myth to Christian Mysticism* and Denys Turner's *The Darkness of God: Negativity in Christian Mysticism* (Cambridge: Cambridge University Press, 1998).

[68] "Frequenter Magister in spiritu rapitur, cum aliqua contemplatur, sed nunquam tanto tempore sicut nunc uidi ipsum sic a sensibus alienatum" (*Ystoria sancti Thome de Aquino de Guillaume de Tocco* §47, quoted in Torrell, *Thomas Aquinas*, 289). The legendary *abstractio mentis* of Thomas is not

In spite of how busy he must have been to have written such mighty works in so short a time, we find him described as *miro modo contemplativus*, "wondrously contemplative." Nor did this make him an ivory-tower intellectual, cut off from his neighbors, for he readily helped hierarchs of the Church, brother Dominicans, blood relatives, and other laypeople, and vigorously engaged the pressing issues of his day.[69] The "Dumb Ox" took an interest in the biology of animals, because they are God's gifts to mankind, to aid his life and enrich his wonder; the Angelic Doctor mounted upward like the Seraphim, who are "named from the burning of charity" (*nominata ab incendio caritatis*) — such gifts only intensifying his desire for their Giver.[70] In the character of Thomas, the world-embracing wonder of Aristotle and the mystical eros of Pseudo-Dionysius are not opposed; they are contained in each other.

Pondering these well-known facts of the life and work of the Angelic Doctor, Etienne Gilson rightly concludes:

> If we want to recapture the true meaning of Thomism we have to go beyond the tightly-woven fabric of its philosophical doctrines into its soul or spirit. What lies back of the ideas is a deep religious life, the interior warmth of a soul in search of God…. The burning desire of God which in a John of the Cross overflows into lyric poems is here transcribed into the language of pure ideas. Their

---

the mark of an absent-minded academic; it is the mark of one whom his contemporaries referred to as "*homo magnæ contemplationis et orationis*," a man of great contemplation and prayer (*Processus canonizationis S. Thomæ*, Neapoli §40, in *Fontes* fasc. 4, p. 317, quoted in Torrell, *Thomas Aquinas*, 284, n. 81; see 283–95).

[69] See Torrell, *Thomas Aquinas*, 141; Josef Pieper's biography (*Guide to Thomas Aquinas*) is good on this point, as is Thomas Gilby, O.P. (see *Blackfriars Summa*, vol. I, Appendix 4). In "St. Thomas Aquinas and the Profession of Arms" (*Mediæval Studies* 50 [1988]: 404–47), Edward Synan discusses Thomas's views on social and military issues of his day.

[70] On the material creation as a gift of divine *amor amicitiae*, see *Summa theologiae* I, qu. 20, art. 2, ad 3; the phrase regarding the Seraphim is from *In II Sent.*, dist. 6, qu. 1, art. 5, notitiæ.

impersonal formulation must not make us forget that they are nourished on the desire for God and that their end is the satisfaction of this desire.... Only a complete giving of himself can explain his mastery of expression and organization of philosophic ideas. Thus his *Summa Theologiae* with its abstract clarity, its impersonal transparency, crystallizes before our very eyes and for all eternity his interior life.... Only that will to understand [reality], shared between ourselves and St. Thomas the philosopher, will serve to make us see that this tremendous work is but the outward glow of an invisible fire, and that there is to be found behind the order of its ideas that powerful impulse which gathered them together.[71]

It is as if Gilson were saying: there is no "secret life" of Thomas beneath the writings, no esoteric mysticism cordoned off from the public products of reasoning. His total dedication to the truth of creation and of revelation, in which he submerged his ego into nothingness and aspired to maximal lucidity and cogency, shows a soul ravished out of itself into God.

Thomas's submission, at the end of his life, of all of his teachings on the sacraments to the authority of the Roman Church is the act of a teacher *par excellence*: in humble deference to the heavenly Teacher, he places himself at the disposal of a Truth that is neither his handiwork nor his possession. He is and always was its servant, never its master. Thus he provides to worshipers, choirmasters, liturgists, rubricians, masters of ceremonies, clergy — indeed, to all of us — a perfect model of *disponibilité*: the capacity to give of oneself for the sake of others, and ultimately, for the sake of Him who gave Himself for us. "Christ died for all; that they also who live, may not now live to themselves, but unto him who died for them, and rose again" (2 Cor. 5:15, DR).

---

[71] Etienne Gilson, *The Christian Philosophy of Saint Thomas* [1924], trans. Laurence K. Shook, C.S.B. (Notre Dame, IN: University of Notre Dame Press, 1994), 375–76.

Part 2

Approach with Faith and Fear of God

6

On Worthily Receiving the Lord

The Council of Trent expressed with incomparable brevity and clarity the reason why we must be concerned to present ourselves "worthily" for Holy Communion:

> It is unfitting to take part in any sacred function without holiness. Assuredly, therefore, the more that Christians perceive the sacredness and divinity of this heavenly Sacrament, the more must they take every care not to come to receive It without reverence and holiness, especially since we have the frightening words of St. Paul: "For those who eat and drink unworthily, eat and drink damnation to themselves, not discerning the Lord's body" (1 Cor 11:29). Those wishing to receive Communion must be reminded of St. Paul's command: "Let a man examine himself" (1 Cor 11:28).[72]

The collective and indiscriminate reception of Holy Communion by all or nearly all Catholics who attend Mass, even by those who are not properly disposed to receive the Lord to their benefit, is a major problem straightforwardly acknowledged by the previous two popes. For example, John Paul II wrote:

> Sometimes, indeed quite frequently, everybody participating in the Eucharistic assembly goes to Communion; and on some such

---

[72] Session 13, chapter 7.

occasions, as experienced pastors confirm, there has not been due care to approach the sacrament of Penance so as to purify one's conscience.[73]

While this passage might win an award for understatement, its meaning is unambiguous. Purifying our conscience through sacramental Confession on a regular basis — certainly whenever a grave or mortal sin has been committed — is the very least we can do to ensure that we are showing proper reverence to Our Lord Jesus Christ, the Holy One of Israel, really present in the Most Blessed Sacrament as the food for our pilgrimage to heaven.

As the Church teaches, the Eucharist is not a remedy for those whose souls are *dead*, but a food for those who, being alive, need to be strengthened for the life of charity.[74] You can put food all day long into a corpse and it will never do any good. In the spiritual life, it is worse: when a spiritually dead man takes the bread of life, he becomes *more* guilty; he dies again. And the giving of such food to unrepentant public sinners (as when priests or bishops give the Lord to politicians who vote in favor of abortion) heaps burning coals upon the heads of both the recipient and the minister.[75] There's no escaping this unanimous teaching of every Father, Doctor, and pope who holds the Catholic Faith.

Pope Benedict XVI noted in an interview that it disturbed him to see crowds coming to Communion at big events at the Vatican, when it was clear that many were tourists or visitors, or otherwise indisposed (e.g., by lack of fasting). He therefore reintroduced the use of kneelers and had the Host distributed to kneeling faithful on their tongues in order to remind people that this is a sacred ritual involving the Most Holy, the *Sanctissimum*:

---

[73] Apostolic Letter *Dominicæ Cenæ* (February 24, 1980), §11.
[74] See John Paul II, *Ecclesia de Eucharistia* §§35–36, quoted below in chapter 13.
[75] See chapter 16.

There is a great danger of superficiality precisely in the kinds of mass events we hold at St. Peter's.... In this context, where people think that everyone is just automatically supposed to receive Communion — everyone else is going up, so I will, too — I wanted to send a clear signal.... This is not just some social ritual in which we can take part if we want to.[76]

Catholics need to know what it means to "take every care not to come to receive It without reverence and holiness."

Conditions for fruitful and frequent reception

The answer was given authoritatively in the 1905 decree *Sacra Tridentina Synodus* of the Sacred Congregation of the Council, which reflects the mind and will of Pope St. Pius X. This pope, in response to lingering forms of Jansenism that discouraged the faithful from approaching the altar, lowered the age for First Communions and encouraged frequent reception of the Lord. The conditions are as follows.

First, one who wishes to approach the sacred banquet must be morally certain that he is in a state of grace, not burdened by the guilt of any unconfessed mortal sin.

Second, he must have a "right and devout intention." The decree defines this as follows: "that he who approaches the Holy Table should do so, not out of routine, or vainglory, or human respect, but that he wish to please God, to be more closely united with Him by charity, and to have recourse to this divine remedy for his weakness and defects." In other words, the communicant should be conscious of what he is doing and Whom he is approaching (hence, not from routine), and that he is doing it to please the Lord and sanctify his soul through a closer union with Him, not because of what others may be thinking (hence, not from vainglory or human respect).

[76] *Light of the World: The Pope, the Church, and the Signs of the Times: A Conversation with Peter Seewald*, trans. Michael J. Miller and Adrian J. Walker (San Francisco: Ignatius Press, 2010), 156.

The Holy Bread of Eternal Life

Third, while it is fitting that he should be free of fully deliberate venial sins and any affection for them, he should at least be free from mortal sin—and in such a way that he has the intention of never sinning mortally in the future. This is a particularly important point today, in the huge mess created by Pope Francis's Post-Synodal Apostolic Exhortation *Amoris Laetitia*. As long as a Catholic intends to continue living in sin, that is, cooperating in an objectively sinful situation, such as a civil marriage with another partner while the original spouse is still alive, he or she may not receive Holy Communion.[77]

Fourth, while it is not absolutely required that a communicant have spent time in careful preparation or that he spend time afterward in thanksgiving, *both* of these—the preparation and the thanksgiving—are vital to obtaining the full benefit of reception of the Holy Eucharist. As the decree puts it: "the sacraments…produce a great effect in proportion as the dispositions of the recipient are better." Apart from the hidden intentions of God who wills to elevate some souls higher than others, it is, on *our* part, the exercise of a lively faith and the stirring up of actual devotion in approaching the altar and communing with the Lord that accounts for the difference between those whom frequent Communion transforms into saints and those who seem to be left relatively unaffected even by daily contact with the Lord.

In brief, the four conditions for frequent and fruitful reception of Holy Communion are: (1) being in a state of grace, (2) having a right and devout intention, (3) being free from attachment to sin, in the sense of intending not to sin in the future, (4) making due preparation and thanksgiving.

What will be the result if we follow the wise counsel of Holy Mother Church? The same decree puts it beautifully: "by the frequent or daily reception of the Holy Eucharist, union with Christ is strengthened, the spiritual life more abundantly sustained, the soul more richly endowed

---

[77] See *Remaining in the Truth of Christ: Marriage and Communion in the Catholic Church*, ed. Robert Dodaro (San Francisco: Ignatius Press, 2014).

with virtues, and the pledge of everlasting happiness more securely bestowed." What a privilege — and what a challenge to us to order our lives so that we may grow in grace, purity, faith, and devotion!

On the discipline of fasting before communing

The decree summarized above does not mention fasting, but fasting before partaking of the Bread of Angels has been a custom practiced universally since ancient times, and required by canon law in its various forms. When we fast from earthly food, the resulting hunger reminds us of how God alone is the nourishment of our souls, the source of our health, the giver of our joy. Just as a full stomach naturally clouds our minds and inclines us to rest, an empty stomach clarifies inner sight and opens the ear of the heart. In spite of how little reference is made to it nowadays, asceticism — that is, the practice of self-denial — is a non-negotiable element in Catholic spirituality, and therefore in the spirituality of couples and families. As sinners in constant need of purification, all of us must examine our consciences, do penance, and carefully prepare ourselves for the reception of the sacraments.

The worst problem of modern times, already lamented by Pope Pius XII, is *the loss of the sense of sin*.[78] Our problem is, however, made worse by the loss of many of the customs by which Catholics once reminded themselves of their sinful condition and their need for penance: Friday abstinence throughout the year; fasting *daily* in Lent rather than merely on Ash Wednesday and Good Friday; and the all-night Eucharistic fast, later reduced to three hours, then finally to one hour.

When in 1953 Pius XII lowered the Eucharistic fast from midnight onward to *three hours* before Mass, it was hailed as a remarkable concession

---

[78] Pius XII's exact words: "Perhaps the greatest sin in the world today is that men have begun to lose the sense of sin." Radio message to the participants in the National Catechetical Congress of the United States in Boston, October 1946.

of the Church to modern needs, but all could recognize that it still required forethought and dedication. In 1964, Pope Paul VI lowered the fast from three hours to *one hour* before Communion, which in many cases amounts to: don't eat something on the way to Sunday Mass. Does this leave intact *any* substantive or meaningful fast? A single hour is so easy to observe that it has resulted, ironically, in many Catholics simply ignoring it altogether, since, as Aristotle observes, "the little by which the result is missed seems to be nothing."[79]

A significant Eucharistic fast shows our respect for Our Lord, and our desire to receive Him as the most important nourishment of our lives. It also makes a moral demand on us that underlines the obligation of worthy reception: be attentive, Christian man or woman, to what you are proposing to do; think deliberately about whether you are in a state of grace such that you may worthily approach the Lord Jesus Christ and receive Him in so intimate a way. The three-hour fast was simultaneously about the Lord, giving *Him* honor, and about me, taking *my* state into account. It was a discipline that discouraged unthinking, indifferent, "social" Communions.

The surroundings of worship in far too many parishes are enough to destroy true faith in the Blessed Sacrament, which the Catholic Church confesses to be the Body, Blood, Soul, and Divinity of our Lord Jesus Christ, and with whom one must be in a union of faith and charity prior to consummating a one-flesh union. The Novus Ordo lectionary *totally excludes* St. Paul's plea to examine one's conscience before receiving the Eucharist (1 Cor. 11:27–29), which was and still is read several times each year in the traditional Latin liturgy.[80] Laity, men and women, handle and distribute the Blessed Sacrament with informality. Lounge-like or emotionally charged music fails to set off the sacred mysteries *as* sacred and fails to stir up the response of prayerful adoration in the faithful. The discipline of fasting is, as we have said, lightweight. Preparation before

---

[79] *Physics*, Bk. II, ch. 5, 197a30.
[80] See chapter 13.

Mass or thanksgiving afterward is almost non-existent. All these things taken together render the reception of Holy Communion so banal, so commonplace, that it would seem insane to deny it to anyone.

In traditional Latin Mass communities, the faithful tend to be acutely aware that they must examine their consciences and, if they are conscious of any mortal sin, must go to Confession before receiving the Eucharist. In the same communities, Confessions are often heard before and *during* Mass on Sundays and Holy Days—an arrangement well suited to the spiritual needs of ordinary Catholics. One priest will celebrate the Mass while the other hears Confessions. At the consecration, Confessions are momentarily suspended; at Communion time, the confessor joins the priest to help distribute the Hosts. One does not see everyone going up automatically, pew after pew. Those who are *ready* to approach the mystical banquet go forward, kneel in adoring reverence, and receive Him on the tongue, from the consecrated hand of the priest. It is all done in a manner proper, just, and right. Man comes before God and, having removed whatever obstacles it is in his power to remove, begs to receive the awesome gift of His divine life.

Could our lack of training in (for lack of a better term) *Eucharistic temperance* and reverence for the Lord's Body be related to the destruction of the virtue of chastity as it relates to marriage—temperance in the sexual plane, and a reverence for the spouse's body? Just as it seems to many that there is no need to prepare and wait and beg the grace to be worthy of the Lord's gift of self to us in Communion, so there would likewise seem to be no need to prepare and wait and beg the grace to be made worthy to receive the gift of another person indissolubly in marriage while making a worthy gift of oneself to that other.

In our society, even lamentably in Catholic circles, people see no need to be chaste before marriage or during marriage. It's all "free love." But free love is cheap and false. Is it not the same with Eucharistic Communion? It is the supreme mutual gift of love—of Christ to me, and of myself to Him. Am I "chaste" in preparation for this mystical marriage with the Savior, and chaste in taking no other master of my soul? Am I ready to give myself wholly to Him, in obedience to His commandments and teachings? Am I ready to put aside eating and drinking to make room for the one food without which my soul will perish for eternity? There can be no doubt that He is and will always be worthy of my love; but am I, will I be, worthy of His?

The recovery of the discipline of fasting, the abolition of ushers who step from aisle to aisle as if signaling for the entire row to get up and go, and the reintroduction of the custom of clergy alone distributing the Blessed Sacrament on the tongues of kneeling communicants are three obvious ways to combat the pandemic of irreverence and the plague of unworthy Communions. Such steps may, over time, prompt couples to think differently about themselves and their own bodies, too—about the care and respect with which one should treat *any* Christian body that is a temple of the Holy Spirit, and about the reverence, altogether free of manipulativeness, that is due to the beloved's body. Married sexual intimacy is, after all, about mutual self-giving under *God's* conditions, not about consensual exploitation.[81]

Making a thanksgiving after Mass

One of the most outstanding acts of piety and devotion open to Catholics in their daily lives is to remain after Mass for a time of thanksgiving.

This custom did not take long to develop among the Christian people, who knew the special Guest they had received into their bodies and souls with the gift of the consecrated bread and wine—no mere earthly food but the food of immortality, Christ Jesus Himself, "the resurrection and the life" (John 11:25). No greater honor could the baptized enjoy than approaching this fearful banquet in a state of righteousness and welcoming the Lord of heaven and earth, who deigned to "become flesh and pitch his tent" among them (see John 1:14).

---

[81] It is no surprise that St. Paul treats of both sexual ethics and Eucharistic ethics in 1 Corinthians. See chapter 4; cf. chapter 12.

Over time, the worthy reception of Holy Communion was seen as intimately bound up with giving thanks to Our Lord, who is really, truly, substantially present in the Most Holy Eucharist—a word that *means* "thanksgiving," as we are often reminded. Would it not be strange if we spent a lot of time preparing for the arrival of One who is both a great dignitary and a best friend, as we do in the Holy Mass from its start until Communion time, and then having met Him, rushed away to other business of far lesser importance?

It is not always possible, of course, to remain after Mass. Sometimes the children are fussing, or the Mass took longer than expected, or we are subject to a tight work schedule. Nevertheless, if we are *able* to take a quarter of an hour or so after Mass, we *ought* to do so; it is a true requirement for advancing in holiness, gratitude, virtue, conquest of sin, and friendship with God. This is why, as mentioned above, the decree *Sacra Tridentina Synodus* of 1905 specifies adequate preparation and thanksgiving as conditions for the *frequent* and *fruitful* reception of Holy Communion.

No one, to my mind, has written more touchingly of this loving duty and indeed this intimate privilege than Sir (and Saint) Thomas More, who suffered greatly for his fidelity to the Catholic Church, and who surely could not have endured the psychological torment of his lengthy incarceration and the many allurements constantly brought against him, had he not been deeply wedded in spirit to the Eucharistic Lord, Whom he had received with such immense devotion. Here is an excerpt from More's *A Treatise: To Receive the Blessed Body of Our Lord*:

> Now, when we have received our Lord, and have him in our body, let us not then let him alone and get us forth about other things, and look no more unto him (for little good could he that so would serve any guest); but let *all* our *busyness* be about *him*. Let us by devout prayer talk to him, by devout meditation talk with him. Let us say with the prophet, "Audiam quid loquatur in me Dominus"—"I will hear what our Lord will speak within me" (Psalm 84:9). For surely, if we set aside all other things and attend unto him, he will

not fail with good inspirations to speak such things to us within us as shall serve to the great spiritual comfort and profit of our soul.

And therefore let us with Martha provide that all our outward busyness may be pertaining to him: in making cheer to him, and to his company for his sake; that is to wit, to poor folk — of which he taketh every one … not only for his disciple, but also as for *himself*. For himself saith, "Quamdiu fecistis uni de his fratribus meis minimis, mihi fecistis" — "That that you have done to one of the least of these my brethren, you have done it to myself" (Matthew 25:40). And let us with Mary also sit in devout meditation and hearken well what our Savior, being now our guest, will inwardly say unto us.

Now have we a special time of prayer: while he that hath made us, he that hath bought us, he whom we have offended, he that shall judge us, he that shall either damn us or save us, is, of his great goodness, become our guest, and is personally present within us, and that for none other purpose but to be sued unto for *pardon* — and so, thereby, to save us. Let us not lose this time, therefore; suffer not this occasion to slip which we can little tell whether ever we shall get it again, or never. Let us endeavor ourselves to keep him still, and let us say with his two disciples that were going to the castle of Emmaus, "Mane nobiscum, Domine" — "Tarry with us, good Lord" (Luke 24:29), and then shall we be sure that he will not go from us, but if [i.e., unless] we unkindly put him from us.[82]

Expanding our view of what Mass is about

It should be added that it is fitting to remain for a time and give thanks even when we have *not* received Holy Communion. This might strike

---

[82] Published in *The Yale Edition of the Complete Works of Thomas More*, vol. 13, ed. Garry E. Haupt (New Haven, CT: Yale University Press, 1976), and available online: www.thomasmorestudies.org/docs/ TreatiseBlessedBody2016-etext.pdf.

the reader as puzzling. What's there to stick around and give thanks *for*, in that case?

One of the widespread errors of our age is the belief that Mass is more or less a fancied-up Communion service for the sake of getting the Eucharist — so much so that it is thought strange to attend Mass *without* communing. This view has surely contributed to the common practice of nearly everyone going forward to receive, when it cannot be assumed that nearly everyone is in a state of grace, having examined their consciences and confessed their sins.

Undoubtedly, the union of the members of the Mystical Body with their Head is *included* in the purpose of the Mass: Our Lord gave us His flesh and blood so that we could be united with Him most intimately. But we can receive Communion also *outside of* Mass, as when It is brought to the sick in the hospital, or to soldiers on a battlefield. The primary and inherent purpose of the Mass *as such* is to adore, praise, placate, and supplicate the Most Holy Trinity. It is the perfect act of divine worship, by which the Father is well pleased with the Son; through it, the Church Militant receives an outpouring of grace, the Church Triumphant an increase of joy, the Church Suffering an alleviation of pains.

The truth of the inherent value of the Mass was better understood in olden times, when people spoke of "*assisting* at Mass." We *assist* in this outpouring, this increase, this alleviation, by our presence and our personal prayer united to the Holy Sacrifice. We are already mightily blessed simply to *be* there for this august Mystery, this all-worthy Offering. Even if there were nothing else "in it for us," so to speak, the Holy Sacrifice of the Mass, all by itself, would give us matter for a lifetime and, indeed, an eternity of thanksgiving. In heaven, the communion we enjoy with God is so perfect there is no need any more for sacraments, yet the worship of the Mystical Body still continues — the Son still offers His divine humanity and His holy wounds to the Father, and we offer ourselves with Him.

In light of the problem of indiscriminate reception of Communion, it might be time to consider anew Joseph Ratzinger's provocative proposal of a "Eucharistic fast." He said that Christians should sometimes consider "fasting" from Communion in order to be in solidarity with other Christians who are prevented from receiving the Lord either because of persecution or because of sin.[83] Now, whatever we make of this idea of solidarity, we can appreciate how there could be times when, in order to avoid the danger of taking this awesome sacrament for granted, we might abstain although we *could* receive—for example, when we are tired or distracted, or have not been able to prepare with a more substantial fast than the one-hour fast currently mandated by canon law, or have missed too much of the service.

We don't need to see this ascetical restraint as being in tension with Pope St. Pius X's encouragement of frequent Communion, or, indeed, as being in tension with the institution of the Holy Eucharist for our spiritual nourishment: "He who eats my flesh and drinks my blood abides in me, and I in him" (John 6:56); "Unless you eat the flesh of the Son of Man and drink His blood, you have no life in you" (John 6:53). St. Augustine and St. Thomas Aquinas, among others, wrote about the question of frequent Communion and pointed out that there is no hard and fast rule about this matter in the Christian life, except that we must follow whatever rule is imposed by Holy Mother Church; and she says we must receive at least once a year.[84] No one should *always* go or always *refrain* from going; the frequency is something we need to discern prayerfully, and we should become aware of the conditions for communing as well as legitimate reasons for holding back. As a general rule, it's fair to say that those who are properly disposed, with living faith and actual devotion, and conscious of no impediment, *ought* to receive: thirsty men in a desert should drink the water provided for them. No doubt Augustine, Aquinas, Pius X, and Ratzinger would concur.[85]

---

[83] See *Behold the Pierced One: An Approach to a Spiritual Christology*, trans. Graham Harrison (San Francisco: Ignatius Press, 1986), 96–98.

[84] See St. Thomas, *Summa theologiae* III, qu. 80, art. 10; the *Roman Catechism* or catechism of the Council of Trent, in its section on the Eucharist, devotes several beautiful pages to the subject of frequent Communion.

[85] See also Mectilde de Bar, *The Mystery of Incomprehensible Love: The Eucharistic Message of Mother Mectilde of the Blessed Sacrament* (Brooklyn, NY: Angelico Press, 2020), 33–57.

There is a parallel here with the question of daily Mass attendance. Some Catholics will go to Mass every day no matter how bad the liturgy at their local parish might be. They are not using discernment or discretion. Precisely because the Mass is so much more than a Communion service, the *way* it is offered has an enormous influence on our interior life and on the quality of the offering we make to God, as well as the fruit we can derive from the liturgy and from Communion itself.[86]

An *addendum for priests*

By the grace of God I've been a Catholic all my life, and during these decades, I've known and observed many priests going about their duties. One of the most fascinating differences among them is how they bear themselves before and after Mass. It took me a long time to realize how great an impact for good or for ill this can have.

Let us take as our point of departure a weighty line in the *Code of Canon Law*. Canon 909 reads: "A priest is not to omit dutifully to prepare himself by prayer before the celebration of the Eucharist, nor afterwards to omit to make thanksgiving to God." As if commenting on this canon, Bishop Marc Aillet writes:

> Tearing us away from the secular world and thus from the temptation of immanentism, [the liturgical rites] have the power to immerse us suddenly in the Mystery and open us to the Transcendent. In this sense, one can never stress enough the importance of the silence preceding the liturgical celebration, an inner narthex, where we are freed of the concerns, even if legitimate, of the secular world, in order to enter the sacred space and time where God will reveal his Mystery; one can never stress enough the importance

---

[86] For an approach to this question, see Kwasniewski, *Reclaiming Our Roman Catholic Birthright*, ch. 21, "Sorting Out Difficulties in Liturgical Allegiance," 281–88.

of silence in the liturgy to open oneself more readily to the action of God; and one can never stress enough the appropriateness of a period of thanksgiving, whether integrated into the celebration or not, to apprehend the inner extent of the mission that awaits us once we are back in the world.[87]

Consider first the time prior to Mass. Shawn Tribe urges the recovery of a spirit of reverence, respect, and quietude in the sacristy before the celebration of Mass.[88] He notes that many sacristies have a sign reading SILENTIUM, and recalls the very old custom of the priest reciting hallowed prayers as he dons each separate garment in preparation for offering the Holy Sacrifice. Before a High Mass, a Solemn Mass, or some other major liturgy, the platoon of servers will be very busy, but there is no reason why they cannot be *quietly* busy, learning to move in an atmosphere of prayerful preparation and anticipation, keeping their voices down and their conversations useful to the matters at hand.

The holiest priests I've known (although there are exceptions to any rule) have tended to arrive in the sacristy early so that they could prepare in an unrushed spirit. I have noticed that they would review the missal, carefully say the vesting prayers, and then be ready, waiting, often gazing at a wall-mounted crucifix, before the servers had finishing pulling themselves together. When the bell rings or the clock strikes, such a priest is ready to process in, with a "Procedamus in pace" on his lips. What a profound "ripple effect" his earnest, calm, and focused mind can have on the entire sacristy atmosphere, and on all who are working in it!

Contrast this with the priest who rushes in at the last minute, in a whirl and a tizzy. He's looking here and there, maybe stealing a quick glance at the Ordo, racing against the clock. He throws open the closet

---

[87] "The Wounded Liturgy," a talk at the Pontifical Lateran University, March 11, 2010; translation published at *New Liturgical Movement*, March 22, 2010.

[88] See "Reclaiming the Sacristy as a Place of Prayer and Preparation," *New Liturgical Movement*, November 8, 2008.

and grabs the alb and the chasuble, scarcely taking time to straighten them before walking out into the church. Where is the "dutiful preparation" of Canon 909? Do the servers imbibe a true spirit of reverence toward this most awesome of all human actions—indeed, do they see that the priest is embarking on a *divine* action of which he is, and they are, totally unworthy, and before which we stand in fear and trembling? Or take the other contrast, Father Foghorn, whose arrival *everyone* knows because you can hear him yacking away in the sacristy before Mass, about the weather, or football, or something in the news, or someone's sick aunt, or whatever the topic *du jour* may be. Indeed, he might even be giving out commands about liturgical preparations, but the generalissimo manner is enough to debar anyone from recollection.

The truth is simple: Father Foghorn and Reverend Roadrunner are not edifying. We need clergy who, before Mass, conscientiously pursue the spirit of recollection, prayerfulness, humility, and peace. At the end of the day, this is not merely for the benefit of a bunch of rag-tag servers or half-asleep pewsitters; it is for the benefit of the clergy themselves, who stand to win or lose their vocations based on how they approach the very work for which they have been set apart. The devil never omits to prepare for whatever dark business he has in hand, and it seems he targets those who have forgotten their dignity. We must not omit to prepare ourselves for ascending the mountain of the Lord in the company of the angels.

Let us turn to the time after Mass. Although I don't remember ever seeing this custom while growing up in a mainstream American parish in the 1970s and 1980s, I began to notice in college and afterward that more conservative or traditional priests, having returned to the sacristy, would say "Prosit" and then give a blessing to the kneeling altar servers. This is a laudable custom that surely deserves to be retained wherever it exists or revived wherever it has fallen into desuetude.

But what should happen next? The best way I can answer that question is to describe a particular priest friend of mine, whose example in this regard was as luminous as can be. After blessing the servers, he would quietly divest (no indulging in sacristy banter and very little of the "post-game debrief"), and then immediately step out to the sanctuary, kneel on the side, and pray for several minutes. He sometimes used the traditional prayers of thanksgiving from the *Missale Romanum*, other times not. It was clear that he was not doing this to be seen by men, yet everyone saw him nonetheless—and this is as it should be. "So let your light shine before men, that they may see your good works, and glorify your Father who is in heaven" (Matt. 5:16, DR). The priest who offers the Holy Sacrifice of the Mass, the most sublime act of worship on the face of the earth, the ecstasy of angels and the terror of demons—how can he possibly return immediately to secularity, light chit-chat, text messages, voicemails, or emails, or rush away to do something else (unless it is a genuine emergency)?

The holy priest just described is the polar opposite of the priest who seems unable to get away fast enough when Mass is over. He zips out of the sanctuary or nave (depending on the planned or available route of escape), whips off the garments, and is out the door quicker than you can say: "Father, do you have a minute to hear a confession?" To a layman, this is a dismaying experience. I was taught in grammar school to stay a bit after Mass and make thanksgiving. Why isn't our priest, our leader, doing the same? We always say that example speaks louder than words...

Then there is the priest who obviously thinks that the time after Mass was custom-designed for socializing, often at great length, in the atrium or right outside the main doors of the church. I'm not saying that greeting people, shaking hands, and asking "How's your mother doing?" or questions of that sort is a bad idea; in fact, on Sundays it seems to be an especially good opportunity for making the sort of "horizontal" connections that ought to be avoided *during* the Holy Sacrifice of the Mass. Nevertheless, when the post-liturgical bonhomie is conducted with such vim and vigor that the faithful who are trying to pray in the church can hear the guffawing and backslapping pouring through the entrance, or when the extent of the socializing crowds out any real prayer of thanksgiving on the priest's part, we are dealing with mixed-up priorities.

When we have received Our Lord in Holy Communion, He is, for some precious minutes, substantially present within us. If we are in a state of grace (and we'd have no business receiving Communion otherwise), He is always with us spiritually; but He is *not* always with us in the miraculous mode of His Eucharistic presence. This is a special time, a time of unique intimacy and love, when our praises to God and His favors to us are poured out more abundantly, when we are most of all abiding in Him and He in us. Let us not squander this gift from the Lord—and let the clergy lead the way in setting a strong and sincere example of how to rejoice and give thanks. I am reminded of the saying recounted by Dom Jean-Baptiste Chautard: "If the priest is a saint, the people will be fervent; if the priest is fervent, the people will be pious; if the priest is pious, the people will at least be decent. But if the priest is only decent, the people will be godless." He then adds his own observation: "The spiritual generation is always one degree less intense in its life than those who beget it in Christ."[89]

As a parting thought, the impression has grown on me more and more over the years that one of the strongest merits of the *usus antiquior* is that it has preparation and thanksgiving already "built in." Yes, there is still a brief period for each in the Novus Ordo, but nothing comparable to Psalm 42 and its accompanying versicles and prayers, or to the Placeat and the Last Gospel. One feels that one has decisively *begun* and decisively *ended*. There is a suitable psychological and spiritual transition from the secular world to the sacred, and again from the sacred to the secular. And yet, paradoxically, it is among *usus antiquior*-celebrating priests that I have tended to find the greatest recollection and prayerfulness *before* and *after* Mass, too. What this suggests to me is that the very reduction

---

[89] *The Soul of the Apostolate*, trans. A Monk of Our Lady of Gethsemani (Trappist, KY: The Abbey of Gethsemani, 1946; repr. TAN Books, n.d.), 39. I first heard this saying in another form: "If the priest is an angel, the people will be saints; if the priest is a saint, the people will be good; if the priest is good, the people will be mediocre; and if the priest is mediocre, the people will be beasts."

of the rituals of preparation and thanksgiving within the Ordinary Form has had a bleed-over effect on the time before and after the liturgy itself.

This is why we should adamantly oppose any "reform" of the 1962 *Missale Romanum* that involves the abolition of the prayers at the foot of the altar and the Last Gospel. Those who speak of the value of the 1965 *Missal*—the supposed implementation of *Sacrosanctum Concilium*—as if it's the fulfillment of legitimate liturgical reform are not thinking carefully enough about why these introductory and conclusory parts became popular in the first place and why, under the influence of the Holy Spirit, they were eventually integrated into the Tridentine missal. We will often find, if we are patient enough to absorb the lessons of tradition, that our ancestors were wiser than we are.

7

Why We Should Receive Communion
Kneeling and on the Tongue

If we are to worship God not merely out of routine or habit, but with an intelligent love and a loving intelligence, we need to understand why we are doing what we do. For example, why do we kneel? What is so important, so meaningful, about this posture that we use it before and after Mass, during the Eucharistic Prayer, and at other times in the liturgy, including—as once was the universal custom—when we receive Holy Communion?

In his *Commentary on the Epistle to the Ephesians*, St. Thomas Aquinas underlines the intimate connection between kneeling and humility:

Humility makes a prayer worthy of being heard: "He hath had regard to the prayer of the humble: and he hath not despised their petition" (Ps. 101:18). And, "The prayer of him that humbleth himself shall pierce the clouds: and till it come nigh he will not be comforted" (Sir. 35:21). Therefore, he [the Apostle] immediately starts his prayer in humility, saying: "For this cause," that you fail not in the faith, "I bend my knees to the Father."

This is a symbol of humility for two reasons. First, a man belittles himself, in a certain way, when he genuflects, and he subjects himself to the one he genuflects before. In such a way he recognizes his own weakness and insignificance. Secondly, physical strength is present in the knees; in bending them a man confesses openly to his lack of strength. Thus external, physical symbols are shown to God for the purpose of renewing and spiritually training the inner soul, as in the prayer of Manasse: "I bend the knee of my heart"; and "for every knee shall be bowed to me: and every tongue shall swear" (Isa. 45:24).[90]

We will understand better the importance of this training of the inner man in humility before the infinite holiness of God if we reflect on the fundamental problem of fallen man. The serpent's tactic in the Garden of Eden was to suggest to Eve that she should think of God as being "on the same playing field," as "one of us"—and, therefore, as one who is in competition with us, jealous of our status, eager to keep us down. When Eve surrendered her mind to this primordial lie, and Adam submitted his mind to hers, they became custodians of the lie, estranged from the true God, from each other, from their own selves, and from the whole of nature. Thus had begun the downward-spiraling self-alienation of man, where every step away from God was a step of greater misery, a loss of divine likeness and human integrity at one and the same time. The one and only cure is to submit to God in total trusting obedience, for He alone can give us freedom and happiness, just as He alone gives us our living, moving, and being (see Acts 17:28).

Traditional Christian liturgies of East and West dramatically emphasize God's transcendence over us, His benevolent reign, His rightful demand of our whole heart, soul, mind, and strength, and our corresponding duty to worship Him by offering sacrifice with contrite and humble hearts. In spite of the illusions fostered by modern democracy, we are *not* equals before Jesus Christ our God; He is our Lord and Master, and we are His disciples, servants, and adorers. Yes, He lovingly calls us His friends; but He is not just *any* friend, He is the Lord of heaven and earth who

---

[90] *Commentary on the Letters of Saint Paul to the Galatians and Ephesians*, trans. Fabian R. Larcher, O.P., and Matthew Lamb, vol. 39 in the *Latin/English Edition of the Works of St. Thomas Aquinas* (Green Bay, WI: Aquinas Institute, 2018), ch. 3, lect. 4, n. 166, p. 248.

has called us out of darkness into His marvelous light (see 1 Pet. 2:9), and who deserves (and rewards) our absolute self-surrender, which no creature can rightly demand or receive. This is why kneeling, within a tradition that has long expressed and cultivated the attitude of humility by means of it, is no mere incidental or external feature that we can take or leave. It is part of our fundamental spiritual discipline. Kneeling is a vivid and heartfelt expression of worship, of the adoration that is due to our Lord and God.

As Cardinal Malcolm Ranjith rightly points out:

> To prostrate oneself or to kneel down before the majesty of the divine presence, in humble adoration, was a habit of reverence that Israel always practiced in the presence of the Lord.... The same tradition can also be found in the New Testament, where we see Peter kneeling before Jesus (see Lk 5:8); Jairus, who knelt to request the healing of his daughter (Lk 8:41); the Samaritan who returned and knelt to give thanks to Jesus (Lk 17:16); and Mary, the sister of Lazarus, who, on her knees, asked the favor of having her brother brought back to life (Jn 11:32). The same attitude of prostration before the stupendous divine presence is found throughout the Book of Revelation (Rev 5:8, 14; 19:4).... The Eucharist, bread transubstantiated into the Body of Christ and wine into the Blood of Christ, God in our midst, had to be received with awe, with the greatest reverence, and in an attitude of humble adoration.[91]

The converse is also true, as Bishop Thomas Olmsted relates:

> According to Abba Apollo, a desert father who lived about 1,700 years ago, the devil has no knees; he cannot kneel; he cannot adore; he cannot pray; he can only look down his nose in contempt. Being

---

[91] Malcolm Cardinal Ranjith, preface to Most Rev. Athanasius Schneider, *Dominus Est—It Is the Lord!*, trans. Nicholas L. Gregoris (Pine Beach, NJ: Newman House Press, 2008), 13–14; translation slightly modified.

unwilling to bend the knee at the name of Jesus is the essence of evil (cf. Is 45:23, Rom 14:11).[92]

In addition to the posture of kneeling, there is the question of receiving on the tongue, rather than in the hand. The Instruction *Memoriale Domini* of the Congregation for Divine Worship (May 29, 1969) explained the fittingness of this practice — an opinion with which the majority of the world's bishops, when polled at that time by Paul VI, concurred:

> In view of the state of the Church as a whole today, this manner of distributing Holy Communion [viz., on the tongue] must be retained, not only because it rests upon a tradition of many centuries, but especially because it is a sign of the reverence of the faithful toward the Eucharist. The practice in no way detracts from the personal dignity of those who approach this great Sacrament, and it is a part of the preparation needed for the most fruitful reception of the Lord's body.
>
> This reverence is a sign of Holy Communion not in "common bread and drink" but in the Body and Blood of the Lord....
>
> In addition, this manner of communicating, which is now to be considered as prescribed by custom, gives more effective assurance that Holy Communion will be distributed with the appropriate reverence, decorum, and dignity; that any danger of profaning the Eucharistic species, in which "the whole and entire Christ, God and man, is substantially contained and permanently present in a unique way," will be avoided; and finally that the diligent care which the Church has always commended for the very fragments of the consecrated bread will be maintained: "If you have allowed anything to be lost, consider this a lessening of your own members."[93]

[92] Most Rev. Thomas J. Olmsted, "Knees to Love Christ," *The Catholic Sun* (Phoenix), February 17, 2005.

[93] The text is cited here from Joseph Shaw, ed., *The Case for Liturgical Restoration: Una Voce Studies on the Traditional Latin Mass* (Brooklyn, NY: Angelico Press, 2019), 61; the original Latin is quoted on p. 318.

Note how well everything fits together in the Roman liturgy as it developed over the millennia. As long as Communion is given on the tongue, there is good reason to kneel—not only for its symbolic and formative value, but also because kneeling makes it easier for the priest or deacon to place the Host on the tongue. And once this becomes the practice, a communion rail is obviously helpful, not only to affirm the symbolic distinction between the sanctuary and the nave, but also to offer bodily support to those who are kneeling. Moreover, the priest is always to be accompanied by a server holding a paten, out of respect for the Blessed Sacrament and lest it or any fragment of it fall to the ground.[94] All of these customs grew up in support of each other, once the fundamental principle was allowed to breathe freely: Our Lord Jesus Christ is really, truly, substantially present in the Most Holy Sacrament of the Altar. "At the Name of Jesus, every knee shall bend…" (see Phil. 2:10). The same customs arise anew wherever the same dogmatic truth is not merely acknowledged with a lazy nod but deeply internalized and acted on as a Christian's devotional anchor.

Permission to receive Communion in the hand is something the devil worked hard to achieve by influencing ecclesiastical authorities to relax

---

For a full account of the history of this document, with a translation and commentary, see Most Rev. Juan Rodolfo Laise, *Holy Communion. Communion in the Hand: Documents & History; Some Reflections on Spiritual Communion and the State of Grace*, 5th ed. (Boonville, NY: Preserving Christian Publications, 2018), 6–89.

[94] It is worth noting that the Instruction *Redemptionis Sacramentum* of the Congregation for Divine Worship and the Discipline of the Sacraments specifies the use of such a paten even in the context of the Ordinary Form: "The Communion-plate [*patina*, i.e., paten] for the Communion of the faithful ought to be retained [*oportet retineatur*], so as to avoid the danger of the sacred host or some fragment of it falling" (§93). The *General Instruction of the Roman Missal* lists the communion-plate or paten as an item that should be placed on the credence table for the celebration of Mass. See my article "Why We Should Retain or Reintroduce the Communion Plate ('Chin Paten')," *New Liturgical Movement*, November 18, 2019.

a discipline that was longstanding and wise.[95] Satan derives a demented pleasure from seeing the Holy Eucharist profaned and desecrated. This happens in two ways: through negligence, as when people carelessly drop fragments of the Host or spill the precious Blood; through contempt, as when non-Catholic visitors and tourists receive the Blessed Sacrament, or when anti-Catholics deliberately carry them away in order to destroy them, use them in satanic worship, or sell them online. When we ponder the awesome mystery that is the Holy Eucharist, such evils should cause us immense anguish, sadness, and righteous anger.

Our Lord himself, glorified in heaven, is beyond all suffering; He is not directly harmed when the Blessed Sacrament is harmed. He is present in the sacrament as the *Risen Christ* seated at the right hand of the Father; after the resurrection He cannot suffer or die, but lives in the glory of immortality.[96] The person who is harmed by desecration is the *desecrator*—and this shows us why Satan delights in desecration. Anyone who performs this act is committing the sin of Judas, the crime of betraying that which most deserves our fidelity, the crime of hating that which most deserves our love, the crime of holding in contempt the mystery that deserves our heartfelt adoration on bended knee. It is a mockery of Christ. It is a rejection of His adorable Person, and therefore a rejection of the

---

[95] "[T]he history of the reintroduction of Communion in the hand is nothing other than the triumph of an act of disobedience. The consideration of the details of this history makes evident to us the gravity of this disobedience: in fact, it is very serious above all because of the very matter which it concerns; very serious because it implies the open resistance to a clear, explicit and solidly founded directive of the pope; most serious by its universal extension; most serious because those who did not obey were not only the faithful or priests, but in many cases bishops and entire episcopal conferences; most serious, because not only did they remain unpunished but they obtained a resounding success; most serious, in short, because it has succeeded in having the state of disobedience remain hidden, making it such that one might believe, on the contrary, that they were adopting a proposal that came from Rome" (Bishop Juan Rodolfo Laise, *Holy Communion*, 109).

[96] See chapter 5.

Father who sent Him. No wonder the devil is eager to see Hosts treated indifferently, carelessly, disrespectfully, sacrilegiously. These are steps along the same continuum — steps that separate us from the infinitely holy God and push us to the brink of hell.[97]

Apart from such evils, there is the basic question of *reverence*. The priest's hands are specially consecrated with holy oil so that he may fittingly handle the Blessed Sacrament, that he may touch and administer the holy gifts of the altar. In the words of Pope John Paul II:

> One must not forget the primary office of priests, who have been consecrated by their ordination to represent Christ the Priest: for this reason their hands, like their words and their will, have become the direct instruments of Christ. Through this fact, that is, as ministers of the Holy Eucharist, they have a primary responsibility for the sacred species, because it is a total responsibility: they offer the bread and wine, they consecrate it, and then distribute the sacred species to the participants in the assembly who wish to receive them.... How eloquent therefore, even if not of ancient custom, is the rite of the anointing of the hands in our Latin ordination, as though precisely for these hands a special grace and power of the Holy Spirit is necessary! To touch the sacred species and to distribute them with their own hands is a privilege of the ordained, one which indicates an active participation in the ministry of the Eucharist.[98]

A layman's hands, in contrast, are not anointed in this way; no layman represents Christ the Priest in the Mass and serves as His direct

---

[97] On the foregoing paragraphs, see the appendix by Bishop Athanasius Schneider.

[98] *Dominicæ Cenæ* §11. John Paul II unfortunately goes on to say that the faculty of handling and distributing the Blessed Sacrament can be extended beyond its ordinary ministers "to meet a just need," which compromises the theological point he is making, and introduces incoherence between office, sign, and praxis.

instrument, responsible for His body; no layman has, strictly speaking, an *active* part in Eucharistic ministry.[99] It is therefore absolutely fitting that Christ's faithful should go before His minister, *receiving* on bended knee and with open mouth the nourishment of body and soul, like a baby bird fed in the nest by its parent. From this symbolic vantage, it is wholly inappropriate that the priest put the Host into our *hands*, so that we may then *administer Communion to ourselves*. This gesture means: "I'm grown up and can feed myself, thank you very much; the priest's hands are no different, no better than mine." But this is false. We cannot feed ourselves. Only Christ the High Priest can give us the Bread of Life, and His ordained minister acts in His place, set apart by holy orders, and with hands likewise set apart for a task of divine bestowal more fearful and awe-inspiring than anything else that is done or could be done by the children of men. By flattening the divine bestowal into a human transfer, Communion in the hand does much to create and support the fatal atmosphere of egalitarianism, horizontalism, and activism that has poisoned the spiritual life of the Church for half a century.

In fact, so pervasive and profound was the Church's reverence toward Christ our God in His Holy Sacrament that she even forbade the laity to touch the *vessels* that touched Christ. The *Catechism of the Council of Trent*—the Magisterium's first universal catechism, published in 1566 and obviously still authoritative as a witness to the Faith—explained this point with unanswerable logic:

> To safeguard in every possible way the dignity of so august a Sac-
> rament, not only is the power of its administration entrusted ex-
> clusively to priests, but the Church has also prohibited by law

---

[99] This is why the Vatican has clarified that a layman may not be called an "ordinary minister of the Eucharist" but only an "*extraordinary* minister of *Holy Communion*." See *Redemptionis Sacramentum* §156; *Code of Canon Law* (1983), can. 910 and can. 911. The minister of the Eucharist is the one who confects the sacrament, namely, a bishop or priest; by current law, the ordinary minister of Communion is a bishop, a priest, or a deacon.

any but consecrated persons, unless some case of great necessity intervene, to dare handle or touch the sacred vessels, the linen, or other instruments necessary to its completion. Priests themselves and the rest of the faithful may hence understand how great should be the piety and holiness of those who approach to consecrate, administer, or receive the Eucharist.[100]

We must therefore do everything in our power—with patience, yes, but also with a perseverance that never quits—to overturn the practice of Communion in the hand and all the aberrations that have accompanied it, replacing them with worthier customs, such as reception of the Eucharist on the tongue of the kneeling faithful, administered by the clergy. Such customs cannot, in and of themselves, prevent unworthy Communions from happening, but certain evils will be limited or eliminated, and the goods of supernatural faith, interior devotion, and external reverence will greatly increase and multiply.

Digging deeper into the reasons

Why is receiving the Holy Eucharist directly into the mouth the only right way to receive the Lord? To begin with, it has centuries of unanimous

---

[100] *The Catechism of the Council of Trent for Parish Priests,* edited under the guidance of St. Charles Borromeo, issued by order of Pope St. Pius V, trans. John A. McHugh, O.P., and Charles J. Callan, O.P. (Rockford, IL: TAN Books and Publishers, 1982), in the chapter "The Sacrament of the Eucharist," p. 254. Cf. the 1917 *Code of Canon Law,* can. 1306: "§1 Care should be taken lest a chalice, paten, or, before cleansing, purificators, palls, and corporals that were used in the sacrifice of the Mass are touched by any other than by clerics or those who have custody of these things. §2 Purificators, palls, and corporals used in the sacrifice of the Mass shall not be put into the hands of the laity, even religious, unless they have first been washed by a cleric constituted in major orders; and the water from this first washing shall be put into a sacrarium or, in its absence, into a fire." To this day, servers and sacristans in traditional parishes wear gloves or use cloths if they need to move sacred vessels.

practice in East and West behind it. Accordingly, it must be considered a development guided by the Holy Spirit—for otherwise, we would surely have to conclude that the Church of Christ, in both its Eastern and Western spheres, had gone off the rails in its second millennium.[101]

If one really believes that a priest is set aside by a divine act of transformation to be an *alter Christus* ("other Christ") who, at the altar, brings about the same miracle that Christ the High Priest brought about at the Last Supper in anticipation of His atoning sacrifice on Calvary, one will see immediately that the priest is the one authorized by God to handle the most holy gifts and to distribute them to others. While there may be exceptions for emergencies, clearly the ministerial priest will be the fitting imparter of the Bread of Angels into the mouths of Christians.

Again, if one believes that the entire substance of the bread is converted into the entire substance of Christ, with the accidents of bread alone remaining, one will invariably arrive at the conclusion that the distribution of the Holy Eucharist must be done in such a way as to prevent any dispersion or loss of fragments, that is, crumbs or specks. Distribution of larger or crumblier altar breads, and above all distribution into the hand, is directly opposed to the infinitely higher good of honoring God in Himself and avoiding the sin of profanation or desecration against Him.[102]

Let us consider what the Lord Himself has to say about divine food in the Scriptures. In the prophet Ezekiel, we read: "Open thy mouth, and eat what *I* give thee" (Ezek. 2:8, DR). In the Psalms, we read, "Open

---

[101] See my article "Surprising Convergences between an Anti-Catholic Textbook and the Liturgical Reform," *New Liturgical Movement*, August 5, 2019, and my lecture "Beyond 'Smells and Bells': Why We Need the Objective Content of the *Usus Antiquior*," published at *Rorate Caeli*, November 29, 2019.

[102] See chapter 10 for further examples of widespread Eucharistic abuse, especially in connection with the Precious Blood. The traditional Roman Rite contains layers of rubrics to avoid dispersion of crumbs and stray droplets, as well as to ensure a thorough cleansing of vessels and of fingers by the priest (and only by him).

thy mouth wide, and *I* will fill it" (Ps. 80:11, DR). Who is the "I" in these statements? It is the Lord. The Lord alone may feed us. This is the deepest reason why, in the Divine Liturgy, in the Holy Sacrifice of the Mass, it must be the ordained minister who, as acting *in persona Christi* (on behalf of Christ), distributes the Bread of Angels to the communicants.

This mode of receiving—common to East and West—symbolizes and emphasizes several truths at once.

1. The one doing the feeding is Christ. I do not feed myself.

2. I am, in fact, *incapable* of nourishing myself supernaturally; I must be *fed*, like a little child, an elderly person, or someone handicapped. Yes, I am able to come forward to the communion rail, unlike the paralytic carried on a pallet in the Gospel (see Luke 5:17–26); but once I reach the threshold of divinity, it is imperative that I demonstrate—to myself and in the sight of others—that at this threshold I must kneel or take a passive stance and allow myself to be *acted upon*. I am not there to feed myself as an autonomous agent, or to collect something I can add to my personal life portfolio; rather, I am "imposed upon" and thus altered. The divine food is more powerful than I am, and I submit to it.

> This millennium-old practice of kneeling before the Holy One of Israel, truly present in the Sacrament of the Altar, and of receiving Him on the tongue from the hand of an ordained minister, literally *embodies* our dependency on God, our lowliness and unworthiness, our need to fall in adoration before the Lord, and our desire for healing and elevation. As Our Lady's Magnificat proclaims, the creature must first be low—and see itself to be low—in order to be raised up on high by God. In this practice is contained the humility of willing to be fed like a child too small to feed itself.[103]

Mother Cécile Bruyère, a disciple of Dom Prosper Guéranger, tells us how this way of thinking stretches back to the early centuries:

---

[103] Kwasniewski, *Reclaiming Our Roman Catholic Birthright*, 44.

The Holy Bread of Eternal Life

At the time when our fathers in the faith had to observe the "discipline of the secret," they had an admirable way of expressing this teaching. In their paintings and in their writings they represented the divine Eucharist under the symbol of milk. Milk is the child's food, given by God in a mysterious way to the mother. It is the mother's food, adapted to the child's tender age. Thus, as long as we are in this life, we are but children, and our mother the Church has received for us the milk of the Eucharist, that is, divine food suited to our weakness — the food of the angels themselves and of the elect, which is to last until we have attained the age of perfect men, "unto the measure of the age of the fulness of Christ" (Eph 4:13). It is in this sense that certain passages of the Canticle of Canticles are interpreted when applied to the Church. For instance: "We will be glad and rejoice in thee, remembering thy breasts more than wine" (Song 1:3). The milk here spoken of is indeed richer than wine, but still it is milk, and the food of our childhood here below.[104]

3. The food is entering *immediately* into my body — that is, I surrender myself to the coming of the Word from without, and make myself passive and receptive to it: in a word, *vulnerable*. I am not "in control"; I am not the one who determines the conditions or the timing under which Christ will act on me. By coming forward and submitting to the hand of another, I relinquish my mastery. There is no moment between reception and eating; to receive *is* to eat.

4. More particularly, we *wait* for the Lord. "Blessed are those servants, whom the Lord when he cometh, shall find watching. Amen I say to you, that he will gird himself, and make them sit down to meat, and passing will minister unto them" (Luke 12:37, DR). This is exactly what the ministers at the traditional Latin Mass do: *they* vest ("gird") themselves, they make the faithful adopt a position of repose and receptivity, and

---

[104] *The Spiritual Life and Prayer according to Holy Scripture and Monastic Tradition*, trans. The Benedictines of Stanbrook (London: Art and Book, 1900; repr. Eugene, OR: Wipf and Stock, 2002), 62–63.

"passing, minister unto them." On behalf of his Lord and bearing His Body in the ciborium, the priest is the one who moves from communicant to communicant, while we remain steady on our knees, waiting for that anointed hand to bestow its benison. "The eyes of all look to thee, and thou givest them their food in due season. Thou openest thy hand, thou satisfiest the desire of every living thing" (Ps. 144:15–16). Note how well the traditional practice corresponds to the sentiments in this verse: the communicant, kneeling at the altar rail, *waits* for God to come to him, as the priest makes his rounds—he being the primary agent, as God is; he then *gives* us the food at the proper time, opening *his* hand to satisfy *our* desire.

The Synoptic Evangelists drive home the point that Our Lord, when He multiplied the loaves and fishes, commanded the people to sit down, or had the disciples make them do so.[105] This, I believe, was not merely for comfort or convenience. It put them in a position of waiting; they were to be not agents of change but recipients of largesse. They were to be given from above the material bread that symbolized the living bread come down from heaven. Their being seated in groups of fifty, much like the successive rows of the faithful kneeling at the communion rail, emphasizes the orderliness that belongs to the works of God, who creates all things "in measure, and number, and weight" (Wis. 11:21, DR).

5. There is a clear hierarchical distinction between the one giving the divine gift and the one receiving it. Because the communicant kneels down at an altar rail or prie-dieu while the priest or deacon remains standing, there is a strong differentiation of persons and actions. The relationship is reminiscent of streams flowing down from a mountaintop to the lakes below, or the descent of the dove on the baptized. The conferral of the manna "from above" imitates the descent of the Son of God in His Incarnation, in

---

[105] "And when he had commanded the multitudes to sit down upon the grass…" (Matt. 14:19, DR); "And he commanded the crowd to sit down on the ground" (Mark 8:6); "And he said to his disciples: 'Make them sit down by fifties in a company.' And they did so; and made them all sit down" (Luke 9:14–15, DR).

order to lift us up to His heavenly glory.[106] Fr. Réginald Garrigou-Lagrange observes: "To abase ourselves before the Most High is to recognize, not only in a speculative but in a practical manner, our inferiority, littleness, and indigence, manifest in us even though we are innocent, and, once we have sinned, it consists in recognizing our wretchedness."[107]

Communion in the hand, standing, to people lined up in a queue, systematically undermines *all* of these symbolic and ascetical aspects of the act of Eucharistic communion. By getting the Host in my hand, more or less at eye level with the distributor, I become the one who feeds myself. I am now a "grown up" vis-à-vis God, with whom I relate on *my* terms: I determine when I put this Host into my mouth (or, as in well-documented cases, take it away for a rainy day, or make it

---

[106] "Historically, the priest, standing—and acting *in persona Christi*—would lower his anointed hand and place the Eucharist directly on the tongue of the communicant, who would be kneeling upon the ground before the altar. So, per the doctrine, the divine was literally descending from a higher plane to the lower plane of man, who was kneeling upon a still lower plane, the earth. Today's Eucharistic distribution, though, aligns more with the types of lateral structures advocated at the [Amazon] synod. A lay minister (who is not ordained to act *in persona Christi*) stands before the communicant, who is also standing, and the host is exchanged from one mortal hand to the other, moving only horizontally instead of vertically, from person to person (instead of from divine to person), and remaining within one plane. Arguing about Eucharistic distribution may seem like a trifling matter of style, but as literature professors used to teach (back when they taught the classics), style informs content." Honora Kenney, "Amazon Synod Reveals Vatican Bureaucracy Nightmare," *OnePeterFive*, October 15, 2019. Admittedly, the vertical symbolism is a little less manifest in the Eastern practice, where the communicant, who receives in the mouth but standing, usually has to bend his legs or crouch a little to bring his mouth to the right angle for the spoon to deposit its precious freight. Nevertheless, there is still the all-important hierarchical differentiation between the priest who alone wields the chalice and spoon and the layman who lowers himself to receive the Lord. There is never parity of stance and a hand-to-hand exchange.

[107] Garrigou-Lagrange, *Three Ages of the Interior Life*, 2:118.

a souvenir, or put it in the hymnal, or give it to someone else, or use it in a satanic ritual or an act of blasphemy). I am parleying with the Word, rather than suffering It. At the threshold of divinity, I assert my independence and control. In the modern Western context (which is decidedly *not* the ancient context[108]), Communion in the hand, standing, means: I come to Christ and His Church when and as it suits me, in my active, busy lifestyle. "The secular withholds any obeisance / that is aimed upwards."[109]

This is why Communion for the divorced and "remarried" or for non-Catholic spouses has become such a hot topic among progressives: it is ultimately about *who gets to decide the conditions for Communion*. In the Kasperian perspective, it is the individual believer who decides how the world and its Maker will revolve around him or her.[110] Modern Eucharistic praxis approaches *non serviam* asymptotically. In the Catholic tradition, however, it is the feeder (i.e., the one giving the food) who decides the conditions for Communion; and this is not primarily the minister, or even the Church, but Christ Himself, in laying down the natural law and the divine law, from which there are no exceptions.[111]

No one would contend, of course, that these Antichristic meanings are consciously intended by everyone who receives in the hand. But these meanings are *built into the action itself*, even as the opposite meanings are conveyed by the preestablished and still intuitively understood millennium-old tradition of kneeling and receiving Communion on the tongue from the anointed hand of the ordained minister. As at the time of Our Lord, so today, most of the people are like sheep without a shepherd (see Matt. 9:36) — indeed, at this point, most of the shepherds are like sheep without a shepherd.

---

[108] See the next chapter.

[109] The poet Les Murray, quoted in Roy Peachey, *50 Books for Life: A Concise Guide to Catholic Literature* (Brooklyn, NY: Angelico Press, 2019), 10.

[110] See Prof. Thomas Heinrich Stark, "German Idealism and Cardinal Kasper's Theological Project," *The Catholic World Report*, June 9, 2015.

[111] See chapters 13, 14, 16, and 19.

8

The Scandal of Communion in the Hand

On November 21, 2019, the feast of the Presentation of the Blessed Virgin Mary, Cardinal Gerhard Ludwig Müller and Cardinal Robert Sarah were present at the abbey of Kloster Weltenburg in Bavaria for a pontifical Mass followed by the presentation of Cardinal Sarah's book, *The Day Is Now Far Spent*. In his comments, the Prefect of the Congregation for Divine Worship and the Discipline of the Sacraments returned to a favorite theme of many of his speeches and writings: the urgent need to recover a reverent manner of distributing and receiving Holy Communion. Like Pope Benedict XVI, Cardinal Sarah is a strong proponent of reception on the tongue by faithful who are kneeling. The consistent good example and lucid teaching on this matter from Pope Benedict XVI, Cardinal Sarah, Cardinal Francis Arinze, Cardinal Antonio Cañizares Llovera, Cardinal Raymond Leo Burke, and Bishop Athanasius Schneider, among others, have led countless Catholics to return to the traditional manner of receiving Our Lord.

There will never be lacking the objector who trots out the famous passage from the *Mystagogical Catecheses* of St. Cyril of Jerusalem (313–386), quoted again and again to persuade Catholics that Communion in the hand is really just an ancient practice legitimately restored by the Church after the Second Vatican Council:

Coming up to receive, therefore, do not approach with your wrists extended or your fingers splayed, but making your left hand a throne for the right (for it is about to receive a King) and cupping your palm, so receive the Body of Christ; and answer: "Amen." Carefully hallow your eyes by the touch of the sacred Body, and then partake, taking care to lose no part of It. Such a loss would be like a mutilation of your own body. Why, if you had been given gold-dust, would you not take the utmost care to hold it fast, not letting a grain slip through your fingers, lest you be by so much the poorer? How much more carefully, then, will you guard against losing so much as a crumb of that which is more precious than gold and precious stones![112]

We ought to note several things about this passage.

First, the extreme carefulness that St. Cyril demands of the one about to receive the Lord Himself, the King: not a speck of the consecrated bread should be lost — that would be like a mutilation of one's body, a loss of something more precious than any created thing! It was, in fact, this very emphasis on the immense care to be taken toward the Eucharist, together with an ever-deepening appreciation of the sheer magnitude of so divine a gift, that led the Church over time to *abandon* Communion in the hand and to prefer Communion directly in the mouth. This is a primary example of organic development in the liturgy, which pursues the implications of an original belief or attitude until the external expression most perfectly reflects and inculcates that belief or attitude. Conversely, the artificial return to a much earlier but long since discontinued prac-tice — and one that *now*, reappearing in a very different context, carries with it overtones of casualness and lack of faith in the Real Presence — is a primary example of the error of antiquarianism condemned in 1947 by Pius XII in *Mediator Dei*.[113]

---

[112] *Mystagogical Catecheses* 5.21, in *The Works of Saint Cyril of Jerusalem*, vol. 2, trans. Leo P. McCauley and Anthony A. Stephenson, 2nd ed. (Washington, DC: Catholic University of America Press, 2000), 203.

[113] For commentary, see Kwasniewski, *Reclaiming Our Roman Catholic Birthright*, 149–60.

Second, if we look more carefully at what Cyril describes, and combine this passage with other hints from antiquity, we can see that even when Communion in the hand *was* practiced, it involved marks of reverence that (curiously?) never accompanied its re-invention in the late 1960s. Concerning this passage, Professor of Patristics Michael Fiedrowicz observes:

> It is significant that the Eucharist, laid on the right hand, is not then received by means of the less-valued left hand, but rather directly by the mouth. What appears at first glance to be Communion in the hand reveals itself on closer examination to be Communion in the mouth, with the right hand serving as a sort of paten. Bishop Cyril's description shows that the attitude of the communicant is, then, not one of taking and capturing, but rather of reverent and humble reception, accompanied by a sign of adoration.[114]

Bishop Athanasius Schneider—who, like Fiedrowicz, is a specialist in Patrology—goes into greater detail about the ancient ritual:

> The practice had a different form in ancient times than it does today: the Holy Eucharist was received on the palm of the right hand and the faithful were not allowed to touch the Holy Host with their fingers, but they had to bow down their head to the palm of the hand and take the Sacrament directly with their mouth, thus, in a position of a profound bow and not standing upright. The common practice today is to receive the Eucharist standing upright, taking it with the left hand. This is something which, symbolically, the Church Fathers would find horrific—how can the Holy of Holies be taken with the left hand? Then, today the faithful take and touch the Host directly with their fingers and

---

[114] Michael Fiedrowicz, *The Traditional Mass: History, Form, and Theology of the Classical Roman Rite*, trans. Rose Pfeifer (Brooklyn, NY: Angelico Press, 2020), 115–16.

then put the Host in the mouth: this gesture has never been known in the entire history of the Catholic Church but was invented by Calvin—not even by Martin Luther. The Lutherans have typically received the Eucharist kneeling and on the tongue, although of course they do not have the Real Presence because they do not have a valid priesthood. The Calvinists and other Protestant free churches, who do not believe at all in the Real Presence of Christ in the Eucharist, invented a rite which is void of almost all gestures of sacredness and of exterior adoration, i.e., receiving "Communion" standing upright, and touching the bread "Host" with their fingers and putting it in their mouth in the way people treat ordinary bread.…

For them, this was just a symbol, so their exterior behavior towards Communion was similar to behavior towards a symbol. During the Second Vatican Council, Catholic Modernists—especially in the Netherlands—took this Calvinist Communion rite and wrongly attributed it to the Early Church, in order to spread it more easily throughout the Church. We have to dismantle this myth and these insidious tactics, which started in the Catholic Church more than fifty years ago, and which like an avalanche have now rolled through, crushing almost all Catholic churches in the entire world, with the exception of some Catholic countries in Eastern Europe and a few places in Asia and Africa.[115]

---

[115] Bishop Athanasius Schneider, with Diane Montagna, *Christus Vincit: Christ's Triumph over the Darkness of the Age* (Brooklyn, NY: Angelico Press, 2019), 223–24. Msgr. Nicola Bux, a distinguished specialist in liturgical and sacramental theology, has a somewhat different interpretation of the passage in Cyril: "Appeal is made by defenders of communion in the hand to St. Cyril of Jerusalem, who asked the faithful to make of their hand a throne at the moment of receiving communion. I hold, treading lightly in this, that the invitation to dispose the hands in this manner can be understood as not for the purpose of receiving it in the hands, but in order to extend them, also with a bow of the head, in a single act of adoration, and in addition, to prevent the fall of fragments. In fact, on account of

These words afford a backdrop for the disturbing assertions of a close friend and interviewer of Pope Paul VI, the eminent French philosopher Jean Guitton (1901–1999):

> The intention of Paul VI with regard to the liturgy, with regard to what is commonly called the Mass, was to reform the Catholic liturgy in such a way that it should almost coincide with the Protestant liturgy.... Paul VI did everything in his power to get the Catholic Mass, beyond the Council of Trent, closer to the Protestant Lord's Supper.... [T]here was with Paul VI an ecumenical

---

the innate sense of the sacred, very strong in the East, reverence toward the sacrament was affirmed more and more, with the precaution of taking communion in the mouth, for multiple reasons — one among them being the inability to guarantee clean hands and, especially, the safeguarding of the fragments.

"All this renders more comprehensible the statement of St. Augustine: 'no one eats that flesh if he has not first adored.' Benedict XVI recalled this significantly, precisely in the well-known address on the interpretation of Vatican II. Becoming more explicit, Cyril invites us to 'not put the hands out, but in a gesture of adoration and veneration (*tropo proskyniseos kai sevasmatos*), draw near to the chalice of the blood of Christ.' In such a way that he who receives communion makes a *proskynesis*, the prostration or bow, down to the ground — similar to our genuflexion — extending his hands like a throne at the same time, while from the hand of the Lord he receives communion in the mouth. This is what appears clearly depicted by the Purple Codex of Rossano, dated between the end of the 5th and the beginning of the 6th century after Christ: this is a Greek illuminated Gospel book, certainly put together in a Syriac milieu. Therefore we should not be surprised by the fact that the Eastern and the Western pictorial tradition, from the 5th to the 16th century, has depicted Christ as giving communion to the apostles directly in the mouth" (*No Trifling Matter: Taking the Sacraments Seriously Again* [Brooklyn, NY: Angelico Press, 2018], 94–97). Bux speaks here of a classic way of depicting the Last Supper, where Our Lord is either placing a morsel into Judas's mouth, or going around the table to bestow the gift of Communion upon each Apostle in succession. Artistic illustrations may be found in my article "'Eat That Which I Will Give You': Why We Receive Communion in the Mouth," *New Liturgical Movement*, June 17, 2019.

intention to remove, or at least to correct, or at least to relax what was too Catholic, in the traditional sense, in the Mass, and, I repeat, to get the Catholic Mass closer to the Calvinist mass.[116]

As a result, says eminent liturgist Klaus Gamber, Catholics "are now breathing the thin air of Calvinistic sterility."[117]

Moreover, as Bishop Schneider goes on to mention (and as he discusses at greater length in his book *Dominus Est*), in the early Church a communion cloth was, at least in some places and times, laid over the hands of recipients so that they would not directly touch the Holy Sacrament and any fragments could be easily gathered. The Byzantine Rite still utilizes such a cloth, held under the chins of those who are receiving in their mouths from a spoon handled by the priest. Some traditional parishes retain the use of a houseling cloth that covers the communion rail. While the invention of the so-called chin paten renders the houseling cloth no longer necessary, traditional Catholic churches and chapels often retain it as an additional reminder of the sacredness of this Eucharistic banquet and a symbolic link between the people's reception of the Lord and the cloth-covered altar of sacrifice on which the divine Victim has been offered. It underlines that they, like the priest, are partaking of a mystical sacrifice.[118]

In short: the ancient record bears witness to beliefs and attitudes that would, over time, develop into the longstanding Communion praxis of both the Latin West and the Byzantine East. In the West, Communion on the tongue, kneeling, is the natural and suitable result of St. Cyril's Eucharistic piety. The attempt to turn back the clock to antiquity — an

---

[116] In a discussion with historians Yves Chiron and François-Georges Dreyfus on the radio program Lumiere 101, broadcast on December 19, 1993 by Radio-Courtoise, cited by the Very Rev. Dom Gerard, O.S.B., Abbot of Abbaye Sainte-Madeleine, Le Barroux, trans. [likely by Paul Crane, S.J.] in *Christian Order* 35.10 (1994), 454. The original French transcript was published as *Entretien sur Paul VI* (Éditions Nivoit, 2011).

[117] *The Reform of the Roman Liturgy: Its Problems and Background*, trans. Klaus D. Grimm (Fort Collins, CO: Roman Catholic Books, n.d.), 5.

[118] See Kwasniewski, *Reclaiming Our Roman Catholic Birthright*, 321.

antiquity, moreover, deceptively misrepresented and fictitiously recon-structed — is, in the end, nothing but a Trojan horse for Calvinistic sacramental theology.[119]

What is at stake, therefore, is precisely those distinctively Catholic dogmas that a Pew Research survey indicates are rapidly eroding, even among those who still attend Mass.[120] Cardinal Sarah, Bishop Schneider, and many others are pleading for the restoration of a traditional practice that emerged out of and reinforces the Catholic Faith. Will other Church leaders pay heed?

At the very least, right here and right now, every layman and lay-woman can make a firm commitment, for the glory of God and the sanctification of their souls, always to receive Our Lord kneeling and on the tongue, at every Mass they attend, anywhere, at any time.[121]

The art of begging the question

On July 19, 2020, former Anglican and popular author Fr. Dwight Longe-necker tweeted the following: "Which is better? To receive communion reverently and humbly standing and on the hand or to receive kneeling and on the tongue with a heart full of self-righteousness because you are a better Catholic than all hand-receivers?"

He begins by setting up an alternative: "Which is better?" It may turn out that neither option is good, as if one were to say: "Which is better? Dying by cyanide or dying by firing squad?" When he sets up as the first alternative "to receive communion reverently and humbly

---

[119] It is therefore ironic that a Catholic priest online accused proponents of Communion on the tongue of espousing Calvinist views — a claim I will take up later in this chapter.

[120] See www.pewresearch.org/fact-tank/2019/08/05/transubstantiation-eucharist-u-s-catholics.

[121] For full documentation in connection with the "Ordinary Form" or Novus Ordo, see my article "Why Receiving the Eucharist Kneeling Is Always Permissible," *LifeSiteNews*, January 17, 2019.

standing," he begs the very question at issue. Is not the entire debate about whether it is *possible* for Roman Catholics to receive reverently and humbly if they receive standing and in the hand?[122] Having begged the question, Fr. Longenecker sets up the other alternative, which is a classic caricature, custom-made to prove his point: the Catholic who, with self-righteousness, thinks himself better than others because he receives kneeling and on the tongue. Well, naturally, we'd prefer *anyone* to such a person, wouldn't we? It's like asking "Do you prefer the kindly Muslim or the axe-murdering Christian?"

But what of all those Catholics, surely not few in number, who want to receive kneeling and on the tongue because it is more conducive to actual devotion? Who humble themselves physically to help them bear in mind the One Who is feeding us—or rather, the One with Whom we are being fed? Who are not afraid to look odd by lowering themselves or to stand out by not standing up, precisely because they are more concerned with the invisible Lord than with His visible agents? We're talking, in other words, about the kind of Catholics who attend Fr. Longenecker's parish, where Communion kneeling and on the tongue predominates.

The real question of the day should be framed as follows: "Which is better? To receive Communion in a posture dictated by a millennium of exclusive use—a posture that manifestly suggests our creaturely status and our identity as children before God? Or to receive Communion in a posture reintroduced by liturgical experimenters and more or less flagrant Eucharistic heretics in the 1960s, on the basis either of pseudo-antiquarianism or of hyper-modern assumptions about what 'Christian maturity' should look like?" The benefit of putting the question this way is that it places it on objective ground, rather than trying to peek inside of people's hearts, which are notoriously hard to read.

[122] Since this book is intended for Catholics of the Latin Rite, here is not the place to discuss various Eastern Catholic practices; these, in any case, could never be confused with the postconciliar manner in which Communion is given in most Novus Ordo parishes.

Martin Mosebach is the modern author who has expressed with the greatest clarity the meaning of the change from Communion kneeling to Communion standing:

> Kneeling was medieval, they said. The early Christians prayed standing. Standing signifies the resurrected Christ, they said; it is the most appropriate attitude for a Christian. The early Christians are also supposed to have received Communion in their hands. What is irreverent about the faithful making their hands into a "throne" for the Host? I grant that the people who tell me such things are absolutely serious about it all. But it becomes very clear that pastors of souls are incredibly remote from the world in these matters; academic arguments are completely useless in questions of liturgy. These scholars are always concerned only about the historical side of the substance of faith and of the forms of devotion. If, however, we think correctly and historically, we should realize that what is an expression of veneration in one period can be an expression of blasphemy in another. If people who have been kneeling for a thousand years suddenly get to their feet, they do not think, "We're doing this like the early Christians, who stood for the Consecration"; they are not aware of returning to some particularly authentic form of worship. They simply get up, brush the dust from their trouser-legs and say to themselves: "So it wasn't such a serious business after all." Everything that takes place in celebrations of this kind implies the same thing: "It wasn't all that serious after all." Under such circumstances, anthropologically speaking, it is quite impossible for faith in the presence of Christ in the Sacrament to have any deeper spiritual significance, even if the Church continues to proclaim it and even if the participants of such celebrations go so far as to affirm it explicitly.[123]

[123] *The Heresy of Formlessness: The Roman Liturgy and Its Enemy*, rev. and expanded ed., trans. Graham Harrison (Brooklyn, NY: Angelico Press, 2018), 14–15.

The Holy Bread of Eternal Life

In contrast stands (if we may put it thus) the wisdom of Benedict XVI, who said on May 22, 2008: "Kneeling in adoration before the Eucharist is the most valid and radical remedy against the idolatries of yesterday and today." This observation is not limited to times set aside for Eucharistic Adoration or solemn exposition, when a large Host is placed in a monstrance. In the Western tradition, kneeling is the most appropriate response to the Real Presence of the Lord. This is why we kneel for the Eucharistic Prayer, in which the miracle of transubstantiation takes place; this is why we kneel for the most intimate moment of Communion, because—like the Magi, like Jairus, like Mary of Bethany—we know Who it is into Whose presence we are come. We are come to adore, to receive, to abide, and to love.

Fr. Longenecker himself *knows* all this. Indeed, he wrote in a recent book:

> One of the most instrumental factors in developing reverence at Mass is how we receive communion. While the faithful can certainly be reverent in receiving communion in the hand while standing, no one can disagree that receiving communion on the tongue while kneeling is more reverent. Why is this? Firstly, because kneeling in our Western culture is an intrinsic act of devotion, homage, and worship. This is true no matter what the context. Knights kneel to receive their knighthood from the Queen. Bride and groom kneel to receive a nuptial blessing. To receive communion on the tongue is a sign of belief in the real presence of Christ's Body and Blood in the Eucharistic Host, because a sign that you are intent not to profane the Body of Christ by dropping it or soiling it in any way.[124]

Equipped with this knowledge, Fr. Longenecker and other "conservative" or "middle-of-the-road" clergy like him should publicly support, and not subtly undermine, Catholics who wish to honor their Lord and God with all their heart, soul, mind, and bodily strength, in the midst of a Church whose own leaders often seem hell-bent against allowing it to happen.

---

[124] *Letters on Liturgy* (Brooklyn, NY: Angelico Press, 2020), 51; cf. 118.

The internet exposes the most breathtaking ignorance to full public display. It's like a form of intellectual nudism. I suppose this is a good thing, as the errors and vices of the postconciliar Church can no longer hide, like creepy-crawly things in dark swamps, but are being exposed for what they are in broad daylight. This is not to say they will be instantly wiped out. It is only to say that it is easier to fight an enemy who makes himself apparent.

Case in point: the Catholic Boomer priest, trained at St. John's in Camarillo, who posted this nugget on Facebook:

> For the first thousand years of the Church Communion was given in the hand only. John Calvin's influence on the Church, along with the Gnostics preached that the human body was evil and that humans were basically evil and that Communion was only for the holy Clergy. This heresy was condemned, so the Jansenists, who followed a lot of Calvin's heresies, said "You aren't good enough to touch the Body of Christ with your hand, only with your tongue!" as if the tongue is holier than the hand. When someone is Baptized or Confirmed their entire being is Baptized or Confirmed, not just their tongue. They are anointed and consecrated to Christ, their entire body, mind and spirit.

One barely knows where to begin taking apart such a tangled web of misinformation and fantasy.

1. We already have evidence of Communion placed into the mouth from the first millennium.[125] Msgr. Nicola Bux argues there are even indications of it at the Last Supper.[126]

2. The early Christians did not practice Communion on the hand in the way we do it. Our way is novel and desacralizing.

---

[125] See Joseph Shaw, "Ancient Church Doctor Lays Out Why Laity Should Never Touch Holy Communion with Bare Hands," *LifeSiteNews*, July 20, 2020.

[126] See the preceding chapter, as well as note 130.

3. The custom of receiving directly into the mouth, observed for well over one thousand years by all Eastern and Western Christians, has nothing to do with Calvin or Gnosticism or Jansenism, but with humble and adoring reverence toward the Body of Christ, and due respect for the anointed hands of the priest who handles the Body of Christ as his proper office. The custom also predominated for practical reasons: it is safer and more efficient.

4. The tongue, as a matter of fact, is specially blessed in the traditional rite of baptism, where a pinch of exorcised and blessed salt is placed on it, with a prayer that looks ahead to the reception of Communion: "N., accipe sal sapientiæ: propitiatio sit tibi in vitam æternam" (N., receive the salt of wisdom: may it be propitious to you unto eternal life), and then:

> O God of our fathers, O God the Author of all truth, vouchsafe, we humbly beseech Thee, to look graciously down upon this Thy servant, N., and as he tastes this first nutriment of salt, suffer him no longer to hunger for want of heavenly food, to the end that he may be always fervent in spirit, rejoicing in hope, always serving Thy name. Lead him, O Lord, we beseech Thee, to the laver of the new regeneration, that, together with Thy faithful, he may deserve to attain the everlasting rewards of Thy promises.

No other part of the body is set aside in this manner for blessed food.[127] It is no wonder that the removal of this precious ceremony from the rite of baptism more or less coincided with the permission, born of disobedience, for Communion on the hand.

Let us consider some important points that one would think should be obvious—but I suppose nothing can be taken for obvious in our era, which combines a staggering lack of common sense with a confounding lack of historical, cultural, and liturgical awareness.

---

[127] The salt can be seen as either a symbolic "substitute" for Communion, or as an anticipation of and preparation for the Eucharist for the one who cannot yet receive it.

1. Hands are seldom clean, which is why we're supposed to be washing them frequently and we're told not to touch our mouths or faces. The modern practice of Communion in the hand can involve frequent hand-to-hand contact; but if the Host is placed gently on the tip of the tongue, there is no contact between the giver and the recipient.[128]

2. Moreover, the hand symbolizes work ("work of human hands"), while the mouth symbolizes speech, thought, judgment, and love. The Book of Revelation doesn't say that Jesus has a sword in His hand; it says "And out of his mouth goeth a sharp sword" (Rev. 19:5, KJV), showing His power and His reign of justice. The Canticle of Canticles does not begin: "Let him touch me with the touches of his hands," but "Let him kiss me with the kisses of his mouth" (Song of Sol. 1:2, KJV). Scripture sees the mouth as closer to the core of the person, more expressive of who and what he is.

3. Building off of these points is the symbolism of receiving in the mouth versus taking with the hand.[129] When someone puts food into our hands, it is being "handed over" and comes into our power. It is our possession. When, in contrast, someone feeds us directly into the mouth, we are basically passive: the feeder feeds, and the one fed is fed, like a small child by its parent. The latter arrangement suits better the divine feeding of us with bread from heaven.

4. While it is true that all of the faithful are baptized into Christ's priesthood, the ordained priest participates in that priesthood in an essentially different and higher way: he can act *in persona Christi capitis*, in the person of Christ the Head of the Church. His ordination has set him

---

[128] Traditionally, the Latin-Rite priest washes his hands in the sacristy just prior to Holy Mass, washes his "canonical digits" (thumbs and forefingers) at the *lavabo*, and rubs the same digits three times on the corporal before the Consecration of the Host, to ensure that his fingers are clean and dry. After Consecration, he holds the canonical digits together for the remainder of the Canon and the Communion rite, separating them only at the ablutions. For more details, see the six-part series "'The Fingers That Hold God': The Priestly Benefits of 'Liturgical Digits'" at *New Liturgical Movement*, published in 2018.

[129] See the more extended discussion in the preceding chapter.

apart essentially, not accidentally, for that office, and for all the activities that flow from it. Therefore it is fitting for him to feed himself and then to feed the other members of the Church, as Christ did His apostles at the Last Supper. In his painting "Communion of the Apostles," James Tissot (1836–1902), who researched his biblical art with exceptional care, envisions the Lord feeding the apostles as is customary in the Middle East, where a friend may place food in his friend's mouth, or a lover in that of his beloved, at least on special occasions (think of the custom of the bride and bridegroom feeding cake to one another at the wedding reception).[130] Msgr. Bux points out that the Gospel of John implies this manner of feeding:

> The text of John is understood in this way: "Jesus then answered him [John]: 'It is he to whom I shall give a morsel of dipped bread.' Then, having dipped a morsel of bread, he gave it to Judas, son of Simon Iscariot. And as soon as he had taken the mouthful Satan entered into him" (13:26–27).

---

[130] Msgr. Nicola Bux observes: "Not a few people hold that it was only in late antiquity or the early Middle Ages that the Churches of the East and the West began to prefer administering it directly in the mouth. But did Jesus give communion to the apostles on the hand or asking them to take it with their own hands? Visiting an exhibition of Tintoretto in Rome, I observed some 'Last Suppers' in which Jesus gives communion to the apostles in the mouth. One could think that this has to do with an interpretation by the painter after the fact, a little like the posture of Jesus and the apostles at table, in the cenacle of Leonardo, which 'updates' in the Western manner the Jewish custom, which was, instead, to be reclining at table. Reflecting further on this, the custom of giving communion to the faithful directly in the mouth can be considered not only as a Jewish tradition, and therefore apostolic, but also as going back to the Lord Jesus. The Jews and the peoples of the East in general had and today still have the custom of taking food with one's hands and placing it directly in the mouth of the lover or the friend. In the West this is done between couples in love and by the mother toward her little one, who is still inexperienced" (*No Trifling Matter*, 94–95). See my article "The Possibly Dubious Liturgical Legacy of Leonardo's *Last Supper*," *New Liturgical Movement*, December 16, 2019.

But what should be said about the invitation of Jesus: "Take and eat.... Take and drink"? *Take* (in Greek, *labete*; in Latin, *accipite*) also means *receive*. If the mouthful is dipped, it cannot be taken with the hands; rather it is received directly into the mouth. It is true that Jesus consecrated bread and wine separately. But if during the "mystic supper" (as the East calls it) or Last Supper, the two consecrating gestures happened, so it seems, in different phases of the Paschal supper, nevertheless after Pentecost the apostles, aided by Jewish priests who had converted (cf. Acts 6:7), and who were, as we would say, experts in religious worship, united the gestures within the great Eucharistic prayer. The distribution of the consecrated bread and wine was then placed after the anaphora, thus originating the rite of communion.

The conclusion to be drawn is not that *all* Communion was given this way in ancient times, but rather that we cannot *exclude* that Communion was at least sometimes given directly into the mouth from the beginning, before it became the universal norm later on.

5. It was precisely centuries of opportunity to internalize these truths—together with lots of practical experience, good and bad—that prompted the Church *universally*, in all her Eastern and Western rites, to move *exclusively* to Communion in the mouth, preceded or accompanied by a manifest sign of adoration.

6. Therefore, against this millennial tradition, the abrupt return of Communion in the hand in the 1960s sent one and only one signal: the Eucharist and the priesthood aren't such a big deal after all. Don't worry about kneeling or bowing profoundly before it; don't worry about being fed with the bread of angels. It's just a symbol of our communal belonging and how great we already are by our baptism. And that brings us full circle to the Facebook post with which we began.

Stepping back, then, we see that *one consistent set of symbols*—developed over time by a Church that, guided by the Holy Spirit, believed profoundly in transubstantiation and the Real Presence—has been replaced by *another set* contrary to it, erosive of these beliefs. How hard is it to see that this "swap" has, in fact, taken place; that it *cannot* have been caused by the same Spirit, but rather, an opposing spirit; and that the Church must return, in sackcloth and ashes, to her eminently sensible and sacred tradition?

Is it really "a big deal" to receive in the hand?

Many bishops around the world are attempting to compel Catholics, rightly disposed to approach the Holy Eucharist, to receive Our Lord in the hand, contrary to their well-formed consciences about the risks involved in that method, and contrary to their canonical rights to receive on the tongue. I have received many questions from worried Catholics asking if the bishops really have such authority and if it is ever right for the faithful to go along with such decrees. I will quote three sets of inquiries, followed by my answers.

> While thankfully I have regular access to the Blessed Sacrament, my sons are currently residing in a diocese where the bishop, like so many others, has "mandated" Communion in the hand. I discussed with my sons how the bishop has no authority to mandate such a thing, and shared articles (including your own), which my sons discussed with their priests. These priests, however, are going to "just do what the bishop says," and for the past few weeks my sons have refrained from receiving Communion at all rather than have to receive on the hand. Should my sons continue to refrain from receiving? To me, it seems like it would be just the capitulation the Devil desires if we were to say "okay, whatever—I need Communion, so I'll go ahead and receive on the hand for now, since it's my only choice." I hate to "give in" to this destructive progressivism in any way, but would it be actually wrong to receive on the hand if there was no other way available?

This is a painful cross that so many Catholics have to bear in these days of upside-down priorities. A few considerations.

1. Inasmuch as the bishops are abusing their authority (and that they are doing so is beyond doubt, given universal law which they cannot simply put aside), it is wrong to capitulate to their requests, since this would only confirm them in their contempt for law, tradition, and the legitimate rights of the faithful. The same is true for the priests: they want to be "obedient," but they are actually being enablers of episcopal overreach.[131] We may pardon their weakness, but we shouldn't applaud it by "falling in line." Remember the Austrian Catholics at the time of the Third Reich? They fell into line except for Franz Jägerstätter: they all said "Oh, we can square this National Socialist oath of allegiance with Catholicism," and he said: "Not so fast: I don't see how I can." The Church honors him as a martyr. We can hope the Lord had mercy on the rest who caved in.

2. "Is it a big deal to receive in the hand?" Well, for starters, if we were doing it in the ancient manner, we would receive in the *right* hand (not the left!), and bow down in adoration to take up the holy bread with our tongue, and then would lick our palm to make sure no fragments would be left over. (One still sees Byzantine priests licking their fingers as they clean the antimension after Communion.) In other words, not at all what is being done today since the *faux* "revival" of Communion in the hand in the 1960s and '70s. It *might* be possible to receive in the truly ancient manner without sin, but by adopting it one would very obviously "stick out" from the rest of the people — and one would still be licking one's hand, which is hardly sanitary by today's standards, especially if there is a danger of harmful germs. Put differently, the ancient manner of receiving in the hand would have twice the disadvantage, from a hygienic point of view, that receiving directly on the tongue has.

3. It seems to me that there is a great risk of consequentialism here: "We want sacrament X…therefore we are willing to receive it less reverently." If sacrament X were one of absolute necessity, that would be more understandable; but the only such sacrament is baptism. The sacraments are not just for my personal benefit, but for the adoration of God in Himself, and

---

[131] See chapter 19.

for His glorification in me. So, I must not simply dismiss as unimportant the manner in which the Holy Spirit has led the Church to perfect her expressions of reverence — above all when it comes to the reception of our divine Savior, Jesus Christ, in the Most Blessed Sacrament of the Altar.

4. Practically speaking, we should try to find priests who are willing, at least privately, to give Communion in the traditional and still normative way, i.e., on the tongue, and if this is not to be found in one's vicinity, then perhaps one could, once a month, drive to a place where that is possible, and make a half-day of it, praying the Rosary or some part of the Divine Office, and treating the Eucharistic Lord with the honor He deserves. In the meantime, we know that saints have not only recommended spiritual Communion but have emphasized its power. At the end of her life, St. Thérèse of Lisieux was compelled to make spiritual Communions because she could not keep food down, and she turned that into yet another means of purification and sanctification.

It seems to me that this dire situation cannot last forever. There will always be clergy who will see clearly their solemn duties before God and man, and will take these duties seriously. Meanwhile, we must keep up our prayer life in all the ways that are open to us as laymen. In this way we will be strengthened for the journey through the desert.[132]

Is it sinful to receive in the hand?

There has been a big debate between some of my friends and me over the matter of receiving Holy Communion in the hand. One young man believes that it would be wrong to say it is sinful

---

[132] For further discussion of how to sanctify life in the home and develop a prayer routine, see David Clayton and Leila Marie Lawler, *The Little Oratory: A Beginner's Guide to Praying in the Home* (Manchester, NH: Sophia Institute Press, 2014); cf. Kwasniewski, *Reclaiming Our Roman Catholic Birthright*, 281–88, and my article, "The Office of Workers and Fighters: Praying Prime," *OnePeterFive*, February 5, 2020. There are many articles online about how to recite (or sing!) the Divine Office.

if "the living Magisterium has allowed it" (he has *Redemptionis Sacramentum*, no. 92, in mind). To me, however, this sounds like a positivistic and ultramontanist approach. There *is* an objective liturgical tradition that the living Magisterium must adhere to. It seems to me that Communion in the hand could be a sacrilege, and if so, we know that sacrilege is a sin. I think the broader question is, can the living Magisterium promote something sinful through official documents?

It would be difficult to maintain that it is *necessarily* a sin to receive the Eucharist in one's hand, if adequate precautions were taken. After all, if it were sinful in itself, it could never have been practiced in the early Church. If one followed the ancient method, one would place the *right* hand above the left hand, and when the Host is in the palm, one would bow down to the hand (not moving the hand) and take up the Host with one's mouth, licking the area on the palm in order to make sure no particles remained. This is not a form of "self-communication" but is, one might say, making the right hand into a substitute paten, showing adoration by the bow, and exhibiting due care by the licking.

All the same, we do not live anymore in the fourth century; we live in the twenty-first, after a millennium (and more) during which the Church, moved by the Holy Spirit, abandoned Communion in the hand everywhere because of ever-growing reverence for the Most Holy Sacrament, a deepening appreciation of the special anointing conferred on the hands of the priest for handling sacred things, and a realization of the dangers connected with hand reception. Something that might have been acceptable in one age comes to be seen as unacceptable in another, precisely because the Church's practice develops, even as her insight into revealed mysteries develops. One who interprets this development as a corruption has essentially espoused Protestantism or its close relative, false antiquarianism.

For those who realize, as every well-catechized Catholic should, that the Church's traditions are to be revered and trusted, and who know that Communion on the hand had long been abandoned and replaced for fitting reasons with Communion on the tongue, it *would* be sinful to receive on the hand, because one would be acting against one's conscience and against one's understanding of the Faith. However, there are very many Catholics who are so poorly trained and so ignorant that they actually do not know what the tradition was, or why it was that way—or even that we should trust our traditions to begin with. Such a Catholic, if in a state of grace and attempting to do what he believes the Church is asking him to do, would not (necessarily) be committing a sin.

Obviously, saying this doesn't cancel out in any way the serious *problems* with Communion in the hand. It is unfitting for unanointed hands to handle the Body of Christ. It risks profaning Our Lord by the loss of fragments. It is contrary to organic tradition. The living Magisterium itself, as you rightly say, has an obligation to adhere to the tradition and not to contradict it, which would be equivalent to telling the Holy Spirit to get lost. Even Paul VI, who was colorblind and tone-deaf when it came to liturgy, seems to have recognized this (see the strangely contradictory document *Memoriale Domini* of May 29, 1969, from the Sacred Congregation for Divine Worship, approved by Paul VI), but he was too weak and self-doubting to uphold what he knew to be true. We, on the other hand, should not be weak and self-doubting in following the wisdom of tradition.

Rubrics, conditions, and conscience

Some people say Communion in the hand can be sinful in the context of the traditional Latin Mass, because it is forbidden there, yet not sinful in the Novus Ordo, where it is permitted. Could something be sinful in one rite but not in another? Or are you saying the act in itself is not a sin, but the knowledge of the receiver can determine culpability, and thus the weight of the sin? Also, is it always wrong to go against one's conscience? Let's say someone's conscience bothers him about receiving in the hand; should he confess it?

It can indeed be a sin to go against *required* rubrics.[133] Since Communion on the tongue is required in the traditional Latin Mass, to distribute in any other way would be a sin. For the Novus Ordo, Communion on the tongue remains the norm, while Communion in the hand is permitted in countries that have obtained a "rescript," that is, an exception from the norm. The norm remains intact; hence, provided one was in a condition to approach the Sacrament, it could never be seen as disobedient to *refuse* to receive Communion in the hand or to *insist* on receiving on the tongue.

According to the Instruction *Memoriale Domini*, an overarching condition has to be met before Communion in the hand can ever be allowed: there must be no "risk of lack of respect or of false opinions with regard to the Blessed Eucharist" and an avoidance of "any other ill effects." In the *Acta Apostolicae Sedis*, the Instruction was accompanied by a sample letter that fleshed out this condition: "the new method should not be imposed in a way that would exclude the traditional usage"; the faithful "will perform it with the respect due to the sacrament"; there shall be catechesis ensuring no "suggestion of wavering on the part of the Church in its faith in the Eucharistic presence" and removing "any danger or even suggestion of profanation"; the new mode "should not suggest to him [the layman] that this is ordinary bread, or just any sacred object... His respectful attitude should be proportionate to what he is doing."[134] It is impossible to reread this optimistic language from fifty years ago without seeing that these conditions were never met, are still not being met, and in fact will never be *able* to be met. They are, on the contrary, habitually

---

[133] See my article "How Sinful Is It to Disregard the Rubrics?," *New Liturgical Movement*, November 17, 2014.

[134] Text available at https://www.ewtn.com/catholicism/library/instruction -on-the-manner-of-distributing-holy-communion-2195.

violated. The moment clergy awaken to this disturbing fact (and there is a moment of awakening for many), they have a solemn obligation before God, based on natural law, divine law, and ecclesiastical law, to curtail Communion in the hand and to replace it as soon as may be with the normative traditional practice.[135]

In general, once one becomes aware of the problems surrounding Communion in the hand — that it allows for easy and repeated profanation, that it has contributed to a loss of faith in the Real Presence and the special nature of the ordained priesthood, that it contradicts a fitting tradition of many centuries, that it is contrary even to the stipulations that are supposed to regulate it, that it facilitates the theft of the Host for satanic rituals, etc. — then it would be contrary to a well-informed conscience to receive in that way, and so, it would be sinful.

This is not, after all, a unique sort of moral situation. Many times, people are badly (in)formed about the nature of certain actions, and they may not be culpable for their ignorance in a given situation. People can do objectively wrong things while not being subjectively guilty of choosing them *as* evil. However, once they "wise up," they are obliged to follow their better-informed consciences, and they will regret their mistakes and make reparation for them. We know from Scripture and the writings of the saints that God is displeased by objectively wrong actions, even when their perpetrators are ignorant or deceived about what they are doing.

Moreover, regardless of their intentions, people will still suffer negative consequences from the evil actions they do. For example, those who use contraception, having been deceived into thinking it morally acceptable, will nonetheless suffer injury in their personal lives and relationships by using it, and, to some extent, they thwart the will of God, Creator and Lord of life, for their sanctification. Looking back over their lives, they will *regret* what they have done, rather than shrugging their shoulders and saying, "Oh well, we didn't know, so it made no difference." That is why

---

[135] See chapter 19.

the Catholic tradition places such a premium on the correct formation of conscience, and why it makes sense for the faithful to confess anything that seems to them to be a sin against what is known or believed to be pleasing to God.

9

The Wisdom of Tradition

*The following is a lightly edited transcript of John-Henry Westen's interview
with Dr. Peter Kwasniewski at Voice of the Family's online conference "Love
and reverence due to Our Lord: Let us always receive Holy Communion on
the tongue," held on July 16, 2020. The video is available on YouTube.*

John-Henry Westen: Could you give us, first of all, a short history
of the manner in which Holy Communion has been received in the
Church?

Dr. Peter Kwasniewski: The early centuries of the Church don't give us
as full a picture as we would like to have. We have a lot of fragmentary
evidence. It seems that there was a diversity of manners of receiving. Communion was received in the hand but in a very reverent manner, not in
the way it is done today. However, we also have evidence from St. Ephrem
the Syrian, from the liturgy of St. James, from St. Gregory the Great, and
from some other Fathers of the Church that Communion was given in
the mouth as well and that the clergy were the ones who most properly
communicated with their own hands. The regional Council of Rouen
in 878 mandated Communion in the mouth; the canons of the Coptic
Church say "God forbid that any of the pearls," by which they mean the
consecrated fragments, "should adhere to the fingers or fall to the ground."
And even St. Cyril of Jerusalem, who is often quoted as a proponent of
Communion in the hand, says the fragments are more precious than

gold dust and that we should sooner lose one of our own members than lose any fragments. So, there is a very heightened awareness early on of the awesomeness of the Sacrament and in fact it is this growing sense of reverence that leads the Church over time, progressively, to restrict and, finally, to abolish Communion in the hand, except of course for the clergy.

By the beginning of the second millennium, Communion in the mouth is universal for the laity, which goes along with a decrease in Communion under both kinds. That is, the Host is received kneeling and on the tongue, and the chalice becomes more and more reserved just for the celebrating priest or bishop. Essentially, for the second millennium of Catholic history, it is always Communion on the tongue for the laity, out of honor for Our Lord and in the spirit of adoration. It is remarkable how universal the practice is in the second millennium, to the extent that it simply isn't discussed anymore among Catholics in the West or the Orthodox in the East. What we are seeing here is, in my opinion, a clear example of organic development—that is, the Church under the guidance of the Holy Spirit responding more and more appropriately to the gifts that she has received. This is not to say that for the Christians in the third or fourth century it was wrong to do things the way they did, but they had not yet arrived at the most reverent, the safest, and the most efficient way of giving Communion.

We also have to bear in mind a practical question: there were fewer communicants in the early Church. As the Church grew and spread and there were more and more faithful, the question arose: How are we going to give Communion to so many people? And as anyone can see who has been to a traditional Latin Mass, where all the faithful are lined up along a communion rail, kneeling, and the priest goes right along and gives Communion to each one in turn, it is a much more efficient way of giving Communion, in addition to being safer and more reverent.

JHW: So, after doing this universally for over a thousand years, the Church goes back to the practice of Communion in the hand in 1969. How did this even happen?

PK: It is a very sad story. It has been told very well by Bishop Juan Rodolfo Laise. He wrote a book on the history of Holy Communion and the manner of giving it.[136] He documents this in detail as a case of rank disobedience, because the Church had a clear policy about what was to be done (and not done). However, in the '60s there were priests who were experimenting in every direction. And towards the end of the '60s there were priests who, unauthorized, were giving Communion in the hand and there were Bishops' Conferences agitating for it.

Initially, Paul VI opposed Communion in the hand and in fact opposed it very strongly. In 1968 he sent out a questionnaire to all the bishops in the world, asking them whether the traditional manner (receiving Holy Communion kneeling and on the tongue) should be retained, and Communion in the hand allowed. The overwhelming majority of bishops responded "yes, we should retain the traditional manner; no, Communion in the hand should not be allowed." Those results, as well as the actual votes, were published along with the rationale for retaining the traditional practice in a 1969 instruction called *Memoriale Domini*, which was initiated by Paul VI, and approved by him for publication by the Sacred Congregation for Divine Worship. *Memoriale Domini* is a remarkable document, which says (and I quote): "In view of the state of the Church as a whole today, this [the traditional] manner of distributing Holy Communion must be observed[137] not only because it rests upon a tradition of many centuries but especially because it is a sign of the reverence of the faithful toward the Eucharist. The practice in no way detracts from the personal dignity of those who approach this great Sacrament" — you see, there were some people saying that it is not dignified to get down on your knees and act like a slave or a servant; but this document says no, it does not detract from dignity — "and it is a part of the preparation needed for the most fruitful reception of the Lord's Body. This reverence is a sign of Holy Communion being not in 'common bread and drink' but in the Body and Blood of the Lord."

---

[136] See the bibliography.

[137] The Latin could also be translated "preserved."

The Holy Bread of Eternal Life

The document continues: "In addition, this manner of communicating, which is now to be considered as prescribed by custom, gives more effective assurance that Holy Communion will be distributed with the appropriate reverence, decorum, and dignity; that any danger of profaning the Eucharistic species in which 'the whole and an entire Christ, God and man, is substantially contained and permanently present in a unique way,' will be avoided; and finally, that the diligent care which the Church has always commended for the very fragments of the consecrated bread will be maintained."

This is *Memoriale Domini* of 1969, initiated and approved by Paul VI! The odd thing is that in the same document, after laying this out and giving the results of the vote and saying the traditional manner should be retained, Paul VI says: Nevertheless, since there are some places in the world where Communion in the hand has already been introduced, in order to regulate it better, the Episcopal Conferences *of those places* are allowed to permit it, but under certain conditions. So, it is an odd document, because it first persuades us to keep the traditional manner and then it says that certain Episcopal Conferences can decide otherwise. (Unfortunately, a lot of hot-button issues were being pushed off to the Bishops' Conferences in the '60s and '70s—and we have seen the same things happen more recently with *Amoris Laetitia*.) That is an unfortunate contradiction within this document.

However, *Memoriale Domini* does say there is a condition for giving Communion on the hand: it cannot be done if "any possible lack of reverence or false ideas about the Eucharist" are being engendered in the attitudes of the people. Perhaps Paul VI was thinking naively that this change could somehow take place without lessening reverence and devotion, without lessening the faith of the people in the Real Presence, but he was wrong. When we look with hindsight today, we *know*, factually, that he was wrong. I would say they should have known back then, had they been thinking it through, that this would have profound consequences. But nevertheless, *now* it cannot be denied that there have been these profound consequences. As far as *Memoriale Domini* is concerned, we should not be giving Communion in the hand anymore because the very problems that it pointed to have occurred.

JHW: One of the arguments from those who promote Communion in the hand is that this is a restoration of a legitimate, ancient Christian practice. Why can't we do it? Are we not getting back to the roots? How do you respond to them?

PK: This is a problem that Pope Pius XII dealt with in his 1947 Encyclical *Mediator Dei* on the sacred liturgy where he defined an error that he called "false antiquarianism" and condemned it. He said it is a mistake to try to restore later in the Church's history practices that occurred much earlier on, because it was not without the guidance of the Holy Spirit that the Church developed in the way that she did. He gives these examples: it would be dangerous to turn the priest around and have him facing the people; it would be wrong to get rid of black as a color for liturgical vestments. He gives various examples which unfortunately all came to pass only about fifteen or twenty years later! He says this would be a mistake because the Church does in fact deepen her understanding over time. The liturgy does not stop developing in the fifth or the sixth century, neither does the piety of the Christian people, nor the theology. When you look at the Council of Trent in the sixteenth century, it offers one of the most magnificent expositions of Catholic doctrine, and there are things clarified by that council that were unclear prior to it.

If we were to disagree with Pius XII on that point, we would end up saying with the Protestants that the Church got corrupted; that for many centuries—the "Dark Ages"—the Church went off the rails and if we want the authentic Christian Church, we have to go back to the apostles or at least to the apostolic period. That is a characteristically Protestant error. It is something that Luther, Calvin, Zwingli, and Melanchthon said. And lo and behold, there were liturgical reformers in the twentieth century saying exactly the same thing: we have to go back before what the Church did in the Middle Ages, because somehow that is corrupt.

The Holy Bread of Eternal Life

I also wanted to comment that the ancient manner of receiving Communion in the hand was much different, and it would look today much more reverent, than what is done in the Novus Ordo. In the patristic period the right hand was placed forward because you always received in the right hand, never in the left hand (the left symbolizes sin and the devil). Once the holy bread was placed in your hand, you bowed down in adoration and took it up with your mouth. You licked it up with your tongue to make sure there were no particles there. We even have records that sometimes a cloth was used. A cloth would have been put in your hands, the holy bread placed on the cloth, and then you would bow down and receive it and that way whatever fragments might be there would be retained in the cloth which would be held by acolytes. So, there are ways—at least theoretically—in which Communion in the hand could be done with reverence and without danger, or without as much danger. But even so, the Church decided to stop doing it, and what is being done now bears very little resemblance to what I just described.

JHW: So, what then are the basic problems with Communion in the hand?

PK: The number one problem is that it is contrary to at least a thousand years of tradition. The Council of Rouen that I mentioned before took place in 878. It is not an ecumenical council; it is a regional council, but it is indicative of the thinking and of the practice. So, for at least a thousand years the Church has seen fit to give Communion to the faithful kneeling and on the tongue. That is not accidental. That has everything to do with the Church's intensifying faith, especially in the Middle Ages, when the first heretics rose up who denied the Real Presence. For the first thousand years of Christianity nobody denied the Real Presence. The heretics denied other things, but nobody denied that. Once there were heretics actually denying the Real Presence, the Church emphasized in every way she could: this is *really* the Body and Blood of our Lord Jesus Christ and His Soul and Divinity. Therefore, we should do everything in our power, not only spiritually to be ready to receive and not be in a state of sin, but also physically, to show that we adore the Word made flesh in the Blessed Sacrament. This is also the reason why the genuflections that priests do during the traditional liturgy developed in the Middle Ages: to affirm over and over again our faith in the Word made flesh, present on the altar. So that is the number one problem: contempt for tradition.

The number two problem is a practical problem: particles are lost when Communion is given in the hand. Research has been done to show this. There is an article available online in *The Latin Mass* magazine from many years ago where somebody did experiments using black gloves, so that it would be very obvious where the particles were.[138] If you put a Host in someone's hand, especially considering that some of the altar breads are a bit crumbly and not as compact as they traditionally used to be, it is not surprising that little crumbs might remain and fall onto the floor and be scattered. This is something that the Church Fathers would have beheld with horror. They would never have tolerated anything like that. In fact, that is exactly one of the conditions that the Church lays down in *Redemptionis Sacramentum*: "If there is a risk of profanation, then Holy Communion should not be given in the hand to the faithful." Frankly, there is always a risk of profanation if it is given in the hand, even just because of what I described, so this seems to be a very basic problem. That is why the rubrics of the traditional liturgy governing how the priest cleans off the paten and how he cleans the corporal on the altar are very detailed and thorough, because we do not want to lose one pearl, as St. Ephrem the Syrian says. When you give the Host on the tongue to someone kneeling, that danger is almost completely removed. According to the rubrics, there is supposed to be a hand paten or a chin paten placed underneath so that if a fragment were to fall, it would fall right onto the

---

[138] See Father X, "Losing Fragments with Communion in the Hand: Estimating the Problem with Unconsecrated Hosts," *The Latin Mass* 18.4 (Fall 2009), 27–29, available at www.latinmassmagazine.com/pdfs/Losing-Fragments-LM-2009-Fall.pdf.

paten, which the priest will clean afterwards. So the Church has thought of everything, she has left nothing to chance.

Among other problems are that Communion in the hand, especially as it is done nowadays, standing up, lessens reverence for the Lord. When the Magi got to the manger, they did not just stand around and politely distribute gifts as if they were at some kind of convention. They got down on their knees — that is what it says in Scripture. In the Gospels, when people come up to Our Lord to be healed, they fall on their knees. When Peter says "Depart from me, Lord, I am a sinful man" (see Luke 5:8), he is on his knees. It is the most obvious and the most natural sign of adoration and reverence and that is why, even in the Novus Ordo Mass, we are kneeling during the Eucharistic Prayer. Why would we do that if we don't then kneel for Communion? When we go up to Our Lord, this is the most sacred moment for us, because we come into contact with Him. So, there is a real incoherence. The traditional practice was (and is) perfectly consistent.

In connection with all of these things, Communion in the hand lessens the belief in the Real Presence. If you really believe that Our Lord is present in the Eucharist, then you are not going to treat Him like an ordinary cracker, a wafer; you cannot imagine that. Various surveys and polls have been done, which show how even Catholics who go to Mass do not believe in transubstantiation anymore. I think that Communion standing and in the hand bears a lot of the blame for that.

Let me just mention one other thing: it lessens our awareness of the dignity of the ordained priesthood as well, because the priest is ordained not only to offer sacrifice but also to convey the sacraments to the faithful. St. Thomas says it belongs to the same one to consecrate and to distribute the Eucharist.[139] The priests' hands are anointed with sacred chrism in the

---

[139] *Summa theologiae* III, qu. 82, art. 3: "The dispensing of Christ's body belongs to the priest for three reasons. First, because...he consecrates as in the person of Christ. But even as Christ consecrated His body at the supper, so also He gave it to others to be partaken of by them. Accordingly, just as the consecration of Christ's body belongs to the priest, so likewise does the dispensing belong to him. Secondly, because the priest is the

ordination rites, so that he can worthily handle the body of Christ. The faithful's hands are never consecrated that way. We are not set apart for the service of the Eucharist in the same way. Lay people receiving in the hand sends the subtle message of a kind of egalitarianism between the faithful and the priest. A lot of people do not necessarily formulate that in words but it has definitely lessened the respect and the honor that we owe to the priest. If lay people can distribute, it just introduces all kinds of confusion about why the priest is special and what his role is.

JHW: So, can we say then that Communion in the hand is wrong, even sinful, for the faithful who see it that way?

PK: I would answer this question by first saying that the Church clearly stipulated conditions, as we discussed before, for Communion in the hand. Just to reiterate, the two conditions are 1) that no lack of reverence or false ideas about the Eucharist be engendered in the people and 2) that no risk of profanation be present.

I would say that those conditions are never met. Universally neither one is met and most of the time both of them are flagrantly violated. And so, I would say it is wrong on a legal level because we cannot fulfill those conditions. Those conditions were set down, I think, somewhat naively, but they were set down and now we can look back and say we cannot actually fulfill them.

In terms of our particular situation, if we can see in the year 2020 how much damage this has done to faith in the Real Presence, to the adoration

---

appointed intermediary between God and the people; hence, as it belongs to him to offer the people's gifts to God, so it belongs to him to deliver consecrated gifts to the people. Thirdly, because, out of reverence towards this sacrament, nothing touches it but what is consecrated; hence the corporal and the chalice are consecrated, and likewise the priest's hands, for touching this sacrament. Hence it is not lawful for anyone else to touch it except from necessity — for instance, if it were to fall upon the ground, or else in some other case of urgency."

we should give to Our Lord, to the dignity of the priesthood; if we see that it allows Satanists access to Hosts; if we know these things — and it is not difficult to know them — then it would be wrong to receive in the hand, because we would just be augmenting the problem. We would be contributing to it, we would be saying: I agree with this, I consent to this, it should keep happening this way. I think that is wrong. Speaking for myself, in my conscience, I could not receive in the hand.

JHW: I agree. I wonder, though, whether that has to be parsed a little bit because the faithful are being told they should receive this way, and some are being told — especially now during the coronavirus pandemic — that they may not receive any other way. So, for those people who do not know, is it still a sin? And if the bishop or the priest is saying this, is it a sin for them?

PK: These are obviously controversial questions.

I think that many bishops are abusing their authority right now. First of all, they are supposed to uphold canon law, which is really clear on the point that the faithful have the right to receive Communion on the tongue. That is spelled out without any exceptions. As long as the faithful are properly disposed to receive the sacraments, they cannot be denied the sacraments. Some have invoked canon 223, about how a bishop can decide how the rights of the faithful are to be exercised, but this is not a blanket statement. The bishop cannot tell me that I am not allowed to get married or that I have to become a monk. Those are my rights, but he cannot determine the exercise of those rights. So that's a general statement, but without a clarification it would not apply in this case, where the default position is that the faithful should be able to receive on the tongue.

However, more deeply than that, I think what this coronavirus period is bringing out is a real crisis in the bishops' faith in the Real Presence of Our Lord and in the reverence and adoration we owe *Him*. Why do I say that? Because they have been acting for months as if physical health is the highest good, as if it is the *summum bonum*: the number one thing we have to do is to protect ourselves from the coronavirus and therefore how we treat the Eucharist is to be dictated by preventing the coronavirus. That is such a backwards way of thinking, it is completely upside-down. It sends to the faithful the signal: this Sacrament is a means to some end that the Church gets to determine; it is not God Himself Who is the end, the ultimate good, but it is just one more negotiable item in Catholic life. It is in a certain sense like saying that Mass is a "non-essential service." The groceries are essential, food for your body is essential, but food for your soul is not essential. That is the message that has been sent: the Blessed Sacrament is a very special thing, it is a really important symbol for us—but it is not Almighty God, and therefore, it takes the second place to physical health.

I think this is a terrible message to send. Reverence is more important, and there is a paradox here. The faithful are hungry for the Blessed Sacrament, they desperately want to receive, they want to go back to Mass. I feel the same way. Where I live, we have been able to go back to Mass and Communion, thanks be to God. But we should never place our own private good over the common good of the Church and over the homage and worship that we owe to God. Even if that meant sacrificing reception of Communion, I think it is more important. We will actually merit more in the sight of Our Lord if we defend His right to be treated with due honor than if we insist on receiving Him "at any cost."

JHW: Just to make that point clear: Is it then the case that a bishop cannot really refuse or forbid Holy Communion on the tongue?

PK: Yes, that is my position and I have tried to document that. I have collected all the quotations from different Vatican documents that make it clear that the normative and universal manner of reception is on the tongue.[140] That remains the case; that has never been changed.

[140] See chapter 17; cf. chapter 7.

Communion in the hand is the *exception* to the rule. It is an indult, a permission—one that, in my opinion, should never have been granted. However, all it says is: you do not have to do the universal norm, you are allowed to practice this particular exception. The bishops are flipping that around and saying: the universal norm now is Communion in the hand and, by exception or by permission, on the tongue. That is completely to invert all that the Church documents have ever said about this.

JHW: That being said, could a bishop legitimately forbid Communion on the hand completely in his diocese?

PK: Yes, absolutely. That's possible because it is only a permission. The permission has to be requested from the Vatican and nobody needs to take advantage of a permission. In fact, there have been a few bishops in the world who actually said: "In my diocese we are only receiving on the tongue; we are following the Church's universal norm with no exceptions." That is a quite different situation.

I also wanted to mention the importance of receiving Communion not only on the tongue, but also *kneeling*. St. Augustine at the end of the fourth century said: if we do not adore the Eucharist before we receive it, we sin. That is why, technically on the books, even in the Novus Ordo, everyone is supposed to make a sign of adoration towards the Blessed Sacrament before they receive. Some people genuflect, some people bow, but they are supposed to make some sign of adoration, otherwise they sin. Now, they may not know, nobody has ever told them, so they might not be personally culpable, but it is objectively wrong not to show a sign of adoration towards Our Lord in the Sacrament. Kneeling was the traditional way of doing that—to adore and worship God. In the context of the Church, we all understand that this is what it means. But practically speaking, it is much easier for the priest to give Communion to someone who is kneeling because the priest is standing and his hand is at just the right level to put the Host on the tongue without any contact of the tongue. I have been receiving this way for decades and I think I've noticed a priest's finger touch my tongue twice. It is a very safe way of giving Communion but that is because there is a perfect height relationship between the minister and the recipient. In the Novus Ordo when people are queuing up in lines as if they are going to buy bus tickets or something—there is a weird relationship then between the dispenser and the recipient. Often the priest or the minister is shorter than the one receiving and they have to reach up. That is not really a safe way to give Communion on the tongue. So, if you are going to receive Communion on the tongue, kneel. That is what makes it work practically, and it's also the sign of adoration that we owe.

JHW: People also talk about being unworthy to receive altogether and say "is my tongue any more worthy than my hand?"

PK: It is an absurd objection because indeed, metaphysically speaking, every creature is unworthy of God, so that is why we say *Domine, non sum dignus*—Lord, I am not worthy that you should enter under my roof but only say the word and my soul shall be healed. And that is true. We say that even if we are in a state of grace. Even St. Thomas Aquinas said *Domine, non sum dignus.*

However, we are talking about something else. We are talking about fittingness, the way we show our humility and our love and our submission and our worship of the Lord. We want to show that in the best way we can and in that sense make ourselves more worthy. St. Thomas says, a worthy Communion means that you receive in a state of grace with lively faith and actual devotion. So, what he means is that you do not just go up by routine, because everyone else is going up and you receive because your parents or your neighbors are receiving, and you don't even know what it signifies. That would be without faith. We need to have real conscious faith that we are going to receive the Lord Jesus and actual devotion—not just habitual devotion: I was devout last week, or I am capable of being devout—by actually encouraging myself right now to make acts of faith, hope, and charity and asking God to sanctify me, cleanse me, and transform me. So, freedom from the guilt of mortal sin, lively faith, and actual devotion are what we need for a worthy Communion. In that sense we can have a worthy Communion or an unworthy Communion.

There is something very interesting concerning the tongue. In the traditional rite of Baptism that was used in the Church from ancient times all the way until it was changed around 1970, the priest blesses and exorcises some salt and puts a little of the salt into the mouth of the child or the adult being baptized and he says "receive the salt of wisdom, may it be unto thee a sign of reconciliation unto life everlasting. Amen." (As you know, blessed salt is used in the making of traditional holy water and it is also used by exorcists.) After doing that he prays:

> God of our fathers, O God, the source of all truth, humbly we implore thee to look with mercy upon this thy servant, and no more to let him hunger who now tastes this first nourishment of salt: but let him be enriched with heavenly food so that they may ever be inflamed with zeal, joyous in hope, constant in serving Thee. We bid Thee, Lord, lead him to the bath where one is born anew, that in the company Thy faithful he may deserve to win the everlasting reward which Thou hast promised. Through Christ our Lord. Amen.

The meaning of this ceremony in the baptismal rite is that the tongue is being blessed for the eventual reception of the Bread of Life. And so if you are baptized in the traditional rite, your tongue is blessed so that it may properly receive the Host, just as in the rite of Ordination the priest's hands are properly blessed and consecrated so that they may handle it. The *lex orandi* of the Church said yes, this is important. Just as the Church consecrates patens because the Host will be put on them, so she blesses the tongue of the one being baptized, because it, too, will receive the Host.

JHW: One of the arguments that is being made now in a time of pandemic is that because Communion on the tongue is less hygienic than

Communion in the hand, we have to receive Communion in the hand for the time being. How do you respond to that?

PK: I responded earlier on the theoretical level that we should not make health into our God and we should not make human life, this mortal life, into the ultimate standard of every decision we make.

But practically speaking, there are experts who disagree that Communion on the tongue is less hygienic. There have been a number of medical doctors, as well as bishops, who have come out and said it is no less hygienic to give properly onto the tongue than to put the Host in someone's hand. Our hands are quite dirty and that is why they are always telling us to wash them. You can hardly live for 15 minutes without getting germs on your hands from somewhere. I won't even go into some of the studies that have been done about how dirty things are that people are touching. So, I am not at all convinced it is more hygienic to give Communion in the hand, especially if a priest's hand comes into contact with the communicant's hand, which often happens — unless you are going to drop the Host or you use machines as the Germans are doing, or allow other kinds of irreverent, unfitting, unworthy, mechanistic treatments of Our Lord, because of this panic and craze. In fact, if a priest knows what he is doing and the people are kneeling, as I explained before, it seems to be much more hygienic to give on the tongue.

JHW: A priest friend of mine said something very similar. He said that for many years he has been giving Holy Communion on the tongue and he can count on his hand how many times he has touched the tongue of a parishioner. But with Communion in the hand, it is every Mass.... So what advice do you have for Catholics in dioceses where the bishop has forbidden Communion on the tongue?

PK: That is a very painful cross to have to bear. I think there are a few things the faithful can do.

The Holy Bread of Eternal Life

First, they can try to find a priest who is willing to give Communion to them outside of Mass. There is a little ritual for it, it is permissible. This is what I would start with because there are many priests out there who are fully aware of the problems and sympathetic to the plight of the faithful.

But it may not be possible to find a priest who is willing to do that. Another thing that could be done is to intensify your prayer life in other traditional ways: embrace the Rosary anew; pray some part of the Divine Office — whether that is Prime, Compline, Lauds, or Vespers; read the missal. If you cannot get to daily Mass then take a traditional missal and just read the prayers, they are so rich. You can make a very heartfelt, earnest spiritual Communion. The saints say that this can bring us as much grace as sacramental Communion. It is not a long-term solution. However, if we are going to do that as a temporary solution, we should really prepare ourselves for it as well as possible. For example, some people light a couple of candles and, early in the morning, they pray through the prayers of the Mass and they make a spiritual Communion and meditate.[141] Maybe once a month they could drive some place, to a different diocese or a chapel, where they can receive Holy Communion on the tongue.

We are in a battle right now where the different dioceses are almost in rivalry with each other because some have good policies and some have bad policies and some are confused. The idea of a monolithic Catholic Church is not the case anymore. There is a lot of diversity right now. I think the lay people are becoming aware of this and instead of despairing about it or becoming angry they should just take whatever concrete steps they can.

JHW: And when you are given the opportunity to attend Mass, but are told that you may receive only on the hand, would you still go to Mass? Or maybe just watch it on TV since you are not going to receive anyway?

---

[141] For suggestions and templates, see my article "Your Local Mass Canceled? Try Meditating on the Texts of the Traditional Mass," *OnePeterFive*, March 20, 2020.

PK: There is a huge benefit just to being present at Mass — "assisting at Mass," as it used to be called. I have an article about this on OnePeter-Five that might help people.[142] There is nothing you can do to glorify God more than to assist at the Holy Sacrifice of the Mass, even if you do not receive, because at that Mass the Lord is being offered up in the all-pleasing, all-sufficient sacrifice and we join ourselves spiritually with that sacrifice. In fact, it is by joining ourselves spiritually to it that we make ourselves ready to receive the sacrament. And so, it is not necessary always to receive sacramentally, as I am sure you know. It is good to receive frequently if one is well disposed with faith and devotion, but there have been long spans in Church history where even saints have received once a week or less. Sometimes we can use that kind of "Eucharistic fast" to intensify our desire to be united to the Lord and to purify our own motivations, but also to make reparation for profanations and sacrileges. We can really offer this up and say: "Lord, you know how much I want to receive you, but I am not going to dishonor you. I am going to offer this up before you now for those who are committing sacrilege and profanation."

---

[142] "Holy Mass: You Cannot Do Anything to Glorify God More," *OnePeterFive*, February 19, 2020.

10

Time to End the Ordinary Use of
"Extraordinary Ministers"

In the great tradition of the Catholic Church — in its Latin and Greek, Western and Eastern rites alike — only clerics or ordained ministers are permitted to distribute the precious Body and Blood of Our Lord. As the priest prays in the Divine Liturgy of St. John Chrysostom:

> Hear us, O Lord Jesus Christ, our God, from Your holy dwelling-place and from the throne of glory in Your kingdom, and come to sanctify us, You who are seated on high with the Father and are invisibly present here with us. Deign to give to us with Your mighty hand Your most pure Body and precious Blood, *and through us, to all the people.*

This tradition remained unbroken until the rash of liturgical experimentation in the 1960s paved the way for an almost indiscriminate multiplication of unprecedented "lay ministries."

The reason for the traditional restriction is that, as the Church's greatest theologian St. Thomas Aquinas explains, it pertains to the same one to bring about a certain effect and then to see that the effect is bestowed on those for whom it is intended. All the more is this true with supernatural effects that may be produced *only* by supernaturally empowered agents; it would simply not be fitting to entrust such effects to anyone who is not set apart for that ministry. That explains why, even under current Church law, the only *ordinary* minister of Communion — the *only* ordinary minister — is the bishop, priest, or deacon, in virtue of his ordination, which consecrates him to the service of God.

Why is ordination so important? Because the Holy Eucharist is the Body and Blood of God Incarnate. *It is God.* The one who holds the Host is in contact with the Author of all life, all reality. This is not something to treat lightly, or to delegate to clerks like an office job. Our Lord Jesus Christ instituted a priesthood with its specific responsibilities, which the deacon shares and the bishop exemplifies.

Never in the recorded history of the Church had laymen (not to say anything about laywomen) been allowed to distribute the precious gifts, until just a few decades ago. This step was part of a larger enterprise of creating a "new" liturgy for Modern Man, where the old rules and customs no longer had to be respected, and where an informal, casual approach was preferred to a solemn, formal one. (This is why Byzantine Catholics, who have not abandoned their own customs and are keenly aware of the reverence due to the awesome mysteries of Christ, are rightly troubled by what they see going on in so many Latin-Rite churches.) Unfortunately, when old rules and customs disappear, the Faith itself, and the life that corresponds to it, also disappear, as our own eyes have seen, and as all the statistics confirm.

Just as the Second Vatican Council said nothing about abolishing Latin, the priest facing the people, or Communion being received in the hand, it also said *nothing* about laymen distributing the Body and Blood of Christ. However, even when this practice began to be permitted, it was expressly limited to rare cases: bringing Communion to the sick when no ordained minister was available, or helping distribute the Host when the celebrant was too old or too weak to do so himself, or assisting when a very great number of people rendered it necessary. This can be easily proved by looking at all the relevant universal disciplinary norms.[143] For this reason,

---

[143] These have been gathered here: www.ewtn.com/catholicism/library/extraordinary-ministers-of-the-eucharist-4225.

as late as 1997, the Vatican issued a document clarifying in no uncertain terms that "the habitual use of extraordinary ministers of Holy Communion at Mass, thus arbitrarily extending the concept of 'a great number of the faithful,'" is among practices "to be *avoided* and *eliminated* where such have emerged in particular Churches."[144]

Please note: There is not a single document from the Vatican, or any other document with legal force, that requires the distribution of Holy Communion under both species *in spite of* the absence of ordinary ministers. In other words, if there *are* ordinary ministers, Communion *may* be given under both species; but if not, *there is no overriding or compelling reason to do so.* Communion under the form of bread alone is, and is considered to be, fully adequate to the purpose for which Our Lord instituted the Eucharist: to unite the faithful fully to Himself—to the One who is really, truly, substantially present in His Body, Blood, Soul, and Divinity under *either* species.

Most of the Western world has turned a deaf ear to the Vatican's repeated requests to limit extraordinary ministers to their intended purpose. According to the Modernist view, this would mean that the Vatican's request is mistaken because the People of God (or perhaps some bureaucratic behemoth called an Episcopal Conference) has decided otherwise.

But the Modernist viewpoint, which is inherently antiauthoritarian, was condemned by Pope St. Pius X. The fact that the Church in the

---

[144] The document was the Instruction *Ecclesia de Mysterio: On Certain Questions Regarding the Collaboration of the Non-Ordained Faithful,* a most unusual document as it was signed by eight dicasteries—the Congregation for the Clergy; the Pontifical Council for the Laity; the Congregation for the Doctrine of the Faith; the Congregation for Divine Worship and the Discipline of the Sacraments; the Congregation for Bishops; the Congregation for the Evangelization of Peoples; the Congregation for Institutes of Consecrated Life and Societies of Apostolic Life; and the Pontifical Council for the Interpretation of Legislative Texts; and then approved by Pope John Paul II *in forma specifica.* It therefore carries much weight. Unfortunately, as we have seen with a continual stream of Vatican documents over the decades, it had almost no practical effect and is a dead letter.

The Holy Bread of Eternal Life

Western world exists *in statu abusus* — in a state of (nearly perpetual) abuse — in no way undermines the law of the Church, or, above all, her wise tradition of two millennia. Neither tradition nor discipline evaporates just because everyone's ignoring it and the Vatican chooses to tolerate this state of affairs, or rather, not to take punitive steps.

Regrettably, we have seen that we cannot expect much help from the Vatican these days on any matter of substance. Hence, if change does not take place at the parish level, it may never happen. Blessed be the pastor who has the conviction, courage, and tactfulness it takes to remove abuses, in keeping with *Redemptionis Sacramentum* §183:

> In an altogether particular manner, let everyone do all that is in their power to ensure that the Most Holy Sacrament of the Eucharist will be protected from any and every irreverence or distortion and that all abuses be thoroughly corrected. This is a most serious duty incumbent upon each and every one, and all are bound to carry it out without any favoritism.

Perhaps more than citizens of any other nation, Americans have simply chosen to be disobedient in regard to extraordinary ministers, creating their own rules as they go along. I ask: Is this a truly *Catholic* attitude? Or is it just one more example of how far the Church in America has drifted into making up its own religion with its own homegrown rules? The land of thirty thousand denominations has a way of de-Romanizing and de-Catholicizing the Church, unless conscientious and determined efforts are made in the opposite direction.

The other pandemic: regular Eucharistic desecration

What price has the Catholic Church paid for the shortsighted decision to allow lay ministers of Holy Communion?

Here is the eyewitness testimony of Emily Sparks. Looking back many years later, she regrets her well-intentioned involvement in this panoply of abuses but wishes to share with readers a sense of "just how bad it is" at a typical Catholic parish in the USA. There is every reason to believe that elements of her description continue to be applicable to many parishes today. Even if the use of the common chalice suddenly stopped in 2020—and that is all to the good—it can be predicted that the same or similar abuses will start up again wherever the underlying poor formation, bad pastoral judgment, errors of doctrine, and lack of supernatural faith are at work.

While many are aware of the Eucharistic abuses that take place *during* a typical parish liturgy, many are unaware of the frequent *behind-the-scenes* abuses that are the consequence of current liturgical practice. When I was still a teenager, I was employed by my parish as a sacristan and assisted (as instructed) for the preparation of Sunday Masses. The account below summarizes my experiences during this time.

My former parish is a typical parish; in fact, it might be slightly better than average. The tabernacle is in the center of the sanctuary, and Confessions were offered several days a week. The priests were well-meaning and not avant-garde or intentionally revolutionary.

There were four Masses every Sunday, the first at 7:30 and the last starting at noon. My job was to arrive before the end of the 7:30 and make sure the vessels were purified (if necessary), cleaned, refilled, and set up for the next Mass. I would do this after each Mass until the noon Mass was over. I believe that this job was originally handled by lay volunteers, but the parish hired me because having one regular person do it made for better and more reliable results.

At each Sunday Mass, the parish had four ciboria for Holy Communion, and either two or four chalices: two for the 7:30 and noon, and then four for the prime-time Masses at 9:00 and 10:30. The priest who said Mass always distributed Holy Communion. Though the parish had two or three deacons, they would help distribute Communion only when it was their Sunday to preach, which was once a month on a rotating basis. So, on Sundays, each Mass had between five and seven extraordinary ministers distributing Holy Communion. Once a month you can subtract one from that number for a deacon.

When the vessels were brought back, the priest's chalice and paten were almost always purified (though occasionally they weren't), but the ciboria and chalices for the faithful almost never were. Each Sunday, at least one ciborium, and often more, was sent back with a generous coating of consecrated crumbs on the bottom. I knew I didn't have permission to consume the Blessed Sacrament outside of Mass, so I would rinse the vessels in the sacrarium sink before washing them in the regular sink. I would bring the vessels back to the sacristy after Mass. I could not tell which were purified and which were not until I started to wash them, since the ciboria had lids, so I would bring them all back together. This often resulted in particles of the Sacred Species being left alone in the sacristy while I gathered up everything needed for Mass, before starting to clean them.

The pewter chalices that were used for the faithful's Holy Communion were customarily purified partly by the extraordinary minister, and then completely by me in the sacristy. The extraordinary ministers would consume the extra Precious Blood, add a swallow of water and drink it, and leave the cups in the back, where I would do a more thorough job at the sacrarium sink. In a large parish, it is very difficult to estimate the correct amount of wine needed, and sometimes there was more than needed. I remember once an extraordinary minister asking for assistance from others in the sacristy, because she was on antibiotics and could not finish what was left. Another time I remember walking into the sacristy to find an extraordinary minister pouring the Precious Blood directly into the sacrarium sink. Additionally, on a few occasions I came to the sacristy to find the extraordinary ministers rinsing the chalice into the wrong sink, the regular sink instead of the sacrarium.

A few times, a chalice more than half full of Precious Blood was brought back and just left there unconsumed. It was very difficult for me to know what to do in this situation, because I was not given permission to consume the Blessed Sacrament outside of Mass, so I did not do it. Instead, I would try to dilute the Sacred Species so that it was no longer wine before pouring it down the sacrarium sink. Looking back, I realize I probably should have attempted to consume it anyway, but I was acting on the instructions I had been given at the time. I hope I diluted it enough so that it was no longer the species of wine, but I was unsure as to how much water would be needed for that, so I made my best effort.

Sometimes a ciborium would be left in the sacristy full of Hosts, with no explanation as to whether they were unconsecrated (because they weren't needed) or consecrated and brought back by accident. On those occasions I had to enlist a priest's help about what to do. The solution was usually to bring them back out into the church to be consecrated at the next Mass, "just in case."

The priest was greeting people between Masses, so this job in the sacristy was overseen by me and the extraordinary ministers. For this reason I had to open the tabernacle before each Mass to see how many ciboria were consecrated already, and then open each ciborium, making sure they were more than half full. If more than one was half full or less, I combined the Hosts into one ciborium and took the empty ciboria back to the sacristy to purify in the sacrarium sink. I did this multiple times each Sunday.

I was not the only layman who would open the tabernacle regularly. Other extraordinary ministers would do so as well. I remember once approaching the tabernacle for my job, only to find my way was blocked by two men who were in the sanctuary having a conversation about golf, right in front of the tabernacle. I had to ask them to please take their conversation somewhere else.

The Holy Bread of Eternal Life

When I was attending Mass in the pews, I remember two times seeing someone walk away with Holy Communion. One time it was a young woman who took Communion in her hand but did not consume it. I saw it, and motioned to her to consume it, which she did as she was heading back to her pew. I approached her after Mass, and she told me she was not Catholic, but her grandmother told her to go to Communion anyway, so she did. She simply walked off with the Host because she didn't feel right about receiving. Later that year, I saw a teenage boy, who was wearing a T-shirt for the heavy metal band Lamb of God, take Holy Communion back to his pew in his hands, where he was fiddling with it in full view of his parents. When I told the pastor about these desecrations, there was no measure taken to address them.

People reading this might assume that the sort of things I'm describing are problems that were limited to my parish. While I have no doubt that these sorts of abuses are rare at the few "Reform of the Reform" Novus Ordo churches where priests are trying to make the Novus Ordo closer to the practice of the traditional Mass, I *do* think problems like these are common in parishes that are of average quality — which would be most of them. Based on what I have seen and experienced, I think there are two reasons for this.

The priests who ran my parish meant well. They weren't trying to be revolutionary or lazy; they were just doing what they thought was appropriate. But the conclusion is inescapable: *the understanding of the priest's role as guardian and caretaker of the Holy Mysteries has been completely eradicated in the Novus Ordo liturgy and its surrounding culture.* Practicing Catholics know that only priests can say the words of consecration, but any sort of exclusive duties regarding the Blessed Sacrament end there. And how can a priest even begin to reclaim this? The moment he were to try to stop something even as egregious as Communion in the hand, he would be crucified by most of his congregation and probably by his own bishop. If a priest cannot take measures to prevent highly visible abuses from occurring during Mass, it will be even harder to stop the sacrileges that occur "behind the scenes," about which few people are even aware.

The second point is one of practical logistics. If a parish is going to use several extraordinary ministers, and as many as ten vessels each Mass (four ciboria, four chalices, plus the priest's chalice and paten), it is *very* hard for the priest to do an effective purification of everything at the altar, or to keep track of the several extraordinary ministers. Purified and unpurified vessels get mixed in the shuffle, or the priest runs out of time or water. Extraordinary ministers can take things to the wrong place or go to the sacristy at the wrong time. (For example, one of the reasons why full consecrated chalices would be left unconsumed in the sacristy was because an extraordinary minister didn't show, due to illness or a scheduling error or something like that. No one realized one was missing until after the Consecration.) With so many people and variables at play, human error is going to happen—and, over time, it will happen on a large scale.

Reviewing the situation, a believing Catholic can reach only one conclusion: extraordinary ministers of Holy Communion must be abolished, once and for all, everywhere, without exception.

Another friend—this time, a seminarian—shared with me the following transcript of an actual conversation that took place at dinner one night:

Parishioner: After the funeral last week, someone found a Host on the ground. Sue came up to me and told me about it. I asked her what she did with it. She said it was in her pocket. I asked her to give it to me, so I took it and ate it. She said, "Sally, that was on the ground." But I didn't know what else I should do with it.

Priest: There's another way to handle that. In the sacristy, there are two sinks. In one of them, the pipe goes straight into the ground. You just crumble up the Host and put it in there. It'll go in the ground, not in the sewer.

Parishioner: Oh, okay. I didn't know. Thank you.

(No comment from three other parishioners present, including a fourth-year in the permanent diaconate program.)

A correspondent wrote to me about something he heard at a parish council meeting — this is not, alas, a parody from *Eye of the Tiber*:

At the last meeting, someone suggested asking people in the congregation to give up beer for Lent and to provide the funds that go towards beer to the Church instead. Nothing wrong with that. But then they suggested actually taking a 6-pack of beer and putting it up on the altar or ambo as a prop during the tithing appeal. Aren't they aware that children would ask, "Daddy, why are they doing that?" Aren't they aware that the altar is sacred, and the ambo's supposed to be sacred, too? What's worse, the pastor said he thought it was a great idea — to which the person who had brought it up replied, "Oh, it's not my own idea, I got it from a pastor of the town where I used to live."

These heart-rending accounts — and, I am sure, they could be multiplied by the thousands — read like so many passages from Old Testament prophets warning Israel to repent or face utter destruction. Such desecrations and sacrileges have been taking place week after week after week, for decades. *A Church that continues to act this way is a Church that has signed its own spiritual death warrant.*

And we are busying ourselves with regulations about hand sanitizer and the handshake of bonhomie? The bishops *dare* to tell people they must receive in the hand and cannot receive on the tongue? All of this is nothing more than instrumentalizing Our Lord. We are making the way we treat His all-holy, all-precious Eucharistic Body dependent on our narrow health interests rather than looking to what is *fitting* for handling and consuming the Bread of Angels. If a virus makes the fitting distribution of the Host impossible, so be it: let the priest alone sacramentally communicate while the people make a spiritual Communion. This shows that we *believe* and we *revere* the holy mysteries. But for God's sake (literally), let us stop abusing the Lord for our own interests, let us stop subordinating Him to our worldly notions, and let us stop the pandemic of Eucharistic sacrilege that has swallowed up the Western Church and made it a kingdom of wrath in the sight of our God. "Wherefore, as I live, says the Lord, surely, because you have defiled my sanctuary with all your detestable things, and with all your abominations, therefore will I also diminish you; neither shall my eye spare, and I also will have no pity" (Ezek. 5:11, ALV).

St. Paul says — look in your Bible if you don't believe me — that *many* of the Christians of Corinth are sick and weak, and some have died, because of their Eucharistic irreverence (see 1 Cor. 11:27–32).[145] Today, the Catholic Church is Corinth, and irreverence is her sickness unto death.

A priest or deacon who comes to understand what is wrong with modern Eucharistic praxis and then does nothing to correct it, even at the cost of his position or his very life, will stand condemned before the awesome tribunal of Christ, whose sacred presence in the Holy Eucharist he has held in contempt. "Verily I say unto you, Inasmuch as ye have done it unto one of the least of these, ye have done it unto me" (see Matt. 25:40) — this is no less true of the particles and drops of His divine, immortal, life-giving mysteries as it is of His people. Indeed, if we have any faith left at all, we shall see that this saying is *most of all* true of His Eucharistic presence, since it *is* the Lord Himself. "I have brought up children, and exalted them: but they have despised me" (Isa. 1:2, DR).

In spite of the fact that the Church's Faith is spelled out clearly in two thousand years' worth of catechisms, sermons, spiritual writings, codes of law, and liturgical rubrics, it may be possible that many priests, due to poor catechesis and formation, do not even hold the Catholic Faith concerning the Real Presence in every particle and drop of the sacred species, or the

[145] See chapter 4.

essential distinction between the ordained and the non-ordained (with the consequent distinction in duties), or the primacy of the worship of God over horizontal social relationships. Are seminarians taught that even particles of the Hosts or drops in the chalice are still the Most Blessed Sacrament? Certainly most of the laity seem to be altogether unaware of this. If that is true, it does not excuse us, but renders the judgment all the heavier, since the baptized are *required* before God to know the fundamentals of their religion, and the Eucharist is at the heart of Catholicism.

The wisdom of the Roman Church's traditional practices—always limiting Communion to one species, having the Host distributed *only* by ordained ministers and *only* on the tongue to faithful who are kneeling (making the sign of adoration without which, says St. Augustine, we commit sin), and having the priest alone thoroughly cleanse the few vessels in use before the Mass ends—has never been so dazzlingly clear, and yet never so unappreciated or despised. Will the Bride of Christ on earth respond with humble repentance and zealous reform? Or will the lament of the prophet Jeremiah continue to resound? "As a woman that despiseth her lover, so hath the house of Israel despised me, saith the Lord" (Jer. 3:20, DR).

Adoration as Optimal Preparation for Communion

The great feast of Corpus Christi honors Our Lord's institution of the Most Blessed Sacrament — already commemorated on Holy Thursday together with other mysteries, yet deserving of a day all to itself.[146] According to Holy Mother Church, on Corpus Christi we are to bear aloft the monstrance in a public procession so that "the King and center of all hearts" may receive the inward and outward homage of Christians. Thanks in large part to the spread of this feast throughout the Christian world, the practice of Eucharistic Adoration received a tremendous boost, reaching its apogee in the Tridentine or Counter-Reformation period.

In the latter half of the twentieth century, Adoration withered under the chilling influence of Modernism. Pope Benedict XVI wrote of the period immediately following the Second Vatican Council: "A few even considered Eucharistic Adoration itself to be obsolete, saying that the Lord ought only to be received in the Eucharistic bread and not adored."[147] Then he immediately ripostes: "But it is not possible to eat this bread like any other food. The Lord in the Sacrament of the Eucharist calls us to 'receive' him in all of the dimensions of our existence."[148] Explaining

---

[146] As a further "echo" of Holy Thursday, the traditional Roman calendar has a feast in honor of the Most Precious Blood on July 1.

[147] "Il messaggio di Benedetto XVI ai funerali del card. Meisner," Fondazione Vaticana Joseph Ratzinger-Benedetto XVI, July 11, 2017.

[148] Ibid.

The Holy Bread of Eternal Life

why this devotion is so important in rebuilding the Church's liturgical life and the prayer life of individual Christians, the same pope said:

> There is an intrinsic connection between celebration and adoration. The holy Mass, in fact, is in itself the Church's greatest act of adoration: "No one eats this food," St. Augustine writes, "if he has not first worshipped it" (*Commentary on Psalm* 98:9). Adoration outside of holy Mass prolongs and intensifies what happens in the liturgical celebration and renders a true and profound reception of Christ possible.[149]

On another occasion, Benedict XVI went further:

> Eucharistic Adoration is an essential way of being with the Lord.... In one of his parables the Lord speaks of a treasure hidden in the field; the man who finds it sells all he has in order to buy that field, because the hidden treasure is more valuable than anything else. The hidden treasure, the good greater than any other good, is the Kingdom of God — it is Jesus himself, the Kingdom in person. In the sacred Host, he is present, the true treasure, always waiting for us. Only by adoring this presence do we learn how to receive him properly — we learn the reality of communion, we learn the Eucharistic celebration from the inside.... Let us love being with the Lord![150]

"To love being with the Lord": this phrase is a perfect encapsulation of what is required of us before we go to Communion. *To love being with the Lord*, we first believe the Eucharist *is* the Lord; then we respond with devotion, an appropriate holy fear and reverence; we desire to be *one with Him*, renouncing whatever obstacles could prevent or impede that union. One of the Psalms says: "Open wide your mouth, and I will fill it" (see Ps. 80:11). Eucharistic Adoration calls us to open wide the

---

[149] Angelus, June 10, 2007.
[150] In a homily at Vespers in Altötting, September 11, 2006.

eyes of our faith; it opens wide the mouth of our desire, and readies us to be filled with the immensity of God Himself. It is a guaranteed path for making our participation in Mass, and our entire lives, more fruitful in every way. That is why the renewal of Adoration outside of Mass is a powerful sign of the work of the Holy Spirit in our times. It flourishes wherever the Faith begins to be believed and lived again. The lesson it teaches is divine intimacy.[151]

Resting in the radiance of His Face

For centuries, Catholics were encouraged to make frequent visits to the tabernacle in any church. We, too, should practice this custom. If you pass a church during a walk or an errand, step inside for a moment to be with Our Lord. If stopping is not possible, make the Sign of the Cross as you pass by, and say a short prayer, like "Jesus, King of Love, I put my trust in Thy loving mercy." Mother Mectilde of the Blessed Sacrament (1614–1698), foundress of the first community of Benedictine nuns of perpetual Adoration, offers this counsel:

> We must never lose sight of our holy tabernacles: it is there that we find our strength and our virtue. If human infirmity and affairs allowed, we should pass our whole life at the feet of our divine

---

[151] *Nota bene*: I am not saying that Eucharistic Adoration is a solution or a substitute for bad liturgy, bad youth ministry, or bad catechetical formation. It cannot solve those problems; indeed, it can sometimes be abused by those who do not understand the proper ceremonial for exposition and the spirit of reverence that should be cultivated around the monstrance. (On this point, see Joseph Shaw, "How Priests Can Help Catholics Believe in Real Presence Once Again," *LifeSiteNews*, September 5, 2019; idem, "Some Worries about Exposition of the Blessed Sacrament," published in two parts at *LMS Chairman*, July 1–2, 2018.) However, Adoration is a God-given and time-tested way for those who are already formed in good habits to grow in friendship with Our Lord, to increase their Eucharistic devotion and hunger, to purge their souls of the errors of utilitarianism, rationalism, and populism, and to make reparation for sin.

The Holy Bread of Eternal Life

Master; at least let us go there as often as possible, and quit so many futile occupations that rob us of precious time claimed for what we owe the love of a God.[152]

In one of my favorite books, *In Sinu Jesu*, Our Lord emphasizes the importance of these visits and expresses His displeasure at churches that are kept locked:

> The Most Holy Eucharist is not only My Sacrifice offered to the Father, although in a bloodless manner; it is not only the sustenance of souls, nourishing them with My very Body and Blood; it is also the Sacrament of My divine friendship, the pledge of My burning desire to remain close to all who seek Me, to all who need Me, to all who would spend time in My company.
>
> This is why it so grieves Me that churches are locked and that I am left for days on end alone in the tabernacle. I would draw souls to My open Heart, I would have them experience what it is to abide in the radiance of My Eucharistic Face, I would give Myself in intimate friendship to souls drawn to Me in the Sacrament of My love, but you priests, shepherds of souls, have forgotten that keeping open your churches is integral to your sacred ministry. I would pasture souls in My Eucharistic presence, but you, by continuing to close My churches to souls, frustrate and contradict the desires of My Eucharistic Heart. There is sorrow in heaven over this. It is not difficult to keep My churches open and to provide for the spiritual needs of those who would readily enter them in search of My friendship. The obstacles are not those of which you think; the obstacle is a lack of faith, a loss of belief in My real presence. My priests will be held responsible for the coldness and isolation that has come to surround Me in the Sacrament of My love. How I desire to see My churches open! Open the doors of

[152] *Mystery of Incomprehensible Love*, 22.

My consecrated houses and trust Me to fill them with adorers in spirit and in truth![153]

Later in the book, Our Lady speaks these words:

How is He [my Son] betrayed? His priests, my own sons, betray Him when they fail to make Him known, when by not teaching the mystery of His real presence they leave souls in the darkness of ignorance, without fire or light. They betray my Son when, by their example, they discourage reverence, and adoration, and a loving attention to His presence. They betray Him when they offer the Holy Sacrifice of the Mass unworthily, and when they hand Him over to sinners who have no intention of giving Him their hearts and seeking His mercy and His pardon for their sins. They betray Him when they leave Him alone in locked churches and when they make it difficult or impossible for souls to approach His tabernacles and rest in the radiance of His Eucharistic Face. They betray Him when they allow His churches to become places of noise and worldly chatter, and when they do nothing to recall souls to the living mystery of His love, that is, His presence in the tabernacle.[154]

It seems quite clear what Our Lord's and Our Lady's "marching orders" would be for the clergy and the faithful today as regards the use of churches and the veneration of the awesome mystery of the Eucharist.

Thanks be to God, some churches did remain open even during the COVID-19 lockdowns, and the faithful went to them to pray. Dutiful priests exposed the Host for adoration. Some were able to offer Mass and hear Confessions. When the history of this strange time is written, these men will be the heroes whose quiet exploits are held up for admiration. In other places, the public life of the Church was all but

---

[153] A Benedictine Monk, *In Sinu Jesu: When Heart Speaks to Heart—The Journal of a Priest at Prayer* (Kettering, OH: Angelico Press, 2016), 54.
[154] Ibid., 184.

extinguished, in a manner eerily reminiscent of prophecies of the end times, when souls will search in vain for priests or sacraments, and the dark prince of this world will gloat as if he had extirpated religion from the face of the earth. There were even locations where bishops shut down Perpetual Adoration chapels, in spite of hitherto uninterrupted years or decades of pious Christians adoring the Lord, and in spite of the obvious truth that in a time of crisis it is *more* Eucharistic Adoration that is needed, not less.

"When the Son of Man comes, will He find faith on earth?" (Luke 18:8). He will find faith at least among those Catholics who have held tightly to the mystery of Corpus Christi—who adore the Lord in the tabernacles of His churches and in the tabernacles of their hearts.

How to behave in the Lord's presence

Historically and currently, there are two basic forms of Eucharistic Adoration in the Catholic Church.

First, there is what might be called *simple adoration*, which is when the faithful adore the Lord present in the Most Holy Sacrament, in the ciborium reserved in the tabernacle. If the presence of the faithful can be assured, the doors of the tabernacle may be left open, or the ciborium removed and placed on a corporal on the altar. In this scenario, the ciborium itself should be covered with a veil. (Sometimes people refer to this as *simple exposition*.)

Second, there is *solemn adoration* or *(solemn) exposition* of the Blessed Sacrament, when a large Host is placed within a glass lunette and this, in turn, is fitted into a monstrance, usually made of gold or silver. At least six candles are placed around the monstrance and kept burning for the duration of exposition. Such exposition can be done at any time when the faithful will be guaranteed to be present (the monstrance may never be left unattended), but it is especially fitting to do so on the Feast of Corpus Christi, during its octave, on First Fridays, and on other great feasts of the Church's liturgical year.

Whenever we enter into the nave of a Catholic church, we should immediately genuflect toward the Blessed Sacrament. Happily, the tabernacle is often on or behind the main altar, so that our genuflection becomes at once a reverencing of the Lord's Real Presence and an acknowledgment of the altar, the greatest (mere) symbol of Christ in the Church. If the tabernacle happens to be located elsewhere than the main altar, however, we should conscientiously genuflect toward the tabernacle, and simply bow toward the altar.

(In the local parish church where I went to Mass growing up, a "renovation" in the 1970s had destroyed the integrity of the building by tearing out the high altar, rebuilding the nave "in the round," and putting the tabernacle off to the side, in the midst of a bunch of padded chairs for overflow seating. I never got to experience the original form of the church — although I saw it once in a heartbreaking black and white photograph, and I remember my parents saying that they couldn't understand why the changes had been made. Looking back on my childhood, I cringe to think of how many irreverences were committed for the simple reason that the tabernacle was absolutely in the wrong place and was basically ignored by all. In a "sign of the times," this church has recently been renovated yet again and restored to a more Catholic layout. A history like this inevitably prompts the question: Why did so much money have to be wasted to wreck a lovely Gothic church, and then more money spent to restore it to something that didn't even equal its former glory?)

Traditionally, the genuflection toward the tabernacle should be on to the *right* knee. For simple exposition, too, it is sufficient to genuflect on one knee like this. During liturgies, ministers also go down on the right knee whenever they genuflect, even toward a presiding prelate. Some people follow the custom of using the *left* knee when kneeling before a bishop or a cardinal to kiss his ring, or before a priest to receive a blessing; this is neither to be enjoined nor scorned. What is important is to understand the difference in symbolism: we kneel before the Blessed Sacrament in adoration or *latria* directed to God, whereas we kneel before a successor of the apostles to give honor (but not adoration) to one who represents Christ to us.

At *solemn* exposition, a special custom of veneration has obtained for a long time: the believer is to fall upon *both* of his knees and make a profound bow toward the floor, even to the point of touching the floor with his head.

In the desacralizing tendencies of the 1970s, an attempt was made to do away with this special form of genuflection. It seems that people were strangely embarrassed about humbling themselves before God. The words of the Lord must have vanished from their minds: "For he that shall be ashamed of me and of my words, of him the Son of man shall be ashamed, when he shall come in his majesty, and that of his Father, and of the holy angels" (Luke 9:26, DR). Thus, in the 1973 document *Holy Communion and the Worship of the Eucharist outside Mass*, we read: "A single genuflection is made in the presence of the Blessed Sacrament, whether reserved in the tabernacle or exposed for public adoration."[155] Yet the custom of a double genuflection before the monstrance arose for good reason. Solemn exposition allows us the privilege of a certain physical *nearness* to the Lord who is truly present beneath the veil of the lowly appearance of bread. The nearness is less than that of Holy Communion, but it prompts us to make acts of faith, trust, and adoration that prepare us better to *receive* Jesus in Communion. Put it this

---

[155] "*Coram sanctissimi Sacramento, sive in tabernaculo asservato sive publicæ adorationi exposito, unico genu flectitur*" (§84). Fr. Edward McNamara, a liturgist at Regina Apostolorum, attempted to defend this modern reductionism: "Since a genuflection is, *per se*, an act of adoration, the general liturgical norms no longer make any distinction between the mode of adoring Christ reserved in the tabernacle or exposed upon the altar. The simple single genuflection on one knee may be used in all cases" ("Tabernacles, Adoration and Double Genuflections," ZENIT Daily Dispatch, July 26, 2005). With all due respect for Fr. McNamara, I cannot avoid the impression that this explanation is contrived and disingenuous. The double genuflection, after all, did not develop because the single genuflection failed to express adoration!

way: as your heart expands, so does your capacity to receive all that He will give.

The difference between the Eucharist in the tabernacle and the Eucharist in the monstrance does not have to do with the *personal presence* of the Lord, for He is fully present whether the Sacrament is hidden or exposed to our gaze. The difference is one of *mode* or *manner*: out of sight, safeguarded, reserved, versus placed under our gaze, available to our senses, honored publicly with the guaranteed presence of someone praying. When exposed in the monstrance, the Lord is the hidden God among us in the visible sign of life-giving Bread. It is this obvious and significant difference in mode that justifies and calls for the double genuflection. Think of the difference between the pope in his private rooms and the pope in a general audience, or the difference between how we think of a church across town compared with how we act as we pass a church or go within it. The *way* in which a reality is present to us, the proximity of the sign itself, also matters, not just the reality that is present; both demand their due.

The attitude we should have before the Holy Eucharist—the attitude so well captured in the double genuflection, with one's head placed against the earth—is described with incomparable vividness by Mother Mectilde:

> When we are before the Most Holy Sacrament, we must not be content merely to adore Him with lip-service; we need to lower ourselves into a profound emptying out of self, and recognize that we are nothing, that we are less than nothing and, in this disposition, offer to the spotless Lamb who immolates Himself for the salvation of the world not only a sacrifice of adoration and of thanksgiving, but again a sacrifice of submission, of abandonment, and of consecration. Let us adhere to His divine will, detach ourselves from creatures, and renounce all human consolation, so as to live in Jesus only, and only for Jesus.[156]

---

[156] *Mystery of Incomprehensible Love*, 21.

The Holy Bread of Eternal Life

Basking in the sun of God's love

Some people who are not already accustomed to going to Eucharistic Adoration may be wondering: What do I *do* during Adoration? Should I bring prayer books with me, or spiritual reading, or my Rosary beads? Of course you may bring those things and use them as you wish. But the best thing to do is to *be still before the Lord,* paying Him the homage of your attention, speaking to His Heart and letting Him touch your heart. I love this quotation from Fr. Willie Doyle, S.J., a saintly Catholic priest who was killed on the battlefield in World War I while performing his duties as a chaplain. He writes:

> Try basking in the sun of God's love, that is, quietly kneeling before the tabernacle, as you would sit enjoying the warm sunshine, not trying to do anything, except love Him; but realising that, during all the time you are at His feet, more especially when dry and cold, grace is dropping down upon your soul and you are growing fast in holiness.[157]
>
> I think the best of all prayers is just to kneel quietly and let Jesus pour Himself into your soul.[158]

In the pages of *In Sinu Jesu,* the Lord Himself says something similar:

> It is enough for Me that you should seek Me out and remain quiet in My presence and content to be with Me. I have no need of your thoughts, no need of your words. It is enough for Me that you should offer Me an adoring heart full of love and grateful for My abiding presence in the Most Holy Sacrament.... For you, there is nothing more beneficial. You need to spend time close to My Eucharistic Heart. In My presence I communicate to your soul all that I want you to have, and all that I want you to know. You may

---

[157] *To Raise the Fallen: A Selection of the War Letters, Prayers and Spiritual Writings of Fr. Willie Doyle, S.J.,* compiled by Patrick Kenny (San Francisco: Ignatius Press, 2018), 132.

[158] Ibid., 152.

not be aware of this as it is happening, but later you will experience the fruit and the efficacy of this time spent in My presence.... This is what I want of you: time "wasted," spent in My presence. Time given to Me for My sake.[159]

As I knelt one day at a public Holy Hour, looking at Our Lord in the monstrance, I felt a tremendous peace, knowing in faith that He is forever the Head of the Church, forever the faithful Bridegroom, forever the Ruler and Judge of all. He holds the Church in His holy and venerable hands, like a victim ready to be offered, and every one of us can be present to Him if we wish, as He is always present to us.

I asked Him why He is allowing the Church to be crushed under the weight of so many sins, so much infidelity, so much betrayal and filth. His presence, His silence of strength and order, His indestructible love, were an answer better than any words, and I knew that He was urging me to greater faith, greater trust, more earnest prayer. Although it was good, later in the Holy Hour, to pray the Litany of the Most Sacred Heart and a number of prayers and chants with others in the church, to me the best part of the hour was the silent adoration. "I look at Him, and He looks at me." Where the Lord is, there is the promise of victory over all the forces of evil, within and without.

At this time in history, with news crashing in upon us from every side — mostly bad news, and some of it frankly scandalous in the extreme, as it reveals the callous complicity with, approbation of, and dedication to evil on the part of many in the hierarchy of the Church, who were supposed to be our guides to holiness and our models of it — nothing could be better than for us to go regularly before the Lord in Adoration. Fair weather or foul, super-busy or at loose ends, it doesn't matter; this is what we should be doing for our Church, for our clergy, for ourselves. This is what Our Lord is waiting for: a sign from us, an unmistakable sign, that we love Him for His own sake, and above all things on earth.

[159] *In Sinu Jesu*, 47, 57, 102.

The Holy Bread of Eternal Life

When enough of us are taking real steps to love Him in exactly this way—with our whole mind, our whole heart, our whole soul, and our whole strength—we may then count on a new flood of graces inundating the Church.

12

Living the Virtue of Chastity
by the Power of Jesus

Young Catholics today—and not only young ones—are experiencing an unprecedented bombardment of sexual propaganda and carnal temptations. Sins of the flesh have always been with us since the fall of Adam, but never before has such a multitude of impure images been so easily available, together with so many provocations to indulge in sin without regard to spiritual health, or even psychological and physical health.[160]

If C.S. Lewis was right to say "chastity is the most unpopular of the Christian virtues," it follows that we may also say: "unchastity is the most popular of the world's vices." Our modern situation was described well in advance by Our Lady of Good Success, who appeared to Venerable Mother Mariana de Jesus Torres y Berriochoa in Quito, Ecuador, from 1594 to 1634, and told her in great detail about a "spiritual catastrophe" that would occur in the Church "shortly after the middle of the twentieth century." Among the many prophecies was this one:

> The third reason the lamp was extinguished is because of the spirit of impurity that will permeate the atmosphere during these times. Like a filthy ocean, it will run through the streets, squares, and

---

[160] See my article "The Duty to Be Chaste: Even Pagan Philosophers Knew It Better Than Some Christians Today," *LifeSiteNews*, January 30, 2018.

public places with an astonishing liberty. There will be almost no virgin souls in the world.[161]

In like manner, Our Lady appeared to St. Jacinta of Fátima several times between December 1919 and February 1920. One of the things she said should give us pause: "More souls go to Hell because of sins of the flesh than for any other reason." She also said: "Certain fashions will be introduced that will offend Our Lord very much." In his book *The Message of Our Lady of Fatima*, Dom Augustine Marie comments:

> Sr. Lucia, the last living Fatima seer, said this [statement] refers primarily to sins against chastity, also called sins of impurity. The reason for this statement is not because sins against chastity are the most grievous sins, but [because they are] the most common and (as Sr. Lucia stated) "because of conscience," since sins of impurity are less likely to be repented of than other sins. Why? 1) because the sense of injustice committed, which is the primary stimulus to repent of one's sins, is not strongly felt when engaging in them, with the exception of adultery; 2) there is a greater sense of shame when committing certain impure acts and hence greater difficulty confessing them in the sacrament of Confession, or even repenting of them in one's heart; 3) sexual activity of all kinds is presented by our post-Christian—even anti-Christian—popular culture as natural and good, and sexual abstinence is even taught to be unhealthy.[162]

Although unchastity, immodesty, and related vices of intemperance are not the worst sins in and of themselves, they are undoubtedly among the most common, especially in certain age groups, and they are still

---

[161] In *Our Lady of Good Success: Prophecies for Our Times*, ed. and trans. Marian Therese Horvat (Los Angeles, CA: Tradition in Action, 1999), 56; cf. Steve Skojec, "400 Years Ago, Our Lady Sent Us a Message from Ecuador," *OnePeterFive*, July 6, 2015.

[162] https://archive.org/stream/TheMessageOfOurLadyOfFatimaWithPicture/ fatimaSelectionspic_djvu.txt.

deadly to the soul and corrosive of society. Whether one goes to hell for unrepented murder or unrepented fornication, for thievery or masturbation, in either case one ends up in hell, a place of everlasting torment and darkness; and even if Dante is right to portray hell as consisting of circles of greater or lesser punishment depending on degrees of malice, *all* of the damned experience the pain of losing God and the pain of sensible fire forever. This is absolutely something we want to avoid at all costs, through honorable self-control, repentance when we fall, humble unshakable confidence in God's mercy, and continual recourse to Confession and Communion.

In quo corrigit adolescentior viam suam? in custodiendo sermones tuos (Ps. 118:9). In this verse, the first half of which some Bibles translate "How can a young man keep his way pure?," King David—who had some issues of his own with sins of the flesh—asks a question as old as the hills. The new answer that Christianity brings is: Christ Himself. *We cannot succeed in being chaste or pure without Jesus.* There is no adequate secular substitute. No educational program, however well designed, will take His place and do His work.

Christ brings us countless gifts, but two are especially precious: the knowledge of the truth by which we must live, and the Holy Eucharist that unites us to the very Lord who purifies us and saves us. We need to know the way, and we need the strength to follow it. How tragic it is to see people trying to live without any sense of what is inherently right and wrong, true and false! Without such a map and compass, one will surely get lost in the wilderness, a prey to wild beasts. But no less tragic is it to see those who, aware of right and wrong, true and false, still falter and fail because they have not life *within them* to live righteously. "He who is united to the Lord becomes one spirit with him" (1 Cor. 6:17). St. Cyril of Alexandria, a Father and Doctor of the Church, exclaims in one of his homilies:

> If you feel the itch of intemperance, nourish yourself with the Flesh and Blood of Christ, who practiced heroic self-control during His

earthly life, and you will become temperate.... If you feel scorched by the fever of impurity, go to the banquet of the angels; and the immaculate Flesh of Christ will make you pure and chaste.[163]

Commenting on this passage, Fr. Stefano Manelli says:

When people wanted to know how it came about that St. Charles Borromeo managed to remain chaste and upright in the midst of other youths who were loose and frivolous, they discovered his secret was frequent Holy Communion.... St. Philip Neri, a priest thoroughly knowledgeable in the ways of young people, remarked: "Devotion to the Blessed Sacrament and devotion to the Blessed Virgin are not simply the best way, but in fact are the only way to conserve purity. At the age of twenty, nothing but Communion can keep one's heart pure.... Chastity is not possible without the Eucharist."[164]

The Eucharist is Jesus Himself—true God and true Man, the God who made us and sanctifies us, the Man who knows our weaknesses and heals them with His flesh. It is He who assures us: "What is impossible with men is possible with God" (Luke 18:27). Let us again and again approach Him with fear and faith, to let the power of His presence work miracles in us.

The reason we benefit so much from Communion is that we come into contact with the holy, pure, immaculate, and life-giving Flesh of Christ, the virginal High Priest who placed His Father's will above all earthly enticements and goods, however great they are (or seem to be). From His Sacred Heart, the burning furnace of charity, we receive the strength of will, the determination of purpose, the restraint of passion,

---

[163] Quoted in Fr. Stefano M. Manelli, F.F.I., *Jesus, Our Eucharistic Love: Eucharistic Life Exemplified by the Saints* (New Bedford, MA: Academy of the Immaculate, 1996), ch. 3, p. 48. This book has gone through many printings that vary considerably in their pagination.
[164] Ibid.

the calm of mind, to seek first the Kingdom of God and His righteousness, rather than deviating along the way.

If we fall into sin, moreover, we know that God has not abandoned us, but has permitted this stumbling for our humiliation and the stirring up of the spirit of repentance, without which no fallen human being will be saved. Even those who are far advanced along the way of perfection in charity must sorrow for their sins and the sins of the whole world. Indeed, as we see in the lives of the saints, it is the most perfect who feel most sharply the ingratitude of even the lightest of venial sins in comparison to the immensity of God's goodness.

The spiritual masters teach that those who conquer sins of the flesh often fall into more subtle vices—above all, pride at being free from lesser sins!—and that the Lord, knowing their danger, will at times permit them to yield to a sin they thought they had conquered. In this way, He teaches them multiple lessons at once: (1) their virtue is not exclusively their own work, but comes first and foremost from God, whom they must humbly beseech for it; (2) pride goeth before a fall, as Scripture says, and those whom God favors with graces must ask even more insistently for humility; (3) the thorn of disordered concupiscence will stick in our flesh until the moment the soul is torn from the body, so we should not be naïve in our thoughts or actions.

✠

As great as the power of the sacraments is—no power is greater in this world of ours!—they are not the only aids provided for us by the mercy of God. The Lord has empowered His Church to institute what we call "sacramentals": "sacred signs which bear a resemblance to the sacraments" and "signify effects, particularly of a spiritual nature, which are obtained through the intercession of the Church. By them men are disposed to receive the chief effect of the sacraments, and various occasions in life are rendered holy."[165]

---

[165] *Catechism of the Catholic Church*, n. 1667.

> Sacramentals are instituted for the sanctification of certain ministries of the Church, certain states of life, a great variety of circumstances in Christian life, and the use of many things helpful to man. In accordance with bishops' pastoral decisions, they can also respond to the needs, culture, and special history of the Christian people of a particular region or time.... Sacramentals do not confer the grace of the Holy Spirit in the way that the sacraments do, but by the Church's prayer, they prepare us to receive grace and dispose us to cooperate with it.[166]

Thus, we should not be surprised to find that Holy Mother Church has instituted several sacramentals intended to help us in preserving chastity.

The one I have been using for many years is the Cord of Purity of the Angelic Warfare Confraternity. It consists of a blessed white knotted cord one wears about one's waist as both a reminder that one's body belongs to Christ and as a silent appeal for grace in the battle for purity. This practice is derived from the original cord that St. Thomas Aquinas was given by angels after he drove away a prostitute with a fiery brand (the approach of "dialogue" was, evidently, not popular back then). To this day, the Dominicans are in charge of the Confraternity and have set up a useful website about how to be enrolled in it.[167] I really cannot recommend this too highly. Many saintly people—including St. Aloysius Gonzaga, Blessed Pier Giorgio Frassati, Blessed Columba Rieti, and Blessed Stephana Quinzani—have belonged to this Confraternity.

Other sacramentals with the same purpose exist in our Catholic tradition. One is the Cord of St. Philomena.[168] Another is St. Joseph's

---

[166] Ibid., nn. 1668 and 1670.

[167] www.angelicwarfareconfraternity.org.

[168] To learn more about St. Philomena and devotion to her, see this excellent sermon from a priest of the Priestly Fraternity of St. Peter: www.stfrancislincoln.org/pdf/Sermon_2019_Pentecost_09_St_Philomena.pdf. A brief summary of the cord may be found at www.truoriginal.com

Cincture, about which FishEaters provides ample information.[169] I have seen mention of the White Cord of St. Francis as well, though it seems much less popular than the aforementioned cords.

The Catholic tradition is practically bursting at the seams with devotions, so we must not let ourselves get overwhelmed by the choices available to us. Because they all enjoy the blessing of the Church and have proved themselves effective over a long span of time, we may freely choose *any* of them, without the need to collect and combine as many sacramentals as possible. The most important thing is that we become aware of the helps placed at our disposal—this would include the crucifix, holy water, the Rosary, the St. Benedict medal, the Brown Scapular, other scapulars, and the chastity cords—and make a point of using at least *some* of them consistently. It is very important, too, that whatever sacramentals you use be blessed by a priest using the *Roman Ritual*, which actually *blesses* the objects, instead of the *Book of Blessings*, which merely says nice things about them and us.

I conclude with a note sent to me by a young man, writing about his experience of the Cord of St. Philomena:

> I have found this very helpful against temptation. Sometimes we are not even aware of the difference it makes to carry or wear a blessed item on our person, but this one, I have to say, was really noticeable in its effects on my thoughts and feelings. Why is it not more talked about? Why don't chaplains give them to students more frequently, given the plague of unchastity in schools? I sometimes feel there is a real failure on the part of those who should be talking about the wonderful treasures of the Church, and with it a failure of young Catholics to have or even *know* about what could help to save their souls.

I couldn't agree more.

/2018/08/the-cord-of-st-philomena.html. There are several places online where one may purchase it.

[169] www.fisheaters.com/stjosephcords.html.

The Holy Bread of Eternal Life

Holy Mary, Virgin Most Pure, *pray for us.*
St. Joseph, Chaste Spouse of the Mother of God, *pray for us.*
St. Thomas Aquinas, St. Francis of Assisi,
St. Philomena, *pray for us.*

Part 3

Eating and Drinking Judgment

13

The Omission That Haunts the Church

In the Church today, many seem to be wholly unaware of the terrifying consequences of approaching the sacred banquet without being in a state of grace, that is to say, receiving the Eucharist in a state of mortal sin. Such a Communion not only does not and cannot help us, it heaps punishment upon our souls and makes our state *worse* than it was before. It is St. Paul who first and most clearly teaches this truth:

> Therefore whosoever shall eat this bread, or drink of the chalice of the Lord unworthily, shall be guilty of the Body and of the Blood of the Lord. But let a man prove himself: and so let him eat of that bread, and drink of the chalice. For he that eateth and drinketh unworthily, eateth and drinketh judgment to himself, not discerning the Body of the Lord. (1 Cor. 11:27–29)

In *Ecclesia de Eucharistia*, Pope John Paul II quotes St. John Chrysostom:

> I too raise my voice, I beseech, beg, and implore that no one draw near to this sacred table with a sullied and corrupt conscience. Such an act, in fact, can never be called "communion," not even were we to touch the Lord's body a thousand times over, but "condemnation," "torment," and "increase of punishment."[170]

The pope explains the reason why:

---

[170] *Homiliæ in Isaiam* 6, 3 (PG 56:139), cited in *Ecclesia de Eucharistia* §36.

The Holy Bread of Eternal Life

The celebration of the Eucharist...cannot be the starting-point for communion; it presupposes that communion already exists, a communion which it seeks to consolidate and bring to perfection.... Invisible communion, though by its nature always growing, presupposes the life of grace, by which we become "partakers of the divine nature" (2 Peter 1:4), and the practice of the virtues of faith, hope, and love.... Keeping these invisible bonds intact is a specific moral duty incumbent upon Christians who wish to participate fully in the Eucharist by receiving the Body and Blood of Christ. The Apostle Paul appeals to this duty when he warns: "Let a man examine himself, and so eat of the bread and drink of the cup" (1 Cor 11:28)....

I therefore desire to reaffirm that in the Church there remains in force, now and in the future, the rule by which the Council of Trent gave concrete expression to the Apostle Paul's stern warning when it affirmed that, in order to receive the Eucharist in a worthy manner, "one must first confess one's sins, when one is aware of mortal sin."... Christ is the truth and he bears witness to the truth (cf. Jn 14:6; 18:37); the sacrament of his Body and Blood does not permit duplicity.[171]

John Paul II goes on to speak of the inseparable relationship between the sacraments of Eucharist and Penance. While it is true that the Eucharist is given as a medicine for the weak, the meaning of "weakness" here is *not* the spiritual death induced by mortal sin, which leaves us incapable of eating (as St. Thomas says, a dead man cannot consume food; he first needs to be spiritually resurrected from the dead through Penance), but rather the fragile health of being in a state of grace while still dwelling in this corruptible flesh, struggling against the wounds of original sin, such as disordered concupiscence. Certainly the Church is a "field hospital," and we must bend over backward to take care of

---

[171] *Ecclesia de Eucharistia* §§35–36.

each wounded person who comes our way. At the same time, a doctor does not apply the same remedy to each disease, knowing that a medicine that cures in one case may kill in another. This is how the Church Fathers speak of the Holy Eucharist: it is food for the wayfarer who is living according to God's revealed law; it is poison for anyone else. Only when we have a well-founded confidence that we are wearing the wedding garment of charity and sanctifying grace (see Matt. 22:11) may we dare to approach "the divine, holy, pure, immortal, heavenly, life-creating, and awesome Mysteries of Christ."[172] Otherwise, as every liturgical rite says before Communion, we eat and drink "judgment and condemnation."

We are dealing here, in short, with doctrine that stretches from the Apostolic age to the present Magisterium in an uninterrupted crescendo of unambiguous affirmation. There is no way around it: Catholics are obliged to heed and follow St. Paul's "stern warning" in 1 Corinthians 11:27–29.

In the cycle of readings used for the traditional Latin Mass, these verses were (and still are) heard at least *three times every year*: once on Holy Thursday, for which the Epistle is 1 Corinthians 11:20–32,[173] and twice on Corpus Christi, where the Epistle is 1 Corinthians 11:23–29 and the Communion antiphon is verses 26–27. Catholics who attend the *usus antiquior* will never fail to have St. Paul's challenging words placed before their consciences. If the faithful happen to attend a votive Mass of the Blessed Sacrament—a popular choice among *usus antiquior* votive Masses—they will encounter these verses yet again. Moreover, 1 Corinthians 11:27–29 is part of the ninth reading of Tenebrae on Maundy Thursday and the third reading of Matins on Corpus Christi.

---

[172] Divine Liturgy of St. John Chrysostom.

[173] On Holy Thursday in the Novus Ordo, the second reading is 1 Cor. 11:23–26, simply narrating the institution of the Eucharist. The longer reading found in the *usus antiquior* provides the full context for what St. Paul is saying and makes clearer the connection between the institution of the Holy Eucharist and the present gathering of Christians for the celebration of the Mass.

The Holy Bread of Eternal Life

One might have assumed, as a matter of course, that when Coetus XI of the Consilium devised a new vastly expanded Lectionary spanning three years of Sundays and two years of weekdays, they would certainly have included *all* of the readings already found in the traditional Roman liturgy (as per *Sacrosanctum Concilium* 23 and 50), and that, in the wide scope allotted to New Testament books, no key passages would be omitted. Instead, in keeping with a programmatic decision to avoid what they deemed "difficult" biblical texts,[174] the new Lectionary *altogether omits* 1 Corinthians 11:27–29. St. Paul's "stern warning" against receiving the Body and Blood of the Lord unworthily, that is, unto one's condemnation, has not been read at any Ordinary Form Mass for half a century.

Consider the following comparison: in a community that miraculously managed to maintain the use of the traditional Latin Mass in the fifty-year period since the introduction of the new Lectionary in 1970, 1 Corinthians 11:27–29 (or vv. 26–27, which deliver the same message) will have been *required* reading at Mass 150 times. In the same period, it has been read *zero* times in the sphere of the Ordinary Form. How could this not make a difference in the formation of the faithful, clergy and laity alike? The same Pauline passage has, moreover, been altogether removed from the Liturgy of the Hours, where it once appeared twice, as noted above.[175] I have noticed in recent years a growing awareness of this glaring lacuna and others like it, but the entire problem deserves to be much more widely known, so that we can begin—or continue—to ask difficult questions in earnest.[176] One particularly apposite question

---

[174] See *General Introduction to the Lectionary*, §76; cf. Matthew Hazell, "On the Inclusion of 1 Corinthians 11:27–29 in the Ordinary Form," *New Liturgical Movement*, April 22, 2016.

[175] See, e.g., Felix Just, S.J., "The Office of Readings: Biblical First Readings," accessed at http://catholic-resources.org/LoH/OfficeOfReadings-Biblical. html.

[176] The work has been made significantly easier because of Matthew P. Hazell's *Index Lectionum: A Comparative Table of Readings for the Ordinary and Extraordinary Forms of the Roman Rite* (n.p.: Lectionary Study Press, 2016). On the history, principles, content, and limitations of the new lectionary,

might be: Why, on the Thursday of week 10 *per annum*, does the reading (2 Cor. 3:15–4:1, 3–6) skip verse 2 of chapter 4, where St. Paul says: "We have renounced disgraceful, underhanded ways; we refuse to practice cunning or to tamper with God's word, but by the open statement of the truth we would commend ourselves to every man's conscience in the sight of God"?[177]

Let us be frank: the concept of an unworthy Communion has disappeared from the general Catholic consciousness, at least in the affluent, self-satisfied West. I recall the surprise of more than a few commentators when the Synod fathers in 2015 were debating whether certain people should refrain from receiving Communion. Surely, doesn't everyone, almost without exception, go forward at Communion time?[178]

---

see Peter Kwasniewski, "The Reform of the Lectionary," in Alcuin Reid, ed., *Liturgy in the Twenty-First Century: Contemporary Issues and Perspectives* (London/New York: Bloomsbury T&T Clark, 2016), 287–320, as well as my foreword to the aforementioned *Index Lectionum*: "Not Just More Scripture, but Different Scripture." Both of these are also available online at *Rorate Caeli* (the former under the title "A Systematic Critique of the New Lectionary, On the Occasion of Its Fiftieth Anniversary").

[177] At the traditional Latin Mass, this verse is read every year on October 9 for the feast of St. John Leonardi; it is not included in any obligatory reading for the Novus Ordo, though it is found in some rarely used optional sanctoral readings (see Hazell, *Index Lectionum*, 138).

[178] Joseph Ratzinger addressed this problem in a somewhat understated manner: "It is one of the happy features of worship in the wake of the Council that more and more people participate fully in the Eucharist by receiving the body of the Lord, communicating with him and, in him, with the whole Church of God. Yet do we not feel a slight uneasiness at times in the face of an entire congregation coming to communion? Paul urgently insisted that the Corinthians should 'discern' the Lord's body (1 Cor 11:29): is this still happening? Occasionally one has the feeling that 'communion' is regarded as part of the ritual—that it goes on automatically and is simply an expression of the community's identity. We need to regain a much stronger awareness that the Eucharist does not lose all its meaning where people do not communicate. By going to Communion without 'discernment,' we fail to reach the heights of what is taking place in Communion; we reduce the Lord's gift to the level of

The Holy Bread of Eternal Life

So far from regarding the message of 1 Corinthians 11:27–29 as peripheral, our forebears in the Faith thought it was crucial to reinforce St. Paul's warning. In one of the innumerable galleries of the Louvre hangs an early sixteenth-century tapestry depicting two miracles — not miracles of healing or salvation, but miracles of dire punishment of unworthy communicants.[179] The left panel tells the story of a man who received the Eucharist in a state of mortal sin, and it burned a hole through his neck. The right panel tells the story of a priest who was celebrating Mass in a state of mortal sin, and his hands burst into flames.

A modern Christian may smile at such "medieval fantasies" and reassure himself that God does not act so harshly. Perhaps we have forgotten the story of Ananias and Sapphira in the Acts of the Apostles (5:1–11), where God strikes two Christians dead for telling lies about their donation of wealth.[180] St. Paul tells us, in 1 Corinthians 11:30, that due to unworthy Communions some have become sick and others have died. Is that a superstitious view, or did St. Paul know something we have forgotten?

In the ordinary course of His Providence, God does not punish sinners immediately; we know this from Scripture, from history, and from

everyday ordinariness and manipulation. The Eucharist is not a ritual meal; it is the shared prayer of the Church, in which the Lord prays together with us and gives us himself. Therefore it remains something great and precious, it remains a true gift, even when we cannot communicate. If we understood this better and hence had a more correct view of the Eucharist itself, many pastoral problems — the position of the divorced and remarried in the Church, for instance — would cease to be such a burden" (*The Feast of Faith,* trans. Graham Harrison [San Francisco: Ignatius Press, 1986], 151–52).

[179] *Deux Miracles de l'Hostie de la tenture L'Histoire du saint Sacrement,* aux armes d'Isabelle de La Jaille, abbesse de 1505 à 1518 de l'abbaye du Ronceray, près d'Angers; made between 1505 and 1518; tapestry, linen.

[180] Acts 5:1–11 is found neither in the old lectionary nor in the new. The difference, however, is that the old lectionary never included much of Acts — one might say it had no intention of doing so — whereas the new lectionary's inclusion of vast swathes of the book makes the skipping of these verses more deliberate.

experience. The vast majority of unworthy communicants or celebrants do not erupt into flames or perish on the spot in groans of agony. This does not, however, mean that their Communions are not unworthy. It means that the Lord, though sinned against, has refrained from punishing them immediately and obviously, in view of their possible repentance, conversion, and restoration to His divine friendship.[181] All the same, each and every Catholic is under a serious obligation to examine his or her conscience prior to approaching the sacred banquet, in order to avoid offending God and incurring further guilt.

It might be thought that I am exaggerating the gravity of the omission of the Pauline admonition in the new Mass propers, Lectionary, and Liturgy of the Hours. In that case, listen not to me, but to the words of St. John Vianney, patron of parish priests. Like other great preachers who took seriously their obligation to prepare the faithful for Holy Communion, the Curé of Ars on the one hand extolled the joy, peace, and glory that come to us through grace-filled Communions, and, on the other hand, warned, in no uncertain terms, of the destruction of soul that results from a wicked Communion. Since the positive side of the Church's Eucharistic doctrine is just about the only thing one hears nowadays, as if the negative side did not even exist, it will be beneficial in our present situation to go straight to St. John Vianney's "Sermon on Unworthy Communion":

> Unworthy Communions are frequent. How many have the temerity to approach the holy table with sins hidden and disguised in confession! How many have not that sorrow which the good God wants from them, and preserve a secret willingness to fall back into sin, and do not put forth all their exertions to amend! How many do not avoid the occasions of sin when they can, or preserve enmity in their hearts even at the holy table! If you have ever been in these dispositions in approaching Holy Communion, you

---

[181] See 2 Pet. 3:9–15.

have committed a sacrilege—that horrible crime, on the malice of which we are going to meditate.

1. *It outrages God more than all other mortal sins.* It attacks the Person of Jesus Christ himself, instead of scorning only his commandments, like other mortal sins.

2. *Whoever communicates unworthily crucifies Jesus Christ in his heart.* He submits him to a death more ignominious and humiliating than that of the Cross. On the Cross, indeed, Jesus Christ died voluntarily and for our redemption: but here it is no longer so: he dies in spite of himself, and his death, far from being to our advantage, as it was the first time, turns to our woe by bringing upon us all kinds of chastisements both in this world and the next. The death of Jesus Christ on Calvary was violent and painful, but at least all nature seemed to bear witness to his pain. The least sensible of creatures appeared to be affected by it, and thus wishful to share the Saviour's sufferings. Here there is nothing of this: Jesus is insulted, outraged by a vile nothingness, and all keeps silence; everything appears insensible to his humiliations. May not this God of goodness justly complain, as on the tree of the Cross, that he is forsaken? My God, how can a Christian have the heart to go to the holy table with sin in his soul, there to put Jesus Christ to death?

3. *Unworthy Communion is a more criminal profanation than that of the holy places.* A pagan emperor, in hatred of Jesus Christ, placed infamous idols on Calvary and the holy sepulchre, and he believed that in doing this he could not carry further his fury against Jesus Christ. Ah! great God! Was that anything to be compared with the unworthy communicant? No, no! It is no longer among dumb and senseless idols that he sets his God, but in the midst, alas!, of infamous living passions, which are so many executioners who crucify his Saviour. Alas! What shall I say? That poor wretch unites the Holy of Holies to a prostitute soul, and sells him to iniquity. Yes, that poor wretch plunges his God into a raging hell. Is it possible to conceive anything more dreadful?

4. *Unworthy Communion is in certain respects a greater crime than the deicide of the Jews.* St. Paul tells us that if the Jews had known Jesus Christ as the Saviour they would never have put him to suffering or death; but can you, my friend, be ignorant of him whom you are going to receive? If you do not bear it in mind, listen to the priest who cries aloud to you: "Behold the Lamb of God; behold him that taketh away the sins of the world." He is holy and pure. If you are guilty, unhappy man, do not draw near; or else tremble, lest the thunders of heaven be hurled upon your criminal head to punish you and cast your soul into hell.

5. *Unworthy Communion imitates and renews the crime of Judas.* The traitor, by a kiss of peace, delivered Jesus Christ to his enemies, but the unworthy communicant carries his cruel duplicity yet further. Having lied to the Holy Ghost in the tribunal of penance by hiding or disguising some sin, he dares, this wretch, to go with a hypocritical reverence on his face, and place himself among the faithful destined to eat this Bread. Ah! no, nothing stops this monster of ingratitude; he comes forward and is about to consummate his reprobation. In vain that tender Saviour, seeing that he is coming to him, cries from his tabernacle, as to the perfidious Judas: "Friend, whereto art thou come? What, thou art about to betray thy God and Saviour by a sign of peace? Stop, stop, my son; I pray thee spare me!" Neither the remorse of his conscience nor the tender reproaches made him by his God can stop his criminal steps. He steps forward. He is going to stab his God and Saviour. O heavens! what a horror! Can you indeed behold this wretched murderer of your Creator without trembling?[182]

[182] *Sermon sur la Communion indigne*, quoted in *Eucharistic Meditations: Extracts from the Writings and Instructions of St. John Vianney*, ed. Abbé H. Convert, trans. Sr. Mary Benvenuta (Wheathampstead: Anthony Clarke Books, 1923, repr. 1964), 92–96.

The Holy Bread of Eternal Life

Thus St. John Vianney, who, like St. John Chrysostom, did not flinch when it came to calling out evils and urging their amendment.

Another eloquent witness is Mother Mectilde of the Blessed Sacrament, a spiritual guide from the "golden age" of French spirituality, who was filled by God with a tender and zealous love for the Most Holy Sacrament of the Altar. In her work *The True Spirit of the Perpetual Adorers of the Most Holy Sacrament of the Altar*, a series of conferences she gave to her community of nuns, she describes the horror of unworthy Communions:

> My sisters, let us continue to speak about the humiliations which Jesus bears in us, in our Communions. How great should be our grief on account of ourselves and the many people who receive Communion unworthily and who make Jesus suffer such awful shame and insult? My sisters, we have the glory of being the daughters and the victims of the Most Holy Sacrament. Have we not great reason to weep? I do not even speak here of the external profanations which are committed by the wicked, a single account of which is enough to make one die of sorrow and fear. Sacrilegious Communions, only too frequent among Christians — should we not be overwhelmed with shock?
>
> Oh! Who can understand what injury the Son of God receives from such Communions? I can say nothing to express such a deadly evil. It is the center of all evils, for Jesus in a way receives a kind of death, more disgraceful, more shameful, and crueler than that of His Passion. This evil is so terrible in its reality that it exceeds all human thoughts. It would be necessary to understand something of the infinite dignity, sanctity, and greatness of God to do it justice.
>
> I am very certain, my sisters, that not one of us would want to fall into this disorder. I tell you this only to make you marvel at the excessive humiliations of God when He became man and how He subjects Himself in order to come into our hearts by Holy

Communion. I know that you would not voluntarily allow a venial sin to enter your hearts and that you would rather descend into hell than insult your Spouse in this way; for if we were to be in that infernal abyss, God would not lose any of His glory. But to offend His Majesty in us by a mortal sin is the only evil on earth which a soul ought to fear.

Lest one think that the author of these words had an excessively severe conception of worthiness, I hasten to add that Mother Mectilde was a veritable lieutenant in the campaign against the Jansenists, who were *happy* when people did not go to Communion, because, as they said, no one could be worthy of receiving God. Mother Mectilde would have none of this; she knew that any soul in a state of grace, however imperfect and weak, desperately needs the Bread of Life in order to grow in holiness and charity. She was accustomed to say: "Why would you deprive yourself of the infinite Good?" She encouraged her sisters, as well as laity with whom she corresponded, to receive Holy Communion as frequently as they could, as long as they did so with proper preparation and good dispositions.

At the same time, however, and without the slightest inconsistency, she was inflexibly stern about the evil of going to Communion when one is in a state of discord with the law of God. It does not matter what one's subjective intentions may be; if one is living in a *state* that is objectively contrary to God's will for man, one must never approach the communion rail. This would be no different from Judas betraying the Son of God with a kiss.

The reason for this is simple. God desires our love. But love—the rational, freely chosen love proper to human beings—is not a feeling or an emotion; it is the conformity of our will to God's will, which includes our repentance of sins that are contrary to His will. The ancient Roman Catiline once said: *Idem velle atque idem nolle, ea demum firma amicitia est,* which may be rendered "True friendship is willing and not willing the same things." How can we be said to love the Lord when we are ignoring, contradicting, opposing, or scorning his will? Thus, Mother Mectilde *encourages* frequent Communion for those who are striving to conform to God's will for the very same reason that she *forbids* sacramental Communion for those who are not willing to renounce their lack of conformity to God's will—that is, their attachment to serious sin. The only one who may worthily approach Communion is the one who also grasps how harmful it would be to do so unworthily. To go to Communion casually, routinely, without a thought in the world about the infinitely holy divine Person we are receiving, is *already* to be unworthy and to receive in a sinful way; far worse, then, is it to approach Communion in a state of objective moral disorder, when one is living contrary to God's law, as given to us in Scripture and in the Church's perennial Tradition.

This is why the worldwide debate over the issues raised in chapter 8 of *Amoris Laetitia* is no mere scholarly diversion or pastoral skirmish. As has already been explained countless times by faithful sons and princes of the Church, it is a matter of fidelity or infidelity to the Son of God, the Word made flesh, the King of Kings, the Judge of the living and the dead. Everyone who supports errors concerning admissibility to Holy Communion will have to answer on the dread day of judgment for their part in crucifying the Savior in His Eucharistic Body.

Now, if someone were to ask: Why am I publishing such sobering, fear-inspiring reflections?, here is how I would answer. In communion with the Catholic Church of all times and places, I accept the reality of hell; following Scripture and Tradition, and contrary to the dubious speculations of Hans Urs von Balthasar, I accept that many unrepentant sinners have already gone and will continue to go there to join the devil and his angels in eternal fire.[183] We find the healthy Catholic attitude in a short story by Msgr. Robert Hugh Benson, where a priest is getting

---

[183] See my articles "On Hell: Clarity Is Mercy in an Age of 'Dare We Hope,'" *OnePeterFive*, August 7, 2019; "Purgatory and Hell: Forgotten Destinations," Part I, *OnePeterFive*, December 1, 2015.

ready his holy oils and pyx for a sick call to a Catholic woman who was a public sinner and who had not set foot in a church for over a decade: "I know very well she is out of grace, and I know what will be the end of her if I do not come."[184] In keeping with Christian charity, I do not want to see *any* soul end up in Gehenna by dying in a state of unrepented mortal sin — or, what is worse, by compounding that state with still further sins of "eating and drinking condemnation upon oneself," as St. Paul says (see 1 Cor. 11:29).

The Church and her faithful people always have many needs; but undoubtedly one of those needs today is identifying sin and turning away from it with disgust, rather than compromising with it, condoning it, hiding it, or being afraid to call it by name. We need preachers like St. John Vianney to combat the indifferentism, relativism, universalism, and hedonism in which modern Christians are submerged. Such is the exhortation we receive from Saints Peter and Paul, whose inspired letters proclaim the unadulterated Gospel. On the "hard teachings" of Scripture — passages included in the old lectionary but deemed "too difficult for modern man" and therefore excised from the revised one — Peter Kreeft has some incisive words:

> We want it all. We want God and… But we can't have God and… because there is no such thing. The only God there is, is "God only," not "God and." God is a jealous God. He himself says that, many times, in his word. He will not share our heart's love with other gods, with idols. He is our husband, and his love will not tolerate infidelity. A hard saying, especially to our age, which is spiritually as well as physically promiscuous. But if we find the saying hard, that is all the more reason to look at it again and look at ourselves in its light, for the fact that we find it hard means that we have not accepted it yet, and need to. It's precisely those parts

---

[184] *The Supernatural Stories of Monsignor Robert H. Benson* (Landisville, PA: Coachwhip Publications, 2010), 207.

of God's revealed word that we don't like or understand that we need to pay the most attention to.[185]

Summorum Pontificum has provided to the Church an urgent medicine in this era of misunderstood mercy and forgotten dogma. Pope Benedict XVI recognized that the *usus antiquior* is a treasure for the entire Church, one that must be given its due place for the benefit of all. One of the most valuable contributions it makes, together with the culture of piety it sustains, is to keep alive the integral teaching of Scripture and Tradition precisely on matters that *are* difficult for modern man—and about which he needs to be confronted all the more.[186]

In the ambit of the traditional Mass, one often finds that the faithful are well aware of the requirement to examine their consciences, and, if they are aware of any mortal sin, they will go to Confession first—something rendered far easier by the ready availability of Confession before (and sometimes during) Mass, particularly on Sundays. At communion time, it simply does not happen that everyone goes up, row after row. A number of people remain in the pews; as a result, those who, for whatever reason, cannot or should not receive the Eucharist do not feel oddly isolated or uncomfortably noticed. Finally, the faithful who wish to receive the Body, Blood, Soul, and Divinity of our Lord Jesus Christ —and who are not conscious of any unrepented and unconfessed mortal sin—step forward, kneel down in adoring reverence, and receive the King of Kings and Lord of Lords on their tongues, from the consecrated hand of the priest. It is all done in a manner proper, just, and right. Man comes before

---

[185] *Making Choices: Practical Wisdom for Everyday Moral Decisions* (Ann Arbor, MI: Servant Books, 1990), 151. Even the Anglican Book of Common Prayer, with its defective Eucharistic theology, develops at length St. Paul's warning in 1 Corinthians, in an exhortation meant to be regularly proclaimed to the congregation. For the text, see my article "Christian Wisdom from the Anglican Tradition," *New Liturgical Movement*, April 20, 2016.

[186] See my article "The Reality of Hell and the Fear of God: Banished from a Church Near You," *OnePeterFive*, January 17, 2018.

God and begs to receive the awesome gift of His divine life, of which, as creatures and sinners, we will always, at some level, be unworthy. As we say, three times for emphasis: *Domine, non sum dignus, ut intres sub tectum meum, sed tantum dic verbo, et sanabitur anima mea.* Lord, I am not worthy that Thou shouldst enter under my roof; but only say the word, and my soul shall be healed.

14

Our Progressive Desensitization to the Most Holy Eucharist

In the era of *Amoris Laetitia*, the question of who may or may not receive Holy Communion has been and will remain a contentious issue until the dubia rightly posed by the four cardinals have been definitively resolved in favor of Catholic orthodoxy. Yet we did not wake up one fine day in 2016 to find ourselves suddenly confronted with Eucharistic sacrilege being promoted from on high. There was a long, slow process that led to this moment. It consisted in the gradual dilution of the sacredness of the Holy Sacrifice of the Mass and of the Blessed Sacrament at its heart, with institutionally tolerated sacrilege along the way. Fifty years of desacralization has ended in the temerity of contradicting the entire Catholic tradition about the most holy of all the Church's mysteries.

The first major step was the allowance of Communion in the hand while standing—a sharp break from the deeply ingrained practice of many centuries of kneeling in adoration at the altar rail and receiving on the tongue, like a baby bird being fed by its parent (as we see in countless medieval depictions of the pelican that has wounded her breast in order to feed her chicks). This change had the obvious effect of making people think the Holy Eucharist wasn't so mysterious and holy after all. If you can just take it in your hand like ordinary food, it might as well be a potato chip distributed at a party. The *sense of awe and reverence* toward the Blessed Sacrament was systematically diminished and undermined through this Modernist reintroduction of an ancient practice that had long since been discontinued by the Church in her pastoral wisdom. Nor, as has been well documented, did the *faithful themselves* request the abolition of the custom of receiving on the tongue while kneeling; it was imposed by the self-styled "experts."[187]

The second major step was the allowance of lay ministers of Communion. This reinforced the perception, admittedly imprecise, that the Church had given up all that stuff about the priest's role being essentially different from the laity's, about the Mass as a divine sacrifice and the Eucharist as the Bread of Angels that only anointed hands are fit to handle. True, a priest still had to say the magic words, but after that, Jack and Jill could come up, take bowls and cups, and hand out the tokens of club membership.[188]

The effect of these "reforms" and others like them (the replacement of majestic and mysterious Latin with everyday vernacular, the substitution of guitar and piano ditties for pipe organ and chant, the turning around of the priest to face the people like a talkshow host, the removal of altar rails, the decentering of tabernacles, the uglification of vestments and vessels, and more) was to weaken and corrupt the faith of the people in the Mass as a true and proper sacrifice and in the Eucharist as the true Body and Blood of Jesus. No wonder that after this, the idea of the Eucharistic fast, and of preparing oneself for Communion by going to Confession, went right out the window for the vast majority of people. The Church's own pastors didn't act as if they really believed these things anymore, so why should their flocks?

In short, we have lived through, and suffered under, half a century of ritual diminishment and symbolic contradiction of the Church's faith

---

[187] There is an obvious difference between an original practice, such as early Christians receiving in the hand, and a later *reintroduction* of such a practice when it has long since become obsolete. In the former case, the practice is innocent. In the latter case, it amounts to a repudiation and a symbolic contradiction of the values represented by kneeling before the Host and not handling it oneself. See chapters 7–9.

[188] See chapter 10.

in the sublime mysteries of the Body and Blood of Christ. As John Paul II and Benedict XVI lamented, there is scant evidence in our communities of any awareness of the distinction between worthy and unworthy Communions—one of the most basic lessons children used to be taught in their catechism class.

In those primitive "pre–Vatican II days," children were taught to practice virtue and avoid mortal sin *because* they should desire to be able to receive the Lord and be ever more perfectly united to Him, until they reach the glory of heaven where they will possess Him forever. They were taught that if one receives the Lord in a state of mortal sin, one commits a further and a worse sin. They were taught that making a good Confession, with sorrow for sin and an intention to avoid it in future, is enough to put this bad situation right and restore them to God's friendship. Who could seriously assert that most Catholics believe *any* of this today, or that they would even *recognize*, much less understand, the concepts? Msgr. Robert Hugh Benson wrote this about his Anglican days:

> I was an official in a church that did not seem to know her own mind, even in matters directly connected with the salvation of the soul.... Might I, or might I not, tell my penitents that they are bound to confess their mortal sins before Communion?... The smallest Roman Catholic child knew precisely how to be reconciled to God, and to receive His grace....[189]

Does not this Anglican's description of the problem in his own ecclesial body sound frightfully close to what may be found today in the Roman Catholic Church?

Today, at least in certain Western countries, nearly everyone goes up for Communion when the time comes. It's just "what you do at Mass." Hardly anyone goes to Confession; hardly anyone refrains from receiving, out of a consciousness of sin; and rare is the priest who ever preaches about

---

[189] *Confessions of a Convert* (Notre Dame, IN: Christian Classics, 2016), 60–62. The text was written 1906–1907.

having the right dispositions for Communion. (Contrast this with St. John Vianney, who preached relentlessly about these things, as we saw in the last chapter, and greatly intensified his parish's commitment to the sacrament of Confession and to frequent Communion. It's not for nothing that he's the patron saint of parish priests. Patrons are meant to be imitated.)

Thus was the ground devilishly prepared for the final stage, in which *any* impediments to Communion are theoretically and practically dissolved. In a general situation where the Catholics who still attend Mass all receive, it would seem cruel and unusual punishment to single out a handful of so-called "divorced and remarried" people for special treatment: "*You* are not allowed to go to Communion, but meanwhile, the self-abusing and fornicating teens, the contracepting couples, the families who sometimes skip Sunday Mass for sports events—all are welcome to come forward, as usual!"

This is the big picture that explains, to my mind, why the liberals or progressives in the Church are totally incapable of seeing why anyone would object to chapter 8 of *Amoris Laetitia* with its nuclear footnote 351.[190] They do not really believe that the Mass is a true and proper sacrifice of Jesus Christ offered to the Most Holy Trinity; they do not really believe in transubstantiation and the Real Presence; they do not believe that one is eating and drinking the flesh and blood *of God*; they do not believe that one who eats and drinks unworthily is eating and drinking his own condemnation, just as those who eat worthily are seeding their souls and bodies for a glorious resurrection.

The Amorites, as we might call them, see "the Eucharist" as a fraternal gathering, a social event, an affirmation of human worth, a "celebration" of God's "unconditional love," and whatever other Hallmark slogans come to mind. Within the confines of this horizontal and superficial theology, there is no room for any requirements or prohibitions: everyone is welcome, and anything goes! Since the Eucharist is a meal symbolizing

---

[190] Or perhaps we should say foot*notes*, since there are several that are problematic.

God's welcome of the sinner, there is no reason to exclude anyone, for any reason, from partaking of the "table of plenty."

Amoris Laetitia fits into this larger historical trajectory whereby the Mass has been stripped of its transcendent, mysterious, fearful, and challenging sacrificial realism and pushed continually in the direction of an ordinary meal with ordinary folks doing ordinary things for a this-worldly end (consistent with the love-blind embrace of the United Nations and the "Greenpeace" environmentalism of *Laudato Si'*), with a forced spontaneity and embarrassing banality that has failed to attract the overflow crowds predicted by Paul VI. At such a Mass, is there anything to do *but* receive Communion? Who would ever think of going just for the sake of adoring God and contemplating His beauty? Opportunities and incentives for adoration are practically non-existent in the Novus Ordo, and beauty has fared no better, or rather much worse. In such circumstances, to place a barrier between a free meal and a guest who thinks well of himself for being there is unthinkable.[191]

In truth, the Mass is the unbloody sacrifice of the Cross, made present in our midst; it is simultaneously the heavenly life-giving wedding feast of the now-glorified Christ. The Eucharist is the sacrament of the one-flesh union of a bride adorned with grace and a Bridegroom who is her sole happiness.

I am not surprised to find that, at traditional Latin Masses around the world, including in the United States, one sees two related phenomena:

---

[191] We can begin to see the magnitude of the sea change if we imagine what it would have been like had the Kasper Proposal been floated in 1965 — the last year in which it is possible to argue that the Roman Rite was still intact (albeit already orphaned of its opening and closing portions). There would have been stunned incredulity and righteous indignation. The proposal wouldn't have lasted longer than a lit match. No churchman in his right mind would have countenanced it. Progressives today attack traditionalists equally for our love of the traditional liturgy, our dogmatic intransigence, and our commitment to objective morality. They are right to see a deep and abiding connection between these things — a connection neatly summed up as *lex orandi, lex credendi, lex vivendi.*

The Holy Bread of Eternal Life

a large number of the faithful availing themselves of Confession, before and during Mass; and a fair number of the faithful who remain in the pews and do not go forward for Communion. The interior triumphs of the one, the interior trials of the other, are known to God alone. But this much is obvious: they all came to worship Him. They came in response to His majesty. They came to fulfill a solemn obligation of the virtue of religion. Whether they are personally disposed to receive or not is a question at a different level. This is the sanity that prevails in the realm of tradition; it is the sanity that paves the way for sanctity.

15

Liturgical Abuse, Sexual Abuse, and Clericalism

Every Catholic who can draw upon many years of living the Faith knows that there are good and holy priests, images of the great High Priest and Good Shepherd, who serve us tirelessly, who work earnestly for our salvation, and who are part of the reason why being Catholic is the greatest joy in the world. Many of us may be privileged to count several such priests as family friends. We know that they are often underappreciated, and are subject to undeserved skepticism and suspicion just because of the faults of some of their clerical brethren — faults that they themselves repudiate and condemn just as much as the laity do.

All of us, laity in the pews and clergy in the sanctuaries, must nevertheless ask ourselves hard questions. Perhaps the most important of these tough questions is: What has made it possible for so many "men of God," including bishops, to become pawns of the devil? Apart from general causes like the fall of Adam, disordered concupiscence, and the dangers that accompany positions of authority, can we identify any cause that is specific to the past fifty years — to the period, that is, to which the vast majority of clerical abuse cases are confined?

A systemic cause of clerical deviation from duty, moral laxity, and debauchery is the atmosphere of Woodstockian antinomianism or lawlessness that accompanied the liturgical reforms and deformations of the 1960s and 1970s, a time when self-celebration replaced the Catholic ideal — not everywhere achieved but everywhere required — of a priest who submitted himself to the discipline of a demanding liturgical form with its reverential rubrics and inculcation of the fear of God. The priest used to be a man consecrated to the strict and sober service of the sanctuary. As everything rapidly changed in these decades, he was suddenly the vernacular center of attention, the "presider" who manipulated the congregation. Priests were thrown into the lion's den of vanity, popularity, sentimentality, and relaxation, and not all were Daniels who escaped unscathed. There was no asceticism in sight; whatever evil might have been suppressed by the former code of honor was now given free rein.

Catholics of a certain age know exactly what I am talking about. Born in 1971, I can remember plenty of "creative liturgies"—and not surprisingly, the clergy responsible for such things were among those later investigated for moral corruption. It took me a long time to see the connection (perhaps I'm just slow on the uptake), but it finally crystallized for me: the decades-long abuse of the Holy Mass and all the rest of the sacramental and liturgical rites—and therefore, by extension, the violence done to faithful Catholics who have a right to the sacred liturgy in its fullness, as the Instruction *Redemptionis Sacramentum* expressly acknowledges[192]—constitutes the first and fundamental form of clerical abuse of the laity, of which sexual abuse is a particular and more demented variety. Clerical sexual abuse is linked to clerical liturgical abuse; sexual perversion is a mirror-image of liturgical perversion.

Given the absolute centrality and infinite dignity of the Mass and the Holy Eucharist, abuse of the liturgy and the sacraments is the worst crime against God and man possible. If the highest and holiest thing in existence does not deserve our utmost veneration, why should mere human beings deserve any respect? We are mere dust and ashes compared to the divine Sacrifice of the Altar. On the other hand, if we profoundly reverence and fear Christ, true God and true man, we will acknowledge and care

---

[192] For the pertinent section of this Instruction and many other supporting texts of the Magisterium, see my article "Fidelity to Liturgical Law and the Rights of the Faithful," *OnePeterFive*, July 3, 2017.

for His image in the souls and bodies of all human beings. Reverence for Him goes hand in hand with respect for the little ones.

At his popular blog, Fr. Zuhlsdorf quoted this message from a reader:

> If we can't treat the body of our Lord and Saviour with respect, why would we treat the bodies of our neighbors with respect? Is there a short, slippery slope that runs between sloppiness at Mass and sin?... When we take Mass and the Eucharist seriously and let all our relationships flow forth from that first, essential relationship with Christ, we cannot use other people as objects. When the Mass goes, everything else starts to go too.... I think that a reverent liturgy flows naturally from a love of Christ in the Eucharist and a realization that we're in the presence of God.... Father Z is right. "Save the Liturgy, Save the World." It's not a coincidence that the pope (Benedict) who is focused on cleaning up the filth of abuse in the Church is also focused on cleaning up the liturgy. If we can't respect God, we won't respect each other.[193]

Father Zuhlsdorf himself has said, with characteristic vigor:

> The Eucharist, its celebration and itself as *the* extraordinary Sacrament, is the "source and summit of Christian life." If we *really* believe that, then we must also hold that what we do in church, what we believe happens in a church, makes an enormous difference. Do we believe the consecration *really does* something? Or, do we believe what is said and how, what the gestures are and the attitude in which they are made, are entirely *indifferent*? For example, will a choice not to *kneel* before Christ the King and Judge truly present in each sacred Host, produce a wider effect? If you throw a stone, even a pebble, into a pool, it produces ripples which expand to its edge. The way we celebrate Mass must create

[193] "Connection of Liturgical Abuse and Abuse of Minors?," *Fr. Z's Blog*, September 1, 2010.

spiritual ripples in the Church and the world. So does our good or bad reception of Holy Communion. So must *violations* of rubrics and irreverence.[194]

At times, a Catholic feels the urge to say to the secularizing and liberalizing clergy of the past five decades: You and your minions wrecked theology with modernism; you wrecked the liturgy with your "reform"; and, as the *coup de grâce*, you wrecked the lives of children. This is a ghastly inversion of the Kingdom of God. A time will come when all this evil is purged, if not while yet there is time for repentance, then assuredly when the Lord prepares for us a new heavens and a new earth.

We also say to our good and holy priests: Keep doing what you are doing right. Love the sacred liturgy, celebrate it with awe, devotion, fear, silence, and beauty. Lead us with you, eastward, in pilgrimage to the Lord. Remember and cherish our Catholic inheritance. In this way, you will bring about a real change in the culture of the Church, restoring the institution, its personnel, and its ceremonies to the honor they deserve.

Where clericalism flourishes

We have heard often about the "dangers of clericalism" from leaders in the Church today, as they attempt to steer the conversation away from the primary cause of the vast majority of sexual abuse cases (the psychological disorder of homosexuality) and to lay the blame on structural and institutional factors that feature in their liberal narrative of a Church in need of radical reformation in its teachings connected with sexuality (e.g., ordination of women, optional clerical celibacy, regularization of divorcees, normalization of homosexual relationships).

In a perfect expression of this mentality, Bishop Felix Genn of Münster remarked: "I can tell you firmly: I do not want pre-conciliar clerical

---

[194] In his programmatic statement "Save the Liturgy, Save the World," *Fr. Z's Blog*, January 29, 2007.

guys and I will not ordain them."[195] The language used here connects with a frequent theme in modern-day preaching, namely, that before the Council the Church was segregated into first-class citizens (clergy) and second-class citizens (laity), the former lording it over the latter; and that the phenomenon of traditionalism today is characterized by the same false ecclesiology. Such assertions hark back to the 1970s, when it was fashionable to grant a monopoly to the expression "People of God" in a quasi-Marxist, democratic, secularized sense.

During the procession of the ministers at the start and end of Mass at oratories of the Institute of Christ the King, Sovereign Priest, one will see the faithful first make the sign of the cross as the Cross passes by, and then bow toward the priest — not because he is this or that particular man, wielding authority over other men, but because he represents Christ the High Priest who offers the one saving sacrifice that unites all of us to Him and to one another. The very fact that the priest is clothed with a cope and later with a chasuble, and that he faces eastward at the altar, shows very clearly that he is actively and powerfully standing in for Christ, clothed in the garments of His priesthood, with his own individuality hidden and his office exalted. In this way the faithful are paying homage to their Lord, not to a mere creature.

The same can be said for other pious customs of tradition-loving Catholics, such as kissing a newly ordained priest's hands when receiving his first blessing, or kneeling for any priest's blessing.[196] In so acting, we recognize in the priest in front of us an *efficacious sign* of the One whose

---

[195] "German Bishop Firmly Refuses to Ordain 'Traditional-Minded Priests,'" *GloriaTV*, September 29, 2018.

[196] The abolition in the rubrics of the Missal of Paul VI of the longstanding custom of kneeling for the final blessing at Mass, and, by extension, kneeling any time a priest gives one a blessing, has had a subtly destructive effect. We do not see, do not *feel* the blessing as descending from Almighty God through His minister to the layman, who has his knee planted on the ground. Instead, it is just one more thing that passes over our heads, like the almost non-stop flow of undifferentiated vernacular talk and song.

blessing he has been empowered, by holy orders, to impart. This is not clericalism; this is simply Catholicism.

What, on the other hand, does clericalism *really* look like? Let me suggest six ways it manifests itself in the Catholic Church today.

1. When a priest, contradicting nearly two thousand years of unanimous tradition in the apostolic churches of the East and the West, faces the people at Mass (*versus populum*), he unavoidably imposes himself on them as the principal actor in the liturgy, standing "over against" the passive congregation. In this way the message is transmitted—whether the priest intends it or not—that *he* is the center of attention, the facilitator and even the validator of the assembled faithful. This is an efficacious sign of clericalism if ever there has been one. When a priest faces eastward, on the contrary, the attention is focused more on the liturgical rite and on the altar, crucifix, or reredos that may dominate the sanctuary as a reminder of the supreme Sacrifice of Calvary. All in common, oriented in a single direction, offer a single prayer together. This is the antithesis of clericalism and may explain why clergy inflated with the "spirit of Vatican II" are vehemently opposed to its recovery.[197]

2. When a priest says "call me Fr. Jimmy," acts casually, tells lots of jokes and stories from the pulpit, and "doesn't stand on ceremony," he is in fact promoting a cult of the individual personality, the cult of Jimmy, rather than humbly accepting his God-given office or role in the Church as the impersonal minister of the Lord Jesus, one of a million that God will make use of in the span of history. A certain respect or reverence toward the priest is in fact crucial not only for the laity but also (and perhaps especially) for the priest, if they are to understand the seriousness of their respective tasks in the world and in the liturgy. An informal or casual manner of celebrating the liturgy, which rests on a lack of living faith in the awesome holiness of the sacred mysteries, is a terrible scourge of clericalism that causes countless laity to wince from week to week.

---

[197] See Fiedrowicz, *The Traditional Mass*, "Direction of Prayer," 141–52.

3. On the other hand, when clergy extend traditionally clerical ministries to lay people (e.g., extraordinary ministers of Holy Communion), they are perpetuating the false view that the only worthwhile, validating "work" for a Catholic is to be busy in the sanctuary. This is one of the worst manifestations of clericalism. The proper role of the laity is not to substitute as "straw ministers" but to sanctify the world *outside* of the church building, as many popes have taught and as Vatican II reiterated. The lay faithful are responsible for imbuing family life, their culture, their civil society, with the radiant truths of the Faith—a task that is noble, indispensable, and rewarding. The proper role of the clergy is and has always been to dedicate themselves to prayer, the sacred liturgy, the sacraments, and preaching. When clergy become social activists and laity become mini-priests, all is thrown into confusion, and we lose the beauty of the Mystical Body of Christ with its graceful hierarchical order that reflects the ranks of angels and saints in the heavenly Jerusalem.

4. When priests, bishops, and even popes ignore or hold in contempt the legitimate aspirations and needs of the faithful or of their subordinate clergy; when only a pope, his collaborators, or his allies "know what's best" for everyone else, regardless of education, competency, or expertise—we are facing another notorious form of clericalism, which could be summed up as: "My way or the highway." This, sadly, is something we have seen a lot of in recent years, when the formulation of (understandable!) concerns or critiques by cardinals, bishops, priests, and competent laity have been simply ignored. We also see it in parishes where a young parochial vicar, desirous of reintroducing beauty and tradition, is gagged or hamstrung by an older priest who "knows better." St. Benedict was wise to recognize that "God often reveals what is better to the younger" (*Rule*, ch. 3).

5. When bishops or priests want to intrude their personal theological opinions into their preaching and writing, rather than following and handing down the common and traditional teaching of the Church, we are certainly dealing with a particularly acidic form of clericalism.

The Holy Bread of Eternal Life

6. When a pope appoints ambitious men as bishops and curial officials instead of imitating great reforming popes who scoured observant monasteries and parishes for humble, holy, orthodox candidates, or when people entrusted with proposing episcopal candidates fail in their grave charge, they are flexing the muscles of a clericalism that becomes mightier the more successful the ambitious are. It is like a disease that feeds upon itself. From the "St. Gallen mafia" to the McCarrick scandal exposed by Viganò, we can see how flourishing this form of clericalism is in the Church today — and, ironically, most of all in those who have made an incoherent notion of "clericalism" a diverting screen behind which they think to hide.

Rediscovering the purpose of the priesthood

In the midst of what feels like an interminable and ineradicable abuse crisis, some Catholics will be tempted to pin the blame on the traditional conception of the priesthood, which they poorly understand. In my opinion, the problem is not that we make our clergy *too much*, but that we have cut them down to a mere human job description instead of seeing their work as a sacred mission to which they are called and consecrated by God.

The solution to abuse is not to cast off the ideal but to emphasize it anew, purified of whatever vices it may have picked up in a certain period of history. Our current period is marred by the Sexual Revolution of 1968, as Pope Emeritus Benedict XVI observed in his letter on the abuse crisis. One might add that our period is also marred by egalitarianism, horizontalism, and secularism, a devil's brew that prevents clergy who drink it from aspiring to, and rejoicing in, the full spiritual nobility and self-sacrifice demanded of their vocation.

The figure of the priest as it has been known in the West for nearly two thousand years has been gradually scaled down in the past few decades to something that can hardly be recognized as official, much less as sacred or sacerdotal. Most of the priests I was acquainted with in my youth cut the figure of administrators who handled public relations, luncheons, fundraising, and the like, handing over to laity the responsibilities of "liturgical planning" and even the distribution of Holy Communion, for which the priest's hands have been anointed. What ever happened to the *priest*, that mysterious and majestic representative of God?

Consider for a moment how anti-traditional tendencies, whose bitter fruits we are still reaping, affect the priest's role in the parish and his own perception of the duties belonging to his office. There can be no doubt that priests ought to be shepherds, teachers, and rulers in imitation of their divine model; for there is no doubt that people in all ages need to be shepherded, taught, and ruled. The most important channels for the exercise of this threefold office are the confessional, where the priest can pardon sinners and lead them to holiness; the pulpit, from which he can preach sound doctrine and hold up the saints as our examples; and the sacred liturgy, through which he can unite the faithful to the awesome and life-giving mysteries of Christ.

The false conception of liturgy as a gathering for song and socializing, however, devalues everything the priest is meant to be, turning him into a mere "facilitator" of parish activities scheduled for a Sunday morning.[198] There is no reason why any other person could not "facilitate" those same simple tasks: all it takes is one who can read whatever is printed on a page stuck into a binder. This utilitarian reductionism is part of the reason why some Catholics talk so glibly about "deaconesses." I'll bet if the deaconesses had to be involved in solemn Latin liturgies lasting many hours, they would not be clamoring for the work.

When mysteries of faith and the adoration of God recede into the background, when the doctrine of Christ and His Church receives scarcely a moment's attention, when the confessional is empty, *the priest loses his reason for being.* If men are not really sinners, how could they stand in

---

[198] See my article "Why Mass Is Cheapened When Human Elements Like Socializing Are Emphasized," *LifeSiteNews*, March 29, 2019.

need of sacramental absolution? If men are not really called to work out their salvation in fear and trembling, how could they need—much less hunger for—the Bread of Life? No wonder Reverend Father feels that his days are humdrum. He is no longer governing, healing, and nourishing souls with God Incarnate.

After attending a rapid and vapid parish Mass one morning, it dawned on me why, in some parts of the world, the priesthood is verging toward irrelevance: the priest is no longer a ruler, teacher, and sanctifier. His chief reason for existing, to offer sacrifice to God on behalf of the people, is slipping away. To the extent that Catholics adopt a Protestant view of "ministry," the sole grounds for a sacerdotal hierarchy and ordained priesthood is obliterated. If the congregation is, as the progressive litur-gists say, the *real* celebrant and the priest only a representative who works on their behalf, he becomes no more than a glorified layman who wears a technicolor dreamcoat and sits upon a wooden throne; and obviously there is little attraction to being a pedestaled celibate in an age where good things are measured by carnal comforts. In the absence of genuine spiritual aspirations, the sense appetites reassert themselves—and not surprisingly, we hear incessant clamoring for a married clergy.

Let us not be mistaken about the deeper reason that Protestants re-jected celibacy in the sixteenth century. If the priesthood has not been instituted by Christ in order that the world may be filled with "other Christs," men set apart to carry on the sacred work of the Eternal High Priest, then there is absolutely no basis for any distinction between lay-man and priest, or for any distinctive sacerdotal way of life. The Protes-tants knew from the start that a congregationalist understanding of the Church nullifies hierarchy as well as sacrifice; in an egalitarian society of believers, each member rules and sanctifies himself by personal com-munication with the Holy Spirit.

The abuse crisis and the campaign against celibacy are in fact two sides of the same coin: both result from abandoning the mystical identification of the priest with Christ, and setting aside the "heroism and genius" of this specially favored way of life that is meant to be a blessing for the entire

Church.[199] If we want good and holy priests, and many of them, the one and only thing we must do is recover a thoroughly traditional Catholicism that understands the dignity and demands of the priesthood. Anything short of that will only produce more abuse, be it criminal or subliminal.

---

[199] See William J. Slattery, *Heroism and Genius: How Catholic Priests Helped Build — and Can Help Rebuild — Western Civilization* (San Francisco: Ignatius Press, 2017).

16

The Refusal to Exercise Charitable Discipline

With every election cycle in the United States, invariably the question arises of whether the Eucharist should be given to actively and vocally pro-abortion politicians who present themselves for it. Sometimes, a bishop stands out for courage and clarity. In a statement dated June 2, 2019, Most Reverend Thomas Paprocki, Bishop of Springfield, Illinois, made it clear that pro-abortion Catholic politicians are forbidden to approach and receive the Lord in Holy Communion. Because they have violated the most fundamental requirement of being a practicing Catholic — namely, to adhere to the known teaching of the Church on matters of faith and morals — they are not spiritually capable of receiving the Bread of Life without offending the Lord in the Sacrament and committing additional grave sin. True to his responsibilities as a pastor of souls, Bishop Paprocki was faithfully applying canon law, which serves the good of souls, and interpreting for his flock the admonition of 1 Corinthians 11:27–29, in which St. Paul warns against unworthy reception of the Body and Blood of Christ.[200]

As was to be expected, his brother bishop Cardinal Blase Cupich, Archbishop of Chicago, *defended* giving Communion to pro-abortion politicians. Like Cardinal Donald Wuerl, with whom he has worked closely, Cardinal Cupich decries a supposed "politicization" of the Church's sacramental life. This argument within the American hierarchy goes back many years. Cardinal Burke has always taken the same line as Bishop

---

[200] See chapter 13.

The Holy Bread of Eternal Life

Paprocki, especially when reproaching Nancy Pelosi for her pro-abortion politics. Cardinal Cupich's position stems from an Americanist view of the radical separation of Church and State, by which politics and religion are mutually exclusive domains—the former being public, "neutral," and "non-sectarian," the latter being private, subjective, and particular. This view excludes religion, nay, God's own word, from having any say on matters of public policy. Yet it is obvious that one cannot be a believing Catholic in private life and, in public life, a secularist—or worse, a promoter of murder.

Back in 2009, I attempted to engage Cardinal Wuerl on this issue, challenging his Americanist stance. The response I received was a polite dismissal of the issue. The archbishop's office deemed it sufficient that Wuerl was personally pro-life; the political consequences were left vaguely to individual consciences. It seems that the debates in the Catholic Church in America have a way of getting stuck in a rut, because there has been no effective papal support for the truth and no will among American bishops to correct their erring brethren.

Below is my letter, followed by the letter received from the chancery.

May 11, 2009

Most Reverend Donald W. Wuerl
P. O. Box 29260
Washington, DC 20017-0260

Your Excellency,

I have been following in the news your statements concerning the controversial subject of administering or denying Holy Communion to politicians who assert they are Catholic and yet reject fundamental moral teachings of the Church. I can only begin to imagine the many difficulties you must face every day in ruling your flock in a time of such great intellectual and moral confusion. As a parent of small children and a teacher of college-age students, I know that questions of discipline are always fraught with difficulties. All the same, I am deeply troubled by certain assumptions that seem to be operative in your statements and your approach to these difficulties.

Laity often hear it said that to deny the Eucharist to a politician is to politicize the Eucharist. This is not so. The ones who are politicizing the Eucharist are the politicians who insist on receiving it even though they are manifestly at odds with the well-known teaching of the Church. They make this most holy sacrament a validation of their good standing, an instrument of their reputation. It is a way for them to proclaim: "Look, what I hold and do isn't problematic as far as the Church is concerned. If it was really problematic, then something would be done — but as you see, nothing is being done, so it must be okay, or at least within the realm of disputable opinion."

The Church has the solemn obligation to protect the Sacrament from profanation and to protect the faithful against scandal. Is it any wonder that such a large number of American Catholics appear to think that the morality of abortion is not something about which the Church has a definite, unchanging teaching, and that it is up to each individual to decide for himself? Many American Catholics will continue to be confused until each and every bishop fulfills his task of proclaiming the truth unambiguously *and* taking all necessary, if regrettable, steps to make sure that no one misses or manipulates that truth because of compromises and evasions. A politician who is repeatedly corrected and yet repeatedly signifies no intention of changing his or her public position is manifestly not in a position to receive a Sacrament whose very meaning is unity with the Catholic Church in her faith and morals. This is, after all, what the Catechism teaches us about the *res sacramenti* of the Eucharist — that it is the unity of, and unity with, the Mystical Body. To exist at all, this unity *requires* adherence to the *ecclesia docens*.

Can a Catholic who supports in any way the murder of baby humans be unified with the Mystical Body? We know that Jesus welcomes sinners to His table, for all of us are sinners. But among murderers, He welcomes the repentant, not the unrepentant. If we have mortal sin on our souls, we are obliged to go to Confession, and not just say we are sorry, but have a true purpose of amendment. With Pelosi, Biden, Sebelius, and too many others, where is the evidence of their amendment? As long as that is wanting, they should refrain from going to Communion. And if they insist on going anyway, who, then, is "politicizing the Eucharist"? The priest or bishop who denies it, or the politician who treats it like his/her own personal right "regardless"? The priest who is doing his best to keep the injunction of Jesus Himself—"throw not pearls before swine" (Matt. 7:6)—or the politician who wants to be known as a faithful Catholic *in spite of* persistent public dissent?

Your position, as far as I can tell, does not do justice to the ever-growing problem, or rather scandal, of persistent dissent from Catholic teaching, a dissent that is rarely met with the obviously appropriate response of denial of Communion at some level. Contrary to what you implied in a recent statement, the history of the Church is filled with countless examples of popes and bishops reasonably using the power of the keys to restrict or exclude lay members of the Church (in the old days it was kings and princes) when their behavior ran clearly and danger-ously contrary to the Gospel. I am not saying that Church leaders were right to do this in every instance, but they were surely right to do it in many instances.

What would have happened if St. Ambrose of Milan had not been courageous enough to reprimand the Emperor Theodosius for the slaughter of 7,000 people at Thessalonica in 390? Ambrose refused Communion to Theodosius for several months, urging him to imitate the penance of King David. Finally, the Emperor humbled himself and was readmitted. Here was a great bishop, a Father and Doctor of the Church, who knew that in dealing with the most powerful earthly ruler, he had to use the most powerful spiritual sanction of the Church. Nothing less would suffice. Anything less would have been to capitulate to the powerful of this world, as if the Church is subordinate to the State. In essence, the situation we are facing today is no different; indeed, the stakes are higher, for we are talking about the killing not of 7,000 but of *millions* of unborn children each year in our own country alone.

Is there a time and a place for *public* confrontation? Yes, absolutely, if there are truths worth living and dying for. The Holy Eucharist is the mystery of faith *par excellence*. It symbolizes and effects the unity of the Church for those who, already baptized, adhere to the Church's teaching, which is the teaching of Christ. It therefore strikes at the very meaning of the mystery to allow those who proudly proclaim their dissenting ways to approach unchecked and to profane the Sacrament by their practical rejection of what it *means*. If the Eucharist is not worth defending at all costs from profanation, *nothing is worth anything.* The approach that allows politicians to hold whatever they want and act however they want with no public consequences in Church membership or sacramental access does not have the long-term effect of winning them over but of emboldening them in their dissent, and confusing, scandalizing, and weakening the faithful who are trying to live according to the mind of the Church.

Even our merciful Savior and the "all things to all men" St. Paul recommended severe measures in especially bad situations, so that there might be the hope of a startled awakening followed by repentance and reconciliation (cf. Matt. 18:15–18; 1 Cor. 5:4–5). This would be what Sheldon Vanauken called a "severe mercy": a medicine that may make things worse for a time, in order that there might be healing in the end. As Plato and Aristotle argue, a truly just punishment does not have the purpose of satisfying a private desire for vengeance; its purpose is to restore the order of justice in the souls of the guilty, in the hopes that having been objectively corrected they might also be subjectively reformed.

If the Church does not defend her name, her confession of faith and morals, and her legitimate rights in the public sphere, we have no one but ourselves to blame for the increasing boldness of anti-Christian, inhuman secularism.

Sincerely yours in Christ,
Peter A. Kwasniewski, Ph.D.
Professor of Theology

The Holy Bread of Eternal Life

The reply I received:

May 19, 2009

Archdiocese of Washington
Archdiocesan Pastoral Center
5001 Eastern Avenue
Hyattsville, MD 20782-3447

Dear Dr. Kwasniewski,

Thank you for taking the time to write to Archbishop Wuerl. Although the Archbishop's schedule precludes him from personally responding to every letter, each is carefully reviewed. I would like to respond to the concerns you raise about Catholic politicians who support pro-abortion legislation and who receive Holy Communion.

While abortion is a terrible evil and voting for legislation to support it is wrong, the refusal of Holy Communion to specific politicians for their political actions is a serious matter, rarely done and almost always at the direction of the person's own bishop.

Archbishop Wuerl and his brother bishops continue to speak out strongly against abortion and to point out that legislation supporting abortion is also wrong. Their teaching is intended to change hearts and minds to stop the terrible injustice of the killing of innocent unborn life. I have enclosed a brochure highlighting Archbishop Wuerl's consistent teaching on the sanctity of life and its priority among issues to be considered in exercising faithful citizenship.

Prayers can be a significant force in helping to change hearts and minds, and I invite you to pray with the bishops for the success of their teaching efforts. Of course, our Holy Father has been an inspiration to many in his defense of human dignity, and I have enclosed a card commemorating his visit to our nation's capital last year. Please pray daily for him as he shepherds the Church around the world. Thank you very much for your commitment to defending the sanctity of human life in all its stages.

Sincerely in Christ,
Rev. William Byrne, Secretary

This feeble reply could have many explanations, of course, but subsequent events indicate the most likely explanation: a bishop who covered up clerical sexual predations, who facilitated and was facilitated by McCarrick, and who "lied shamelessly" as he continued to deny knowledge or complicity,[201] is not likely to be a bishop who cares much about the clear proclamation of Catholic truth on sexuality and the consistent implementation of the pro-life message.

Not one to be easily deterred, I made a second attempt in February 2012, sending a letter to the archbishop in the midst of swirling debates over the HHS contraceptive mandate.

February 10, 2012

His Eminence Donald Cardinal Wuerl
Archdiocese of Washington
P.O. Box 29260
Washington, DC 20017

Your Eminence:

In May 2009 I wrote a letter to you concerning the scandalous behavior of Nancy Pelosi, who continues to get away with murder. Her dismissive remarks last November on the effort to introduce clauses allowing providers to refuse to perform abortions have been widely reported:

> When the Republicans vote for this bill today, they will be voting to say that women can die on the floor and health-care providers

---

[201] See Diane Montagna, "Pope Francis Covered Up McCarrick Abuse, Former US Nuncio Testifies," *LifeSiteNews*, August 25, 2018.

do not have to intervene, if this bill is passed. It's just appalling. . . .
I'm a devout Catholic and I honor my faith and love it, but they
have this conscience thing. . . .

We have "this conscience thing." Yes, we do, because we strive to adhere
to the natural moral law and to the divine law as interpreted by the
Catholic Church.

In the immense assault against human life and conscience rights
represented by the HHS decision (and the fake "accommodation" that
has emerged today), Pelosi has shown her true colors again. At a recent
press conference, when asked by a reporter, citing a letter from the U.S.
bishops, "Will you stand with your fellow Catholics in resisting this law
or will you stick by the Administration?," Pelosi replied:

First of all, I am going to stick with my fellow Catholics [?] in supporting the Administration on this. I think it was a very courageous
decision that they made, and I support it.

The former speaker has also said she has "some areas of disagreement"
with the country's bishops, and has claimed that Catholicism does not
necessarily condemn abortion. This cannot be mere ignorance; what we
are seeing is manifest, persistent, stubborn, arrogant defection from fundamental moral teachings of the Faith. John Paul II taught in *Evangelium
Vitae* that the right to life of the human person is absolutely sacred among
men and cannot be compromised for any reason. A Catholic in public life
could never be tolerated who did not consistently and stalwartly defend
this fundamental right, without which no other right has any meaning
or value or even possibility of application.

Commenting on Pelosi's consistent words and track record, a promi-
nent voice in the Catholic world had this to say last week:

Nancy Pelosi considers it consistent with *what Catholics do* to take
a stand *against the bishops* in favor of a policy that would force
Catholic institutions to violate the teachings of her Church.
Pelosi is a highly public figure; there are few more visible. She

is committing the mortal sin of scandalizing the faithful in a matter which is unquestionably grave matter. There has been all manner of discussion concerning her and the issues of abortion, contraception, when life begins, etc. — she can't plead ignorance of the Church's teachings. She continues to be openly, publicly scandalous in these matters. Now she is taking an open stand *against* the American bishops — precisely claiming her catholic identity — in favor of a manifest attack on the Catholic Church by the most aggressively pro-abortion President we have ever seen.

How much longer does this have to go on? What else does she have to do?... Please, somebody, explain to me how we square *doing nothing* about her scandal with can. 915 and the sacred duty bishops have to protect the flock? Can. 915 of the 1983 *Code of Canon Law* authorized that ministers should withhold Holy Communion from those who are "obstinately persevering in manifest grave sin." Can. 915 actually *requires* ministers to withhold Holy Communion in such cases on pain of dereliction of their sacred office (can. 128 and 1389). This isn't a matter of the private conversation of an unknown woman in her living room. I cannot imagine how anyone can question that Pelosi's actions, which are public and clear and defiant and wicked and scandalous when it comes to serious matters of life, qualify her as "obstinately persevering in manifest grave sin." For the good of souls, Nancy Pelosi must be denied Holy Communion and the Catholic people should be *informed* that she is being denied Holy Communion....

Pres. Obama and his administration have openly and aggressively attacked the Catholic Church by trying to force Catholic institutions to perform [or pay for] actions which are evil even by reason alone and natural law, and not just by Catholic doctrine. Nancy Pelosi has publicly chosen sides against the Catholic Church's teachings and against the bishops. Let her choice be publicly confirmed by those same bishops. Nancy Pelosi must not be admitted to Holy Communion until she publicly changes her defiant stance and positions.[202]

These forceful words are truthful and reasonable. In their social encyclicals, the popes call upon Catholics to proclaim and defend their Faith in the public square — even when doing so may bring persecution upon their heads. For a shepherd of the Church to lead his flock in these troubled times, it is not enough to *be* pro-life; it is not enough to support pro-life organizations and initiatives; it is not enough to preach and teach the right to life. It is also necessary to protect the flock from the wolves of error, deception, hypocrisy, and opportunism; it is necessary to have the courage to call a spade a spade, to warn people against losing their souls for the sake of Caesar's favor. Nothing less is demanded as we suffer under the regime of Obama and the culture of death.

It seems hardly necessary to point out that even if Pelosi comes from another diocese, that of San Francisco, she has at least a quasi-domicile in Washington, DC, and therefore cannot be said to *not* be a member of the flock over which you have been given pastoral authority by Jesus Christ.

Sincerely yours in Christ,
Peter A. Kwasniewski, Ph.D.
Professor of Theology

This time the reply threw up a smokescreen of generalities, slogans to cover up a failure of fortitude and governance. I was particularly struck by the implied position that this is only an issue of catechesis and faith formation, and that dedication to the "New Evangelization" (remember that failed concept?) is sufficient. No, it's not, and we can see that more clearly as each day passes.

---

[202] At *Fr. Z's Blog*, February 7, 2012.

February 21, 2012

Archdiocese of Washington
Archdiocesan Pastoral Center
5001 Eastern Avenue
Hyattsville, MD 20782-3447

Dear Dr. Kwasniewski,

Grace and peace to you in the name of Our Lord Jesus Christ.

Although Cardinal Wuerl's schedule precludes him from personally responding to every letter he receives, thank you for sharing your concerns regarding challenges facing the Church in the public square.

As Archbishop of Washington, Cardinal Wuerl understands his episcopal vocation to be one of teaching, sanctifying, and governing his particular Church, and I thank you for taking the time to respectfully express your views related to the subject of governance.

The number of public officials who profess the Catholic faith, but yet who stand in opposition to the Church's highest moral priorities in the legislative arena, is indeed troubling. Cardinal Wuerl recognizes that this phenomenon is a result of failures within the Church over recent decades in the areas of catechesis and faith formation. As such, he has led the Archdiocese of Washington to understand its mission in light of the New Evangelization to which Blessed John Paul II and Pope Benedict XVI have called the Church.

Enclosed is a card commemorating the visit of our Holy Father to the United States. Please remember him and Cardinal Wuerl in your prayers, and thank you for all you do to help others grow in their knowledge of our Catholic faith.

Sincerely in Christ,
William W. Gorman
Associate Moderator for the Curia

We can see what we are up against: a lack of will to engage the most pressing evils of our day, and a pervasive lack of faith in the supernatural mystery of the Most Holy Eucharist. What we must pray for, in truth, is a radical reform, or rather, a general repopulation of the episcopacy, from top to bottom, with zealous orthodox Christians unafraid to preach the full truth, unafraid to confront worldly powers, and unafraid to suffer the consequences. That would be more like the *Old* Evangelization that, in times past, won the world for Christ.

17

Limits to Episcopal Authority over Holy Communion

In this chapter, after a preface about hygienic concerns, I will demonstrate first, in regard to the "Ordinary Form," that bishops, while free to express a preference, have no authority to mandate reception of Holy Communion in the hand or to forbid reception on the tongue (and, *a fortiori*, no pastor of a parish could have such authority), and second, with regard to the "Extraordinary Form," that Communion may be given *only* on the tongue.[203]

Hygienic considerations

Before beginning, it should be noted that there is no evidence that the normative and traditional manner of receiving Communion is less sanitary or in any way more dangerous to public health than Communion in the hand. A canon lawyer wrote to me: "Many have pointed out that germs are spread as easily by frequent hand contact as by placing the Host in the mouth (which, if the priest knows what he's doing, should not involve any transfer of saliva)." Bishop Athanasius Schneider stated on February 28, 2020:

---

[203] I adopt the terminology of Ordinary/Extraordinary from the Apostolic Letter *Summorum Pontificum* (July 7, 2007) for convenience and because it is canonically in force; it can nevertheless be misleading and is not entirely satisfactory. See Kwasniewski, *Noble Beauty, Transcendent Holiness,* 143–49; Fiedrowicz, *The Traditional Mass,* 43–49.

The Holy Bread of Eternal Life

Communion in the hand is no more hygienic than Communion in the mouth. Indeed, it can be dangerous for contagion. From a hygienic point of view, the hand carries a huge amount of bacteria. Many pathogens are transmitted through the hands. Whether by shaking other people's hands or frequently touching objects, such as door handles or handrails and grab bars in public transport, germs can quickly pass from hand to hand; and with these unhygienic hands and fingers people then often touch their nose and mouth. Also, germs can sometimes survive on the surface of the touched objects for days. According to a 2006 study, published in the journal *BMC Infectious Diseases*, influenza viruses and similar viruses can persist on inanimate surfaces, such as (e.g.) door handles or handrails and handles in transport and public buildings for a few days.

Many people who come to church and then receive Holy Communion in their hands have first touched door handles or handrails and grab bars in public transport or other buildings. Thus, viruses are imprinted on the palm and fingers of their hands. And then during Holy Mass with these hands and fingers they are sometimes touching their nose or mouth. With these hands and fingers they touch the consecrated Host, thus impressing the virus also on the Host, thus transporting the viruses through the Host into their mouth.

Communion in the mouth is certainly less dangerous and more hygienic compared to Communion in the hand.[204]

---

[204] "The Rite of Holy Communion in Times of a Pandemic," *Rorate Caeli*, February 28, 2020. A study done in the United Kingdom discovered disturbing facts: "The next time you stop at McDonald's, you may want to skip the new self-order machines, as a recent study found fecal matter on every touchscreen tested at the fast food restaurant. Conducted in November [2019] by U.K. newspaper Metro, the study swabbed screens at eight different McDonald's locations in London and Birmingham. All of the self-order kiosks tested positive for an array of harmful bacteria." Source: "Test Finds McDonald's Touchscreens Are Covered in Fecal Bacteria," *Fatherly*, March 27, 2020.

The Archdiocese of Portland released a statement on March 2, 2020 that includes the following:

> We consulted with two physicians regarding this issue, one of whom is a specialist in immunology for the State of Oregon. They agreed that done properly the reception of Holy Communion on the tongue and in the hand pose a more or less equal risk. The risk of touching the tongue and passing the saliva on to others is obviously a danger; however, the chance of touching someone's hand is equally probable and one's hands have a greater exposure to germs.[205]

The USCCB itself quasi-adopted guidelines from the Thomistic Institute that state: "We believe that, with the precautions listed here, it is possible to distribute on the tongue without unreasonable risk."[206]

Fr. John Zuhlsdorf sums up the view of many priests with whom I have spoken about this matter:

> In my experience of nearly three decades of distributing Communion in both ways, on the hand and on the tongue, to whole congregations on the hand nearly exclusively with a few exceptions, and also to whole congregations on the tongue nearly exclusively with few exceptions during the Novus Ordo and no exceptions at the TLM, is that rarely—rarely—do my fingers come into contact with tongues but very often, nearly always, there is contact with my fingers and hands. Let me repeat: When distributing Communion directly on the tongue, I rarely, rarely, have any contact with the tongue. When distributing on the hand, there is often, quite often, contact with the communicant's fingers or palms.... When both ways are done properly, whereas there is still often contact

---

[205] "Portland Archdiocese: Coronavirus or No, Communion Can Be Received on the Tongue," *Catholic News Agency*, March 4, 2020.

[206] See https://thomisticinstitute.org/covid-sacraments. The precautions are overly elaborate, but we can leave that point to one side.

by Communion on the hand, there is virtually never contact with the tongue.[207]

I will return in a moment to the question of what "done properly" means.

Pertinent legislation on the Ordinary Form

The latest edition of the *General Instruction of the Roman Missal*, issued by the Congregation for Divine Worship and the Discipline of the Sacraments on November 12, 2002, reads:

> If Communion is given only under the species of bread, the Priest raises the Host slightly and shows it to each, saying, "The Body of Christ." The communicant replies, "Amen," and receives the Sacrament either on the tongue or, where this is allowed, in the hand, the choice lying with the communicant.[208]

In support, the Instruction *Redemptionis Sacramentum — On Certain Matters to Be Observed or to Be Avoided Regarding the Most Holy Eucharist*, of the Congregation for Divine Worship and the Discipline of the Sacraments, March 25, 2004, reads in art. 92:

> Although each of the faithful always has the right to receive Holy Communion on the tongue, at his choice, if any communicant should wish to receive the Sacrament in the hand, in areas where the Bishops' Conference with the *recognitio* of the Apostolic See has given permission, the sacred Host is to be administered to him or her [in that manner].

The Congregation for Divine Worship has expressed its mind at least three times in response to situations where attempts were made to enforce Communion in the hand. A letter of April 3, 1985 to the National

---

[207] "Communion in the Time of Coronavirus. Best Practices, Risk, and You," *Fr. Z's Blog*, March 1, 2020.
[208] This is n. 161 as found in the 2011 edition from the USCCB.

Conference of Catholic Bishops (later renamed USCCB) [Prot. 720/85] reads in part:

> The Holy See, since 1969, while maintaining the traditional manner of distributing Communion, has granted to those Episcopal Conferences that have requested it, the faculty of distributing Communion by placing the Host in the hands of the faithful.... The faithful are not to be obliged to adopt the practice of Communion in the hand. Each one is free to communicate in one way or the other.[209]

Here is a response from the Congregation for Divine Worship and the Discipline of the Sacraments, published in *Notitiae* of April 1999:

> *Query*: Whether in dioceses where it is allowed to distribute Communion in the hands of the faithful, a priest or extraordinary ministers of Holy Communion may restrict communicants to receive Communion only in their hands, not on the tongue.

> *Response*: Certainly it is clear from the very documents of the Holy See that in dioceses where the Eucharistic bread is put in the hands of the faithful, the right to receive the Eucharistic bread on the tongue still remains intact to the faithful. Therefore, those who restrict communicants to receive Holy Communion only in the hands are acting against the norms, as are those who refuse to Christ's faithful [the right] to receive Communion in the hand in dioceses that enjoy this indult.[210]

More recently, during the swine flu epidemic of 2009, Fr. Anthony Ward, S.M., undersecretary of the same congregation, wrote in a letter to an inquirer (Prot. N. 655/09/L, dated 24 July 2009):

> This Congregation...wishes to acknowledge receipt of your letter dated 22 June 2009 regarding the right of the faithful to receive

---

[209] *Adoremus*, Online Edition, vol. VII, no. 8 (November 2001).
[210] *Adoremus*, Online Edition, vol. VIII, no. 10 (February 2003).

Holy Communion on the tongue. This Dicastery observes that the Instruction *Redemptionis Sacramentum* (25 March 2004) clearly stipulates that "each of the faithful always has the right to receive Holy Communion on the tongue" (n. 92), nor is it licit to deny Holy Communion to any of Christ's faithful who are not impeded by law from receiving the Holy Eucharist (cf. n. 91).

When the first wave of local directives had emerged in February 2020, I consulted with a canon lawyer, who wrote the following to me:

> From my perspective, a bishop cannot require anyone to receive in the hand. Even in the Ordinary Form, the prescription [i.e., norm] is Communion on the tongue, with the [rescriptive] right to approach and receive in the hand. The norm is the norm, and it is based on the right of the faithful to choose how to worship God at a moment in the Mass that is deeply personal and not communal in nature. My opinion is based on the repeated jurisprudence from the Holy See upholding the rights of a Catholic to receive Communion on the tongue while kneeling during an OF Mass, even if his or her bishop has issued a particular law to the contrary. Such laws are considered suggestive in nature and in no way binding. If this is true for a bishop's law, *a fortiori* it is true of a pastor of a parish. A layman may not be denied the Blessed Sacrament unless he is a notorious public sinner. A priest who, on his own initiative, told the people they must receive in the hand would be violating the law and leading the people into the violation of it.

To avoid all possible confusion, let me reiterate that all of the foregoing legislation applies *only* to the Ordinary Form or Novus Ordo Missae.

Pertinent legislation on the Extraordinary Form

Even as bishops have no authority to change universal ecclesiastical legislation on the manner of receiving Communion at the Ordinary

Form, they have no authority to modify the legislation that governs the Extraordinary Form. The pertinent legislative document, the Instruction *Universae Ecclesiae* of the Pontifical Commission *Ecclesia Dei* (now Section IV of the Congregation for the Doctrine of the Faith), determines as follows:

> 24. The liturgical books of the *forma extraordinaria* are to be used as they stand. All who choose to celebrate according to the *forma extraordinaria* of the Roman Rite are required to know the pertinent rubrics and to follow them correctly in celebrations.

> 28. Furthermore, since it is of course dealt with by special law, in respect of its own subject matter, the Apostolic Letter *Summorum Pontificum* derogates from all liturgical laws that belong to the sacred rites promulgated from the year 1962 onwards, and not coinciding with the rubrics of the liturgical books of the year 1962.

There has never been doubt about what these laws entail: at the Extraordinary Form, laity who approach to receive Communion *must* receive on the tongue; no other way is envisaged or allowed by law. To have a new custom established (*quod Deus avertat*), a bishop or episcopal conference would have to request and obtain a rescript from the Congregation for the Doctrine of the Faith, just as the bishops of different countries had to ask Rome for a rescript to permit Communion in the hand decades ago. Moreover, even if a bishop could obtain such a rescript, it would not change the layman's right to choose the manner in which to receive.

Psychologically, it would be abusive to tell Catholics who love the Extraordinary Form for its pervasive Eucharistic reverence to contradict every instinct and rubric of this older use of the Roman Rite by putting their hands out and taking the Host in a way that (in the traditional understanding) *only* the ordained minister is set apart to do on Christ's behalf.

Everyone understands that emergency situations can arise that may temporarily debar Catholics from the reception of sacraments. However, bishops have a solemn obligation to keep such periods *as short as possible*.

The Holy Bread of Eternal Life

They would be abusing their episcopal authority if they made rules that not only contradicted universal legislation, but also redounded to the disadvantage of some members of the flock, such as those who adhere to the older form of the Roman Rite.

Episcopal oversight, the common good, and useful lessons

Some have claimed that canon 223 of the 1983 *Code of Canon Law* gives bishops the authority to suspend Communion on the tongue and to require Communion in the hand for anyone receiving. Let's have a look.

> Can. 223 §1. In exercising their rights, the Christian faithful, both as individuals and gathered together in associations, must take into account the common good of the Church, the rights of others, and their own duties toward others.
>
> §2. In view of the common good, ecclesiastical authority can direct the exercise of rights which are proper to the Christian faithful.

The first thing we need to consider is a theological fact that has more authority than canon law or any interpretation thereof. As St. Thomas Aquinas teaches,[211] the common good of the entire universe is found in Christ, and Christ is really present in the Holy Eucharist, as the same saint memorably conveys in the Magnificat antiphon for Vespers of Corpus Christi:

> *O sacrum convivium, in quo Christus sumitur: recolitur memoria passionis eius: mens impletur gratia: et futuræ gloriæ nobis pignus datur. Alleluia.*

> O sacred banquet, in which Christ is received, the memory of his Passion is renewed, the mind is filled with grace, and a pledge of future glory is given to us. Alleluia.

[211] See *Super I ad Cor.*, cap. 12, lect. 3.

Therefore, the Holy Eucharist *is* the common good of the entire universe. When we are considering how Communion ought to be distributed, the first and last consideration must be what *we* owe to *God* in loving Him above all others; we owe Him fitting reverence in all that we do and say. The Blessed Sacrament is not just "one more thing" over which a bishop has control, even if there is a limited sense in which he may establish norms for his diocese *not contrary* to universal norms.

If we take seriously the truth of which Aquinas reminds us, we will see that Can. 223 §1 is obliging us to "take into account the common good of the Church"— above all, Christ Himself in the Eucharist— and, in that light, "the rights of others, and their own duties toward others." The faithful have the right to see the Eucharist properly treated *by all*; our duties include building up the Body of Christ in holiness, which is incompatible with any kind of irreverence or unworthy experimentation, such as the German methods of "Coronacommunion."[212]

Inevitably, the question arises: What is and what is not reverent? It seems to me dangerous to say that bishops, all by themselves, get to determine the answer to this question, in a positivist vacuum. That is an anti-traditional nominalism that Catholics should not abide. Meanwhile, it is clear that the current situation shows which bishops have a *supernatural* perspective and which ones have a merely natural perspective.

More interesting is Can. 223 §2: "In view of the common good, ecclesiastical authority can direct the exercise of rights which are proper to the Christian faithful." This canon suffers more than usually from the vagueness that is a necessary fault (as it were) of any code of law, but it is clear that it must be interpreted in light of the general norms of the law. Thus, for instance, Can. 135 §2 states, in part: "A lower legislator cannot validly issue a law contrary to higher law." Given no provision for overruling the liturgical norms in force — which norms are extremely clear and have been repeated numerous times, as demonstrated above — any

---

[212] For illustrations, see my article "Contempt for Communion and the Mechanization of Mass," *New Liturgical Movement*, May 8, 2020.

bishop's attempt to deny the right to receive Holy Communion on the tongue is unlawful on its face.[213]

Having noted that clerical overreach is flourishing and spreading in the coronavirus period, Dr. Joseph Shaw diagnoses the abusive clericalist mentality that is still all too prevalent:

> I would like to express…how outrageous this situation is. There is now a long list of medical experts who have stated that reception on the tongue is no less hygienic than in the hand. The Government is not forcing the issue, and our bishops well know that there are limits to episcopal authority. Parish priests, and even the laity, have rights under Canon Law. This appears to be of no interest or concern to those responsible for many of these documents, because they are expecting it to be enforced, not by due process of law, but by those familiar, informal processes and incentives which make the clerical world go round.
>
> For ten years we have witnessed the public scandal of clerical sexual abuse. As Catholics, we know that lying behind that scandal is one of much longer standing, which has been less exposed to public view: of the clerical abuse of power. Of complaints being ignored, of procedures not being followed, of documents from the Holy See being filed in the bin. This has been going on in the context of our requests for the Extraordinary Form, of what is taught in seminaries, of liturgical abuses, and of course of sexual abuse

---

[213] As a side-note: since we know that canon law can, at times, be poorly formulated—canonists have criticized certain points of both the 1917 and the 1983 codes—I will take this occasion to state that the formulation of Can. 223 §2 is disturbing. How far can it be taken? "Direct the exercise of rights which are proper to the Christian faithful." *All* such rights? For example, could a bishop say "I direct you not to get married" or "I direct you to enter religious life"? After all, those are rights proper to the faithful. Certainly, if a layman had committed a serious public fault, or if he were known to have some impediment, his rights could be curtailed or denied; but to do so otherwise would be arbitrary and tyrannical.

itself. It is clear that the culture of lofty superiority to the rules, to the views of the laity, to natural justice, and even to Divine Law, has not yet been defeated. We should not take seriously claims that the issue of the abuse of minors has been seriously addressed until those wielding authority in the hierarchical Church recognise that they do so within a system of rights and obligations, and for the good of the whole Church.[214]

Practical issues with Communion on the tongue

The perception that Communion on the tongue is not sanitary is caused, in part, by the discontinuation of the traditional manner of receiving: the communicants kneeling shoulder-to-shoulder along an altar rail, with a server holding a paten beneath their chins as he accompanies the priest. This method became universal for good reason. Quite apart from its superior exhibition of reverence and care for particles, it is highly practical in three ways.

First, it was normally done only by a priest, who had gained expertise from daily experience, as opposed to the rotating schedules of extraordinary ministers of Holy Communion who may or may not know how to place the Host properly on the tongue, and who often come across as hesitant, embarrassed, perplexed, or irritated at having to do so.[215]

Second, the priest walking along the communion rail stands at an optimal height at which to place the Host easily on the communicant's tongue. It is awkward to try to give Communion on the tongue to someone standing in front of you, especially if he or she is taller. The traditional method practiced in the West for over a millennium makes it far more likely that a priest will not have *any* physical contact with the faithful, in contrast with Communion in the hand where he will touch many germy

---

[214] "The Abuse of Power," *Mass of Ages* 205 (Autumn 2020), 5; cf. chapter 15.

[215] See chapter 10.

hands — unless he follows the example of some clergy in Germany who are dropping the Host into people's hands like a payload from a bomber, or a trinket gifted to the brightest pupil by an aloof schoolmaster.

Third, because the faithful come up to the altar rail in waves, they have a chance to settle themselves on their knees and calmly prepare for the priest coming to them. By the time he arrives, the communicant can have his or her head tilted back and be ready. There's no unseemly rushing. In the traditional form, the priest is the only one who speaks, saying the prayer: "*Corpus Domini nostri Jesu Christi custodiat animam tuam in vitam æternam. Amen*"[216]; the recipient does not have to move his lips and risk either discharging saliva or accidentally touching the priest's hand.

All Catholics who wish to receive on the tongue should kneel — regardless of which form of the Mass they are attending or from whom they are receiving. They should kneel, first, because it is the Lord God before whom the angels fall on their faces; and second, because, when they kneel, tilt back their head, and protrude their tongue, it will be very easy for the Host to be placed on it.

✠

The reverence owed to Our Lord in the Blessed Sacrament, which the Church's laws are designed to protect and promote, is not trumped by our health concerns. As Bishop Schneider says, the shepherds and the sheep of the Church will stand condemned of worldliness if they are willing to make compromises about the appropriate treatment of the Body of Christ in order to preserve their mortal and perishable lives. We would be justly condemned for seeking first ourselves and not the Kingdom of God:

> If the Church in our day does not endeavor again with the utmost zeal to increase the faith, reverence and security measures for the Body of Christ, all security measures for humans will be in vain. If

---

[216] May the Body of Our Lord Jesus Christ keep thy soul unto everlasting life. Amen.

the Church in our day will not convert and turn to Christ, giving primacy to Jesus, and, namely, to the Eucharistic Jesus, God will show the truth of His Word which says: "Unless the Lord build the house, they labour in vain that build it. Unless the Lord keep the city, he watches in vain that keeps it" (Ps. 126:1–2).[217]

[217] "The Rite of Holy Communion in Times of a Pandemic," *Rorate Caeli*, February 28, 2020.

18

A Powerful Engine of Desacralization

On August 4, 2020, *LifeSiteNews* reported that Archbishop Bernard Longley of Birmingham, caught up in the global fear of contagion, ordered the traditionally minded Birmingham Oratory—founded by John Henry Newman himself, who, as a Catholic priest, celebrated exclusively the traditional Latin Mass and would always have given Communion to the faithful on the tongue—to cease and desist giving Our Lord to the congregation in this manner. The Oratorian Fathers announced they would comply with the directive, but expressed distress and sadness and a keen desire to see this order "rescinded as soon as possible." The Oratory thus became the latest fortress to fall in the ongoing war against tradition, in the name of spurious science and arbitrary determinations of hygiene.

Some readers have asked me why I am so adamant about the manner in which the Most Blessed Sacrament is distributed. In this chapter, I wish to point out the gravity of the situation.

Communion in the hand was introduced by open disobedience in the 1960s—a story told in detail by Bishop Juan Rodolfo Laise in his eye-opening book *Holy Communion: Documents and History*, and summarized in a number of places online.[218] Its beginning was therefore hardly auspicious, and Paul VI, in typical fashion, surrendered to the rebel camp while repeating that he reaffirmed tradition and intended to change nothing.

---

[218] See, for example, Fr. Richard Heilman, "Truth about Communion in the Hand While Standing," *New Liturgical Movement*, March 16, 2014.

The Holy Bread of Eternal Life

Nevertheless, in the dark days of the late '60s and early '70s, Communion in the hand was only ever "permitted," *never required.* The fact that many children were instructed to receive in the hand for their First Communion meant, in practice, a widespread evaporation of the older custom, but the Vatican continued to state in official documents that the traditional manner was normative and could always be chosen by the faithful. Thus, even where the norm became rare, it was always "on the books" *as* the norm—and Catholics were slowly but surely rediscovering it thanks to the good example of Benedict XVI at the Vatican and the spread of the traditional Latin Mass, governed by its own preconciliar rubrics.

What we are seeing today is the first time bishops are attempting to *outlaw* the traditional manner of receiving Our Lord and to *mandate* the novelty—not only in the Novus Ordo but, it seems, in the traditional Mass as well. The difference between Paul VI's tergiversating cowardice and the steely determination of the Novus Ordo Seclorum is well worth pondering. The breezy invocation of Canon 223 to override the rights of the faithful to receive sacraments is symptomatic of a new hyperepiscopal authoritarianism. It is as if bishops have collectively grown spines not to stand up to overreaching secular governments but to reanimate the iconoclasm *ad intra* that had sputtered out during Ratzinger's pontificate.

Those who think that this arrangement is "merely temporary, until the pandemic passes" are being incredibly naive. Our civil and ecclesiastical rulers will extend and perpetuate this "crisis" as long as they can—for years, if possible, and maybe forever, when the "experts" declare that the world is full of so many evil viruses and bacteria that we will never be "safe" again. Within the Church, the point of all this monkeying with rubrics and canonical rights is not to keep people safe, since there is no compelling evidence that we cannot do Communion on the tongue safely, or that reception in the hand is more hygienic. The point is to break people's spirits, to make them violators of the sacred, to shatter the spiritual sensitivity that rightly causes thoughtful laity who believe in the Real Presence to hesitate to take the Host into their own hands as the ordained priest does and to feed themselves.[219]

Whether the bishops pushing these policies are aware of their sinister assumptions and consequences (some, certainly, come across as clueless enough not to be), or whether it is only their underworldly overlords who see the end game, the COVID liturgical claptrap and rigmarole is a powerful engine of disenchantment, meant to stop, once and for all, Benedict XVI's program of liturgical reenchantment. Yes, Ratzinger may have dreamed the impossible dream of reconciling Catholic tradition and the postconciliar reform, but in the realm of action he initiated a powerful movement of recovery and restoration. This was getting to be too successful, especially among the younger clergy and faithful; it had to be stopped.

Someone might say: "You are blowing all this out of proportion. The regulations on Communion are no more than a practical necessity in a difficult situation. It has none of the meanings you're attributing to it, and will pass quickly."

In the liturgy, nothing is merely practical or utilitarian; everything is symbolic. If clergy process solemnly or casually, that is symbolic. If they wear an elaborate vestment or a plain polyester one, that is symbolic. If they speak in an ancient hieratic tongue or a modern vernacular, that is symbolic. If they face eastward with the people or face westward over against the people, that is symbolic. If we are singing medieval plainchant or a folksy refrain from the '70s, that is symbolic. In fact, if there could be an event that was designed to be nothing but practical and utilitarian, *that*, in itself, would be symbolic. Human beings, as rational animals, are not just wielders of tools, they are weavers of symbols. It cannot be otherwise. When we act ceremonially in a church, we signify who we are, who we believe God to be, and how we construe the relationship.

Thus, Communion in the hand for one standing, and Communion on the tongue for one kneeling, are obviously and profoundly different

---

[219] See chapters 7 and 8.

symbols. It doesn't matter whether a bishop who is mandating the first and forbidding the second thinks they aren't, or doesn't care whether they are. "*E pur si muove.... and still it moves.*" The symbol moves the senses, the mind, and the heart. And *we* are moved, either toward greater faith, reverence, devotion, and adoration, or away from them. That is why what is happening is not a trivial matter, a simple temporary "expedient." Nothing in the liturgy is trivial, and nothing should be reduced to expediency, which is not a spiritual or religious value.

These Communion regulations are habituating a generation of clergy and faithful in a form of obedience detached from truth, obedience in service of desacralization, obedience without fidelity to tradition or law. It is an organized antinomianism and a deconstructive mechanization poised against the liberating strictness of traditional worship and its intuitive language of ritual action.

Permission for Communion in the hand was occasioned by a first wave of disobedience in the 1960s. The regulations of 2020—by moving from permission to a spurious obligation imposed with no end in sight—represent a second wave of disobedience to well-established Catholic tradition and canon law. Those who comply with these regulations enter into a double inheritance of disobedience and lose their opportunity to be the "martyrs" or witnesses from whose sacrifice a future truly blessed by God can arise. The least we can do is to forswear any agreement or complicity with these regulations, offering up our "Eucharistic fast" in a spirit of reparation for our own sins and for all sins committed against the Most Blessed Sacrament. May God have mercy on our souls.

Masking Christian worship

A friend sent me the following note.

> Dear Dr. Kwasniewski:
> In our State of _____, masks were recently mandated in public places. Failure to comply with the new order can result in

a petty misdemeanor or fine. Even at Holy Mass, all are supposed to wear masks.

I think that the COVID hype is being manipulated for other ends and I am opposed to mandatory mask-wearing. Yet I do not see how the law is unjust, since it is promulgated under the auspices of protecting the health of all, even if science fails to show that masks do protect health. The order cannot be considered to be simply a penal law, since it is supposed to protect people from disease and death. (For "medical conditions" one may be exempt from wearing a mask and these conditions may be physical or psychological. I could think up some condition which prevents me from wearing a mask, but it seems quite a "mental reservation" to make.)

Have you, as a philosopher, thought about the matter?

My thoughts fall into three areas: (1) Church authority; (2) the scientific/medical domain; and (3) the theology of worship.

The State may not mandate how the Church should do her liturgy or make use of her sacraments. The Church had to fight for many centuries against state encroachments and arrogations, establishing that her ministers have a God-given right to make liturgical and sacramental determinations.[220] On May 7, an open letter, led by Archbishop Carlo Maria Viganò and Cardinals Gerhard Ludwig Müller, Joseph Zen, and Jānis Pujats, and signed by many clergy, reminded politicians that "the state has no right to interfere, for any reason whatsoever, in the sovereignty of the Church."

This autonomy and freedom are an innate right that Our Lord Jesus Christ has given her for the pursuit of her proper ends. For

---

[220] The government has authority over the Church in a certain respect, and circumstances can put an otherwise ecclesial matter into that field. If a bishop were to mandate that his flock celebrate liturgy in the middle of the highway, the government could intervene and say "not on this public road."

this reason, as pastors we firmly assert the right to decide autonomously on the celebration of Mass and the Sacraments, just as we claim absolute autonomy in matters falling within our immediate jurisdiction, such as liturgical norms and ways of administering Communion and the Sacraments.[221]

In a time of infectious disease, bishops may freely decide to issue guidelines similar to those issued by the secular authorities, but they do so by their own judgment and authority, not as subservient to the State.[222] Unfortunately, what we have seen instead is a simple capitulation to health "experts" and civil governors. In some cases, Catholic bishops have imposed even more restrictive and ridiculous conditions than secular leaders. In this way they seem to abdicate their pastoral responsibility of due diligence and evaluation, trample on canon law in regard to the rights of the faithful to worship and sacramental life,[223] and evince a total lack of awareness of what is fitting for sacred rites.[224]

Second, there is the medical/scientific domain. For quite some time now, doctors and specialists have been coming out left and right (well, perhaps, only from the right) saying that the typical face-coverings do little to protect anyone from microbes. Dr. Anthony Fauci initially said masks would not help, then changed his tune when industrial production and supplies were finally in place. Doctors who have found success with simple and inexpensive cures for COVID have been mocked or ignored. It takes little effort to discover that, whatever the truth may be, it is not

---

[221] Paul Smeaton, "Three Cardinals Join Global Appeal Decrying Crackdown on Basic Freedoms over Coronavirus," *LifeSiteNews*, May 7, 2020.

[222] See the clear argumentation of Luis de Molina, S.J., in which he follows the teaching common to all the theological schools: "Molina on Civil and Ecclesiastical Power," trans. Timothy Wilson, *The Josias*, July 8, 2020.

[223] See Anonymous, "An Apologia for the Underground: Objections and Replies on the Subject of 'Underground' Masses during COVID-19," *Rorate Caeli*, July 29, 2020.

[224] See my article "Contempt for Communion and the Mechanization of Mass."

equivalent to the "official line" promoted by powerful factions. From this perspective, it is eminently reasonable to question the *basis* of this kind of state law and, having discovered its irrationality, to conclude that it lacks what is necessary for legality.

The foregoing points have been well covered in commentary. What I have not seen much commented on, however, are the theological and psychological implications of masking in the context of Christian liturgical worship, which has its own specific nature and requirements.[225]

The curse of man under sin and under the Law is to be hidden from God's face, and, in a sense, to be thwarted in one's social intercourse with other men (see Gen. 4:14). In Mark's Gospel, the covering of Christ's face is a sign of contempt, treatment worthy of a wretch: "And some began to spit on him, and to cover his face, and to strike him, saying to him, 'Prophesy!'" (Mark 14:65). Through Christ's sacrifice on the Cross, which tears the veil of the Temple (see Matt. 27:51) and permits us to enter heaven through the veil of His flesh (see Heb. 10:20), the curse begins to be reversed, as St. Paul memorably sets forth in 2 Corinthians:

> Since we have such a hope, we are very bold, not like Moses, who put a veil over his face so that the Israelites might not see the end of the fading splendor. But their minds were hardened; for to this day, when they read the old covenant, that same veil remains unlifted, because only through Christ is it taken away. Yes, to this day whenever Moses is read a veil lies over their minds; but when a man turns to the Lord the veil is removed. Now the Lord is the Spirit, and where the Spirit of the Lord is, there is freedom. And we all, with unveiled face, beholding the glory of the Lord, are being changed into his likeness from one degree of glory to another; for this comes from the Lord who is the Spirit. (2 Cor. 3:12–18)

---

[225] Two articles I would recommend: Maureen Mullarkey, "Prêt-À-Manger Eucharist, etc.," *Studio Matters*, August 2, 2020; Douglas Farrow, "The Health-First Heresy," *Catholic World Report*, August 7, 2020.

The Holy Bread of Eternal Life

While a head covering for a woman symbolizes her honorable subjection, even as the uncovered head of the man symbolizes that he stands within the family *in persona Christi capitis* (in the person of Christ the Head of the Church), Christians do not use *face coverings* in the way strict Muslim women do.[226] The mask seems to be a symbolic cancellation of something deeply true about Christian identity and worship.

When I enter the church, I am going before God as a person: I present my open face to Him, and He sees me as I am, and leads me closer to seeing Him as He is. Although this is primarily a matter of my spirit vis-à-vis the Spirit of God, we depend as rational animals on our bodies as external reminders and supports of what we are aiming to do interiorly. In other words, showing our face to God and to others in church is not altogether disconnected from showing Him and them *myself*. Those who play hide and seek don't say: "3-2-1, here my body comes!" or "You found my body!" When we start looking, we look with body and soul; when we are found, we are found in body and soul.

And when they heard the voice of the Lord God walking in paradise at the afternoon air, Adam and his wife hid themselves from the face of the Lord God, amidst the trees of paradise. And the Lord God called Adam, and said to him: "Where art thou?" And

---

[226] For more on the symbolism of veiling, see my article "The Theology behind Women Wearing Veils in Church," *OnePeterFive*, November 13, 2019. In the ambit of Christianity we find face-veiling only in the specialized context of cloistered contemplative women religious (Carmelites, Cistercians, Capuchins, etc.) who used to pull down a veil over their faces while in private prayer or when going outside of the monastery. St. Teresa of Jesus in 1561 wrote that her nuns should not allow themselves to be seen in the face by outsiders. A gallery of photos of nuns with veiled faces may be found at https://goldenbridgeinmate39. wordpress.com/2013/03/19/veiled-nuns/. This peculiar religious use of the veil is, however, for the sake of preserving a set-apart anonymity, spiritual intimacy, the dignity of a life "hidden with Christ in God"; it is not a sign or effect of the sexual objectification and denigration of women found within Islam.

he said: "I heard thy voice in paradise; and I was afraid, because I was naked, and I hid myself." (Gen. 3:8–9, DR)

So intimate and all-pervasive is the union of body and soul that Adam thought he could hide himself from God by hiding himself bodily; and the omniscient God, who has no need of bodily sight, nevertheless indicated that he wanted Adam to come before him as a man, not hiding his face. *Where art thou?*

When we come into the church to meet the Lord, we fittingly begin with Psalm 42 said at the foot of the altar, before daring to approach Him more closely. We almost turn around the Lord's question to Adam by posing to Him questions of our own: *Quare me repulisti, et quare tristis incedo, dum affligit me inimicus?* "Why hast Thou cast me off, and why go I sorrowful whilst the enemy afflicteth me?" And turning to ourselves: *Quare tristis es anima mea, et quare conturbas me?* "Why art thou sad, O my soul, and why dost thou disquiet me?" The psalmist, model of the Christian, knows the one and only solution: *Spera in Deo, quoniam adhuc confitebor illi: salutare vultus mei et Deus meus.* "Hope in God, for I will still give praise to Him: the salvation of my countenance and my God." The Mass is inherently pointed toward heaven, where we will finally see, and will see that we are seen. "I have seen God face to face, and my soul has been saved" (Gen. 32:30, DR). "O my dove, in the clefts of the rock, in the covert of the cliff, let me see your face, let me hear your voice, for your voice is sweet, and your face is comely" (Song of Sol. 2:14).

The Canticle of Canticles always brings to my mind the members of the Church who are most evidently the brides of Christ: consecrated virgins. The superior of a traditional community of nuns writes concerning one of the most distinctive parts of their clothing:

The wimple always leaves the face uncovered... [A] woman who wears a wimple is not seeking to hide herself *totally*; she is not seeking to exclude or separate herself from others. She is not excluding communication with other persons. Her face is left free; in fact, the wearing of the wimple draws *more* attention to the face, since there is nothing else to draw our eye. The wimple "forces" someone who meets us to focus on our face, not on our body.

In a real sense, our face most fully expresses who we are. Our face reveals who we are more than our body does. Consider that we learn so much more about a person by looking at his or her face than we do by looking at his or her hands or feet. The eyes are called the "windows of the soul," and these eyes are almost highlighted by the wimple. The wimple, then, helps us to relate to other human persons in a way that harmonizes very well with our vocation. The wimple draws attention to the "inner man" which finds expression in our face. Our wimple helps others to look at us in that way.[227]

She then goes on to express the stark contrast between a Christian head covering like the wimple and the modern mask regime:

The mask covers half of the face: the nose and the mouth. It is hard to recognize people when they wear masks; this is why burglars wear masks (the same kind, where only the eyes are visible). We can look from our convent to see people walking the streets who wear masks, but who are otherwise dressed indecently. The symbolic message such people convey is almost an exact inversion of the message we convey. One cannot "see" the "inner man" because of the mask, but one's eyes are drawn, instead, to the body.

The superior completes her analysis with this observation:

The mask is a barrier to truly human communication, for communication is so much more than the exchange of words. We speak with our face, with our expressions. When we add the wearing of masks to the other regulations, especially that of so-called "social distancing," and to the increase in "virtual meetings" and

[227] Anonymous, "A Religious Superior Reflects on Wimples—and on the Current Masquerade," *Rorate Caeli*, August 2, 2020.

"on-line classrooms," we can see the mask as just one element in the dehumanizing tendency of our society.

Even though people may think it "dehumanizing" that we sisters wear all the coverings we do as part of our religious habit, the truth is that the layers we wear can be aids to make our relationship with other human persons "more human," more *personal.* Because the use of masks is an element that frustrates truly human relationships, we have an instinctive aversion to wearing masks. The mask hides the human person; the wimple reveals the human person.

That is why we can speak, with justice, of dehumanization and de-personalization as consequences of the enforcement of masks in public places, *above all* in Catholic churches. Masking clashes with both natural goods of human fellowship and the supernatural reality of what we are doing when we assemble for prayer in the name of and in the presence of Christ. The natural "evil" attached to the wearing of masks—namely, that of obscuring half of the face of the person—is transmitted into the liturgy where, in a symbolically heightened environment, it becomes a *countersign.*

Remember, the logic of symbols in the liturgy is not the same as the logic of arguments with words. Something can be suggested or bodied forth with a symbol that would sound strange in verbal form. So, even if the following statements are not declared outright or intended to be inferred, they are nevertheless suggested or bodied forth by the wearing of masks in church:

1. The Christ whose crucifixion the church building represents and whose life-giving flesh is present for sacrifice and communion is not the all-sufficient Savior of body and soul.
2. The health of the soul is inferior to and less urgent than the health of the body.
3. We are endangering to and endangered by our fellow Christians.
4. We are not willing to take reasonable risks when we do the single most important thing in our lives.

The Holy Bread of Eternal Life

Perhaps there are still other subliminal messages. What they all have in common is a symbolic refusal of *koinonia* or *communio*: natural and supernatural communion in sacred realities, face to face with God and neighbor. If this is not seen to be problematic, I'm not quite sure what disruption of liturgical symbols would ever be problematic. What pastors of souls are allowing or enforcing at this time amounts to a program of radical desacralization and ritual deformation, which is putting the final nails in the coffin of the liturgical reform.

The Covidtide considerations in this chapter will remain pertinent even if the Church returns someday to "normal" operations, because they force us to reflect on the nature of Christian worship and on proportionate or disproportionate responses to problems that arise in a fallen world. We are learning from bitter experience that certain "preventatives" or "cures" can be worse than the diseases they are intended to keep away or to treat, because they subtly or openly undermine the right ordering of man to God, and of members of the Mystical Body to one another.

Resistance to bad policy is not futile, but it will not, alas, come at a light cost, especially to the clergy. The only way forward is to double down on the traditional Roman Rite, celebrated *digne, attente, ac devote* according to its own rubrics, with love and reverential fear—but without the servile fear that corrupts the sense of fittingness and the capacity for good judgment.

The fear of the Lord is the beginning of wisdom

When we enter into a church or do anything liturgical, we ought to have, at some level, an attitude of fear. Will our intentions and actions please the Lord, or offend Him?

As St. John teaches, if our charity reaches perfection, we no longer stand in a slavish fear of God as our master and judge who punishes us for offending (see 1 John 4:18). Rather, we love Him as "all good and deserving of all our love." Precisely in this way, we *do* still fear Him, with what Catholic tradition refers to as "filial fear" or "reverential fear": the fear of sons who, because of reverence for their Father, fear only offending

Him or doing less for Him than they should and could do. Perfect love does not cast out such virtuous fear, but rather intensifies it.

Scripture never lets us forget this fundamental truth of creaturehood: *Servite Domino in timore, et exsultate ei cum tremore.* "Serve ye the Lord in fear, and exult in Him with trembling" (see Ps. 2:11). This is almost certainly the passage St. Paul had in mind when he spoke of "working out your salvation in fear and trembling" (see Phil. 2:12). As it says in another psalm: "In your fear I will worship toward your holy temple" (see Ps. 5:8). The phrase "fear of the Lord" appears fifty-two times in the Douay-Rheims translation of the Bible. Hence, we also find the prophets excoriating the people for their *lack* of fear in the presence of the Lord. One of the most poignant messages comes through the last of the Old Testament prophets, Malachi, who, in verses hauntingly applicable to our times, thunders forth:

> The son honoureth the father, and the servant
>   his master:
> If then I be a father, where is my honour?
> And if I be a master, where is my fear? saith the
>   Lord of hosts.
> To you, O priests, that despise my name, and have said:
> Wherein have we despised thy name?
> You offer polluted bread upon my altar, and you say:
> Wherein have we polluted thee?
> In that you say: The table of the Lord is contemptible.
>   (Mal. 1:6–7)

"Where is my honor?," asks God the Father; "where is my fear?," asks God the Son. The great Advent hymn *Conditor alme siderum* contains this marvelous stanza:

> *Cuius forti potentiæ*
> *genu curvantur omnia;*
> *cælestia, terrestria*
> *nutu fatentur subdita.*

The Holy Bread of Eternal Life

> At whose dread Name, majestic now,
> All knees must bend, all hearts must bow;
> And things celestial Thee shall own,
> And things terrestrial, Lord alone.

Pope Urban VIII's later version, *Creator alme siderum*, conveys the same message:

> *Cuius potestas gloriæ,*
> *Nomenque cum primum sonat,*
> *et cælites et inferi*
> *tremente curvantur genu.*

> Thy glorious power, Thy saving Name
> No sooner any voice can frame,
> But heaven and earth and hell agree
> To honor them with trembling knee.

The liturgical reform tried, in successive waves, to abolish or curtail kneeling wherever it could: our knees will not tremble before majesty. When we worship the god of liberty, we "sit down to eat and drink, and rise up to play" (see Exod. 32:6), as it says of the Israelites disporting before the golden calf. Let's rise up on our own two feet as we queue up for the token of belonging. We're not even as clued in as the demons are, for in his epistle St. James tells us that "the demons believe, and tremble" (see James 2:19), while many Catholics prance right up to the table of plenty and take the communion wafer like a chip at a snackbar. "Wherein have we polluted thee?," asked the prophet Malachi. His answer: "In that you say: the table of the Lord is contemptible."

So much of what we have seen in the past fifty years — so much of what COVID has brought forth in 2020 — is a pollution of the temple, a scorning of the sacred. "You have despised my holy things and profaned my Sabbaths" (Ezek. 22:8). This will not be met with divine approbation, the Word of God assures us. "Because of the wickedness of their doings

I will drive them out of my house; I will love them no more; all their princes are revolters" (see Hos. 9:15).

When Our Lord was praying Psalm 22 upon the altar of the Cross, letting go of His lifeblood for us sinners, He would have prayed these verses: "You who fear the Lord, praise Him; all you seed of Jacob, glorify Him; and stand in awe of Him, all you the seed of Israel." A triple imperative: praise Him, glorify Him, stand in awe of Him...*you who fear the Lord*. May this be the mind *we* put on (cf. Phil 2:5) when we assist at the same sacrifice, and when we humbly approach the sacred banquet of the Lord.

19

Discerning True and False Obedience

The past seven years have demonstrated that the most evident "Francis Effect" is nothing other than a heightened clamp-down on efforts to re-cover and restore Catholic tradition—not just in liturgical practices, but in doctrinal and moral teaching as well. This effort to stymie or suppress the rediscovery of Catholicism on the part of younger generations looking for authenticity, clarity, and beauty is being led by older bishops and clergy who grew up under the hermeneutic of rainbow rupture and who believe that they must remain committed to the "Vatican II program" at any cost.

Here is a letter I received from a reader about what he is seeing in his diocese.

Dear Doctor,

You've written on the link between "conservative" Catholics and philosophical liberalism, but I've recently been thinking, due to an article by Fr. Chad Ripperger, about the link between "conservative" Catholics and philosophical positivism.[228]

In my diocese, I've heard that an effort is being made to defend the practice of Communion in the hand against the reintroduction

[228] See my article "Why Conservatism Is Part of the Problem, Not Part of the Solution," *OnePeterFive*, September 25, 2018; Fr. Chad Ripperger, "Conservative vs. Traditional Catholicism," *Latin Mass Magazine*, Spring 2001, online at http://www.latinmassmagazine.com/articles/articles_2001_sp_ripperger.html.

of Communion on the tongue. People are being told: "Since both are permitted by the Church, you can't say that one is better than the other."

Clearly there is a leap in logic here: if two things are permitted, that doesn't mean one isn't better than the other. Marriage and religious life are both permitted to single Catholics of a certain age, but the Church has always taught that the latter state is better than the former.

Nevertheless, I think the policy line evinces a deeper problem: the presupposition of conservatives that "might makes right"—that a thing's being posited as licit by the competent authority *makes* it morally good (or, at least, in no way objectionable). It seems that recourse to what is stipulated in the law is the beginning and end of any discussion for them, as if there is no need to think beyond legality.

Do you have any thoughts about how to react when we are told that legality is equivalent to goodness (obvious analogies with legalized abortion and euthanasia and the rest of our cultural decay aside!)?

My response:

I know just what you are talking about. Are we supposed to stifle or throw out our mind's ability to see unfittingness, unworthiness, irreverence? This really is the death of reason. How contradictory it is to see a priest donning a cope and humeral veil to handle a monstrance—a metal object holding the Host in a glass lunette—out of respect for the awesome presence of God, and then to have the nice old ladies passing out Hosts like crackers to people sticking out their uncovered hands, with fragments scattered hither and yon. Sheer cognitive dissonance.

Modern Church governance is based on a twisted absolutism of obedience by which everyone is supposed to internalize any command from above, stifling all protests. In an article that should be required reading, John Lamont traces this perverse notion back to the Jesuits.[229] Hierarchs deliberately make clergy swallow contradictions in order to break their will to think and act with good judgment. They must be made to act by the judgment of the superior alone.

It comes down to something rather simple. Either we believe that the Church is guided by the Holy Spirit into the fullness of truth, or we don't. Now, the Church clearly moved unanimously and universally to Communion distributed to the mouths of the kneeling faithful by ordained ministers only. This centuries-old practice was disturbed in the 1960s by European radicals who no longer believed in transubstantiation, and had substituted for it some kind of pseudo-Augustinian horizontal populism. Paul VI, in keeping with his typically weak manner of governance, reaffirmed that the Church's longstanding custom was better—and then allowed for episcopal conferences to make exceptions.

And now here we are, in a situation where a practice which is better, and was even stated to be better by Paul VI, is quite rare, and its return is opposed on the basis of the equality (?) of the two modes of receiving, as well as by the iron will of the local Ordinary who, like the episcopal conferences decades ago, prefers well-established irreverence over the road less traveled.

Legal positivism has *replaced* faith in the Holy Spirit: we are too cynical, too mechanistic, too bureaucratic, and too authoritarian to believe in the Holy Spirit. It has to be the *will* of the pope, of the episcopal conference, of the people, or whatever, but not (God forbid) what the Church humbly and reverently developed over the centuries. This should tell us about which spirit, after all, is guiding the postconciliar process.

Ultimately, it is obedience to the *truth*—not to the wills of individuals who use their positions of authority to dominate and impose

[229] See "Tyranny and Sexual Abuse in the Catholic Church: A Jesuit Tragedy," *Rorate Caeli*, October 27, 2018.

their own opinions—that will set us free. This means the truth of Jesus Christ, Word incarnate; the truth of Catholic dogma authoritatively established for us by *de fide* articles and their accompanying anathemas; the truth of Catholic tradition handed down to us from men of faith. Our polestar is not what is licit, but what is good and right; our goal is not to please the prelate or the populace, but to sanctify sinners and save the lost. In this perspective, we know what to do and how to do it by that supernatural instinct or *sensus fidei* that animates the faithful in all ages, especially in times of crisis.[230]

✠

There is a kind of priest, I'm told, who *always* does what his bishop tells him to do. No matter what it is, he is "obedient" to the bishop. If there is a notorious dissenter from Church teaching but the bishop says "go ahead and give him Communion," then the priest does it. Or if the bishop dislikes the traditional Latin Mass, the priest, citing "obedience," won't celebrate that Mass, in spite of its being a spiritual treasure for himself and the people. If the bishop thinks an eastward orientation (*ad orientem*) for worship is a non-starter, the priest will not break away from the bad custom of *versus populum*.[231]

Is this a problem? Yes.

Obedience cannot absolve us from listening to and following our well-formed consciences. Otherwise, we are reduced to robots. If I were a priest, there is no way in conscience, no matter what a bishop thought, that I could give Holy Communion to a public sinner, or refrain from

---

[230] See Roberto de Mattei, "Resistance and Fidelity to the Church in Times of Crisis," in *Love for the Papacy and Filial Resistance to the Pope in the History of the Church* (Brooklyn, NY: Angelico Press, 2019), 105–30.

[231] And this, in spite of the fact that *versus populum* was never mentioned by Vatican II or mandated in any liturgical book, and its opposite (*ad orientem*) is presupposed by the rubrics of the Novus Ordo. See my article "The Normativity of *Ad Orientem* Worship according to the Ordinary Form's Rubrics," *New Liturgical Movement*, November 23, 2015.

offering the *usus antiquior,* which is a Roman Catholic priest's heritage and canonical right. Nor does a bishop have the authority to forbid any priest to celebrate *ad orientem* or to expect that he will place his ordinary's personal preferences over two thousand years of liturgical orientation, which (*mirabile dictu*) even the new missal allows for.

This path of false obedience is a convenient way to offload one's conscience on to another and to continue on in peace without having to make waves or endure hardship. While no one should go out of his way to *make* waves, and everyone appreciates peace and quiet, at some point one has to stop ignoring the demands placed by the moral law upon *oneself,* not to mention the spiritual needs of the priest and his flock.

As the Abbé de Nantes once said: "The truth is, speaking in general, this attitude of obedience in all things also sits very well with ambition, concern for material goods, a peaceful life and indolence. Whether acknowledged or not, it must be the case that these secondary advantages give rise to a sense of shame and to a confused impression of surrender, as when a man gives himself good reasons to choose a bad path because of the advantages he finds therein." Once a man has compromised so much and traveled so far down that path, it is not easy to turn back. At that point he would need a deep conversion, a grace not everyone will end up receiving or cooperating with.

I know of clergy who fit the description given by the Abbé de Nantes. More often than not, they are classic cases of the "conservative": one who ultimately thinks truth is relative to authority. To be a good conservative is, on this model, to obey most perfectly all the commands given by the superior. Should we be surprised when such conservatives turn out to be evolutionists and opportunists as well?

For example, when Pope Francis attempted to change Catholic teaching on the intrinsic evil of adulterous relations or on the inherent permissibility of the death penalty, we saw certain conservatives lining up to pay obeisance before the ink had even dried on the new versions of the Decalogue and the *Catechism.* No departure from Scripture or Tradition is too great for a conservative, who, depending on which way the wind is blowing, is as ready to wave the magic wand of "development of doctrine" as the nuttiest progressive. One such conservative had this to say: "Theologians have been arguing that we could make this next step, as a true development of doctrine: to intend the death of a human person violates their human dignity and that the death penalty is always and everywhere non-admissible."[232] You see: he simply bends the knee to the master's will, regardless of the implications.[233]

Every Christian is required to know the first principles of faith and reason and to make judgments based on them, rather than letting his or her principles be dictated and manipulated by superiors. A fine treatment of this subject may be found in St. John Henry Newman's *Letter to the Duke of Norfolk* (see Section 5 in particular). To the extent that faith and reason are rejected, we will not fail to see the simultaneous breakdown of theology and of sanity. Those who practice a false obedience give a bad name to a noble virtue.[234] If a pope told them to sell out Jesus for thirty pieces of silver, they would do it; after all, "obedience." And the money could be given to the poor, no less.

There is something extremely sinister about the way this mentality of obedience to whatever the superior says has been used by Catholics against other Catholics and against Catholicism itself. It is Nietzschean, inasmuch as it lives from a cynicism about moral absolutes; Machiavellian, inasmuch as it builds careers and wins promotions. It is the kind of attitude that empowers and protects abusers.[235] False obedience (otherwise

---

[232] Joan Frawley Desmond, "Catechism's New Text on Death Penalty Draws Praise and Concern," *National Catholic Register*, August 6, 2018.

[233] See Peter Kwasniewski, *Tradition and Sanity: Conversations & Dialogues of a Postconciliar Exile* (Brooklyn, NY: Angelico Press, 2018), ch. 12, for a treatment of what those implications are; cf. idem, "What Good Is a Changing Catechism? Revisiting the Purpose and Limits of a Book," *Rorate Caeli*, June 15, 2019.

[234] See my article "Obedience Is Not the Root of All Evil, but the Source of Christian Happiness," *LifeSiteNews*, October 18, 2018.

[235] See chapter 15.

known as compliance and sycophancy), ambition, and worldliness all go together in a sort of witch's brew. *Vade retro Satana*: Go back, Satan.

✠

The Catholic Church on earth is in a state of advanced decadence. Lower clergy and the lay faithful who still believe in the Gospel and in the constant Magisterium, who still have Christian consciences and a sense of duty to Christ the King, will need to prepare themselves for the ecclesiastical equivalent of "civil disobedience" in order to remain obedient to the higher law, the higher sovereignty. They will need holy models to study, imitate, beseech, and be comforted by as they weather the unavoidable storms of conflicting loyalties and unjust punishments.

Although many saints fit the bill, here I would like to propose two female saints—Joan of Arc and Catherine of Siena—who combine in their persons a virile and dauntless commitment to the truth with a childlike openness to God's will, wherever it may lead.

Several aspects of the life and character of the Maid of Orléans hold pointed lessons for us today. First, as a young woman Joan practiced a deep, humble, and serious piety. The age-old practices of the Catholic Faith were enough to take her to the heights of sanctity and the gift of herself for her country and her Lord. She listened to the Lord's voice as He spoke to her through the saints and through circumstances, and she obeyed His will unflinchingly. St. Michael the Archangel addressed her as "Jehanne the Maid, Child of God," for this is what she was and always remained. Instead of allowing herself to be distracted by worldly motivations, she followed the path God set for her, in spite of its difficulty. She is, in other words, the exact antithesis of churchmen today who would dilute the demands of God's law, downplay the necessity of self-denial in adhering to it, and bracket the supernatural motives by which we should act.

Second, Joan boldly stepped into a public role at God's behest, but without losing her femininity. She did not wage war with the soldiers but simply led them in formation. She would not, in principle, kill or wound anyone. There is not the remotest chance that she would ever condone women fighting in the military and being trained to kill — the absurdity of actual or potential nurturers of life taking it voluntarily. In this, she is an example of true Christian womanhood: strong and courageous, willing to stick her neck out, willing to lead (as she herself was willing to be led by her Master), but not stupidly trying to be a man. She did not think equality with maleness something to be grasped, but emptied herself and became a servant. In this way she provided an example of being true to her identity and vocation that is resoundingly necessary for both women *and* men to heed in a world that has become confused about how many sexes there are and who belongs to which "division" of the human race.

(And it is indeed a division — but it need not be an opposition or antagonism, in the way that both male chauvinism and feminism imagine it to be, each feeding off the other. Real difference makes possible a deeper communion and cooperation than uniformity and replaceability, even as, in the Church, the priest's role as mediator is seen to be essentially different from that of the laity, since he acts on their behalf *in persona Christi capitis*, in the person of Christ the Head of the Church. In a similar way, the husband in a family has the calling to imitate and represent the headship of Christ. As St. Paul explained so well, one cannot have a functional organic body if it's made up only of arms or hands or eyes or, for that matter, heads. Real difference and distinction, when embraced in a spirit of servanthood, confer a mutual benefit that far exceeds what one could obtain independently. Hierarchy and unity are correlative, not opposed, as democracy falsely assumes.)

Third, Joan is a model of the virtues of chastity and purity. Feminists like to point out that she donned a man's clothing at a time when this was considered immoral. Yet all historians are agreed that the reason Joan wore a man's clothing during her public service, and later in prison, was to protect herself against the danger of rape from soldiers and enemies among whom she had to dwell. The ordinary women's clothing of the time offered no such defense, and she would not have had the leisure or the talent to create a new and better fashion *de novo*. She complained to the tribunal that an English lord had attempted to violate her in prison. Like

St. Maria Goretti, St. Joan prized the gift of her virginity and defended it. She knew her dignity as a human being, her worth as a woman. From her example, we learn not to sell ourselves cheap, but to remember that Our Lord shed His Precious Blood for each of us—and no one is allowed to trample on the rights that flow from our human nature and from our supernatural dignity as children of God.

Fourth, Joan was condemned by an ecclesiastical kangaroo court presided over by a corrupt bishop, Pierre Cauchon, with the complicity of corrupt clergy. As everyone knows who has read Joan's life, she was falsely charged with heresy and condemned to be burned at the stake. The trial was later re-evaluated by the Church and found to be gravely defective and irregular on numerous counts—indeed, not to mince words, it was a wicked sham, an excuse for murdering an inconvenient and too popular figure who could not be readily controlled by those in power.

We live in a world in which most of episcopacy is corrupt on several levels—doctrinally, through failing to teach the Catholic Faith in its integrity, if not positively adhering to Modernist views; morally, due to practicing sexual abuse or covering it up, while tolerating the *de facto* dominance of the lavender mafia; liturgically, by refusing to model right worship or to correct impious deviations; or, indeed, all three levels at once. Joan sets us an example of a laywoman who refuses to be cowed by threats and intimidations from "authority"—even legitimate authority, abusing its powers—and who would rather die for a right conscience than falsely admit to wrongdoing. She ought to be recognized as the patron saint of those who have been victimized by the Church's hierarchy.

✠

As I read Sigrid Undset's masterful biography of Catherine of Siena,[236] I was simultaneously appalled at the clerical and political corruption of

---

[236] I will be citing the original Sheed & Ward edition from 1954. The new Ignatius Press edition strangely omits the powerful opening chapter, which concludes with the lines: "They [blessed Birgitta of Sweden and blessed

her age and edified by her response to it. How remarkable is her wisdom on every profound question she ever spoke about—this girl who had barely had any education and who said, with simplicity, that the Lord taught her everything she knew! Like St. Thomas Aquinas, she used to dictate two or three letters at a time to her various secretaries and never lost the thread of her thoughts.

St. Ignatius of Loyola gets credit for his discernment of spirits, but we can find in her works a vivid anticipation of the same principles. Jesus says to her at one point:

> My visions are always accompanied at first by a certain amount of fear, but as they unfold they bring a growing feeling of security. First comes bitterness, but later comes strength and consolation. The visions which come from the devil create at first a feeling of security and sweetness, but they end in terror and bitterness. My way is the way of penitence. At first it seems hard and difficult to follow, but the further you pursue it, the happier and sweeter it appears. The way of the devil, on the other hand, is sweet and happy to begin with, but as the soul pursues the way of sin it goes from bitterness to bitterness, and the end is eternal damnation. (44)

Catherine faced a dismal situation: the French-controlled papacy remained comfortably settled in Avignon, perpetuating "the Popes' Babylonian captivity," while the state of the Church went from bad to worse:

> The people lost their love and trust in the Church of Christ since its power to lead souls into the right way and to heal the wounds of the exhausted people had been so sadly weakened. The morals of the clergy, both the higher and the lower, had in many places sunk so deep that the hearts of the faithful were filled with horror and grief. In many parts there was a terrible ignorance of religion;

Catherine] came to play a part in world politics, and to correct, advise and direct—sometimes even order and command—the Vicar of Christ on earth," and consequently numbers Undset's chapter 2 as "chapter 1," etc.

practically no religious teaching was given, men and women knew almost nothing of the faith which they officially professed.... But no place suffered from the absence of the Vicar of Christ from the old capital of the Church so much as Rome itself. (118–19)

Reading such words today can only make us marvel at how history repeats itself, albeit never in quite the same way — for though a leading bishop today dwells in the old capital of the Church, he has dispossessed himself of the title of Vicar of Christ, reducing it to a mere "historical title."[237]

Catherine never sought publicity and, if anything, ran from confrontation. Yet Christ says to her, apropos the alarming situation of her time:

I shall send you to the popes and the leaders of My Church and to all Christians, for I choose to put the pride of the mighty to shame by the use of fragile tools. (102)

In words highly applicable to the fear that has gripped the world and has driven responses to the coronavirus, Catherine writes to a Cardinal Legate, Pierre d'Estaing, in 1372:

A soul which is full of slavish fear cannot achieve anything which is right, whatever the circumstances may be, whether it concern small or great things. It will always be shipwrecked and never complete what it has begun. Oh, how dangerous this fear is! It makes holy desire powerless, it blinds a man so that he can neither see nor understand the truth. This fear is born of the blindness of self-love, for as soon as a human being loves himself with the self-love of the senses he learns fear, and the reason of this fear is that it has given its hope and love to fragile things which have neither substance nor being and vanish like the wind.... Seek for nothing but the honour of God, the salvation of the soul, and the service of the beloved Bride of Christ, the Holy Church. (139–40)

---

[237] See Maike Hickson, "Pope Francis Drops 'Vicar of Christ' Title in Vatican Yearbook," *LifeSiteNews*, Thursday, April 2, 2020.

The Holy Bread of Eternal Life

Catherine writes to another church dignitary, Gérard du Puy:

> Our Lord hates above all things three abominable sins: covetousness, unchastity, and pride. These prevail in the Bride of Christ, that is to say, in the prelates who seek nothing but riches, pleasure, and fame. They see the demons from hell stealing the souls which have been put into their keeping, and are completely unmoved, for they are wolves who do business with divine grace. Strict justice is needed to punish them. In this case exaggerated mercy is in fact the worst cruelty. It is necessary for justice to go hand in hand with mercy to put a stop to such evil. (141)

To three Italian cardinals, she wrote: "You deserve punishment more than words" (247).

In 1375, she addressed to Pope Gregory XI a letter described by Undset as "nothing less than a serious warning." Catherine tells Gregory that "the victim of self-love becomes indifferent to sins and faults among his subordinates.... Either he attempts to punish them so half-heartedly that it is useless, or else he does not punish them at all" (166).

> Catherine tells the pope openly that in the last resort it is he who carries the whole responsibility for the terrible abuses which are draining the life of the Church, even though according to human reckoning he may be a fine person with many good qualities. Nevertheless it is he who is responsible for the bad shepherds and the treacherous monks whose shameful way of living is undermining the faith of believers. (167)

At one moment Undset pauses to speak about the paradox of the papacy—obviously she doesn't belong to that facile school of thought for which a given pope is "the Holy Spirit's choice" and so he must be doing and teaching all the right things:

> As it has been put in the hands of men to appoint a man as the Vicar of Christ, it is only to be expected that the voters will all

too often vote from impure, mean, or cunning motives, for a man who will become an evil to the Church of God on earth. God will nevertheless watch over His Church, raise and restore again what mankind may ruin or soil; it is necessary, for mystical reasons which the saints have partly seen and understood, that the offence should occur. But woe to that person through whom the offence comes. (170)

Catherine nevertheless retained an unshakeable faith in Divine Providence and in the indefectibility of the Catholic Church, in spite of the sins of her members and especially of her shepherds. In the same year (1375), she wrote in a circular letter to the general and elders of Lucca:

The Church is His bride; the faithful sons of the Church are they who prefer to suffer death a thousand times than to leave it. If you reply that it looks as though the Church must surrender, for it is impossible for it to save itself and its children, I say to you that it is not so. The outward appearance deceives, but look at the inward, and you will find that it possesses a power which its enemies can never possess. (172)

In what has to be one of the most remarkable letters ever written, Catherine admonished her spiritual director, Raymond of Capua (who later wrote an important biography of the saint) for his fear of possible ambush and capture in a journey he was to undertake:

My very dear Father in Jesus Christ, I Catherine, Christ's servants' serving-woman and slave, write to you in His precious Blood, full of longing to see you grow out of your childhood and become a grown man.... For an infant who lives on milk is not able to fight on the battlefield; he only wants to play with other children.... But when he becomes a grown man, he leaves behind him his sensitive self-love. Filled with holy desire, he eats bread, chewing it with the teeth of hate and love, and the coarser and harder it is, the better he likes it.... He has become strong, he associates with strong men, he is firm, serious, thoughtful; he hastens to the battlefield with them, and his only wish is to fight for the Truth.... You were not yet worthy to fight on the battlefield, and therefore you were sent behind the lines like a little boy; you fled of your own free will, and were glad to do so, because God showed mercy for your weakness.... Oh bad little Father, what happiness it had been for your soul and mine if you had cemented a single stone in the Church of God with your blood, out of love for the precious Blood.... We have truly reason to complain when we see how our wretched deeds have lost a great reward for us. Oh, let us lose our milk teeth and cut instead the strong teeth of hate and love. (253–54)

Catherine and Raymond had a deep friendship in Christ and their love was only strengthened by the clarity of their candid correspondence. In spite of being chided as "a little boy," Raymond must have been mature indeed to respond so well to such frank criticism! In a letter after this, Catherine continues her advice to her director, whom she knows will be entrusted with more and more responsibilities:

You will not be able to enjoy much of the solitude of the cell, but it is my will that you carry with you everywhere the cell in your heart, for you know that when we are enclosed in it the enemy cannot harm us.... Love the table of the Cross and nourish yourself with the soul's food in holy vigilance and ceaseless prayer; say Mass every day unless you are absolutely prevented.... Cast your weakness and slavish fear from you, for the Holy Church has no use for such servants. (270)

Sigrid Undset concludes with an eloquent peroration to the "martyrdom" suffered by this great Sienese saint in her 33 years of tireless prayer and labors:

It is certain that Catherine voluntarily—and few women have ever had such an inflexible will—chose to suffer ceaselessly for all she believed in, loved, and desired: unity with God, the glory and honour of His name, His kingdom on earth, the eternal happiness of all mankind, and the re-birth of Christ's Church to the beauty which it possesses when the radiance of its soul shines freely through its outward form — that form which was then stained and spoilt by its own degenerate servants and rebellious children. As Catherine expressed it: the strength and beauty of its mystical body can never diminish, for it is God; but the jewels with which its mystical body are adorned are the good accomplished by its sincere and faithful children. (289)

St. Catherine was unquestionably among the most sincere and most faithful Christians the world has ever known — like the ancient saints "of whom the world was not worthy" (Heb. 11:38), and yet who left a decisive mark on the Church and on human civilization. Her spiritual doctrine remains ever fresh and full of life, accurate and relevant. May she intercede for us as we strive to be those "firm, serious, thoughtful" soldiers of Christ who "hasten to the battlefield ... to fight for the Truth."

St. Joan of Arc, the Maid of Orléans,
Patroness of France, *pray for us.*
St. Catherine of Siena, Seraphic Virgin and
Doctor of the Church, *pray for us.*

Appendix

Sins Against the Blessed Sacrament and the Need of a Crusade of Eucharistic Reparation

by Bishop Athanasius Schneider
Auxiliary Bishop of the Archdiocese of Saint Mary in Astana

There has never been in the history of the Church a time where the sacrament of the Eucharist has been abused and outraged to such an alarming and grievous extent as in the past five decades, especially since the official introduction and papal approval in 1969 of the practice of Communion in the hand. These abuses are aggravated, furthermore, by the widespread practice in many countries of faithful who, not having received the sacrament of Penance for many years, nevertheless regularly receive Holy Communion. The height of the abuses of the Holy Eucharist is seen in the admittance to Holy Communion of couples who are living in a public and objective state of adultery, violating thereby their indissoluble valid sacramental marriage bonds, as in the case of the so-called "divorced and remarried," such admittance being in some regions officially legalized by specific norms, and, in the case of the Buenos Aires region in Argentina, norms even approved by Pope Francis. Additionally to these abuses comes the practice of an official admittance of Protestant spouses in mixed marriages to Holy Communion, e.g., in some dioceses in Germany.

To say that the Lord is not suffering because of the outrages committed against Him in the sacrament of the Holy Eucharist can lead to a minimizing of the great atrocities committed. Some people say: God is offended by the abuse of the Blessed Sacrament, but the Lord does not personally suffer. This is, however, theologically and spiritually too narrow a view. Although Christ is now in His glorious state and hence no more subject to suffering in a human way, He nevertheless is affected and touched in His Sacred Heart by the abuses and outrages against the Divine Majesty and the immensity of His Love in the Blessed Sacrament. Our Lord has expressed to some Saints His complaints and His sorrow about the sacrileges and outrages with which men offend Him. One can understand this truth from the words of the Lord spoken to St. Margaret Mary Alacoque, as Pope Pius XI reports in his Encyclical *Miserentissimus Redemptor*:

> When Christ manifested Himself to Margaret Mary, and declared to her the infinitude of His love, at the same time, in the manner of a mourner, He complained that so many and such great injuries were done to Him by ungrateful men—and we would that these words in which He made this complaint were fixed in the minds of the faithful, and were never blotted out by oblivion: "Behold this Heart"—He said—"which has loved men so much and has loaded them with all benefits, and for this boundless love has had no return but neglect, and contumely, and this often from those who were bound by a debt and duty of a more special love." (n. 12)

Frère Michel de la Sainte Trinité gave a profound theological explanation of the meaning of the "suffering" or "sadness" of God because of the offenses that sinners commit against Him:

> This "suffering," this "sadness" of the Heavenly Father, or of Jesus since His Ascension, are to be understood analogically. They are not suffered passively as with us, but on the contrary freely willed and chosen as the ultimate expression of Their mercy towards sinners called to conversion. They are only a manifestation of God's

love for sinners, a love which is sovereignly free and gratuitous, and which is not irrevocable.[238]

This analogical spiritual meaning of the "sadness" or the "suffering" of Jesus in the Eucharistic mystery is confirmed by the words of the Angel in his apparition in 1916 to the children of Fatima and especially by the words and the example of the life of St. Francisco Marto. The children were invited by the Angel to make reparation for offenses against the Eucharistic Jesus and to console Him, as we can read in the memoirs of Sister Lucia:

> While we were there, the Angel appeared to us for the third time, holding a chalice in his hands, with a Host above it from which some drops of blood were falling into the sacred vessel. Leaving the chalice and the Host suspended in the air, the Angel prostrated himself on the ground and repeated this prayer three times: "Most Holy Trinity, Father, Son and Holy Spirit..." Then, rising, he once more took the chalice and the Host in his hands. He gave the Host to me, and to Jacinta and Francisco he gave the contents of the chalice to drink, saying as he did so: "Take and drink the Body and Blood of Jesus Christ, horribly outraged by ungrateful men. Repair their crimes and console your God."[239]

Reporting about the third Apparition on July 13, 1917, Sister Lucia stressed how Francisco perceived the mystery of God and the necessity to console Him because of the offenses of sinners:

> What made the most powerful impression on him [Francisco] and what wholly absorbed him, was God, the Most Holy Trinity,

---

[238] *The Whole Truth about Fatima*, vol. 2, *The Secret and the Church*, trans. John Collorafi (Buffalo, NY: Immaculate Heart Publications, 1989), ch. 3, n. 1, p. 105.

[239] *Fatima in Lucia's Own Words: Sister Lucia's Memoirs*, ed. Louis Kondor, S.V.D., trans. Dominican Nuns of Perpetual Rosary (Fatima: Secretariado dos Pastorinhos, 2007), 172.

perceived in that light which penetrated our inmost souls. Afterwards, he said: "We were on fire in that light which is God, and yet we were not burnt! What is God?... We could never put it into words. Yes, that is something indeed which we could never express! But what a pity it is that He is so sad! If only I could console Him!"[240]

Sister Lucia wrote how Francisco perceived the necessity to console God, whom he understood to be "sad" because of the sins of men:

I asked him one day: "Francisco, which do you like better—to console Our Lord, or to convert sinners, so that no more souls will go to hell?" "I would rather console Our Lord. Didn't you notice how sad Our Lady was that last month, when she said that people must not offend Our Lord any more, for He is already much offended? I would like to console Our Lord, and after that convert sinners so that they won't offend Him any more."[241]

In his prayers and in the offering of his sufferings St. Francisco Marto gave priority to the intention of "consoling the Hidden Jesus," i.e., the Eucharistic Lord. Sister Lucia reported these words of Francisco, which he said to her: "When you come out of school, go and stay for a little while near the Hidden Jesus, and afterwards come home by yourself." When Lucia asked Francisco about his sufferings, he answered: "I'm suffering to console Our Lord. First I make it to console Our Lord and Our Lady, and then, afterwards, for sinners and for the Holy Father.... More than anything else I want to console Him."[242]

Jesus Christ continues in a mysterious way his Passion in Gethsemane throughout the ages in the mystery of His Church and also in the Eucharistic mystery, the mystery of His immense Love. Well-known is the expression of Blaise Pascal: "Jesus will be in agony even to the end of the

---

[240] Ibid., 147.
[241] Ibid., 156.
[242] Ibid., 157; 163.

world. We must not sleep during that time."[243] Cardinal Karol Wojtyła left us a profound reflection on the mystery of Christ's sufferings in Gethsemane, which in a certain sense continue in the life of the Church. Cardinal Wojtyła spoke also about the Church's duty to console Christ:

> And now the Church still seeks to recover that hour in Gethsemane — the hour lost by Peter, James and John — so as to compensate for the Master's lack of companionship which increased his soul's suffering.... The desire to recover it [that hour] has become a real need for many hearts, especially for those who live as fully as they can the mystery of the divine heart. The Lord Jesus allows us to meet him in that hour — which on the human plane is long since past beyond recall — and, just as he did then, invites us to share the prayer of his heart.... The prayer of Gethsemane goes on to this day. Faced with all the trials that man and the Church have to undergo, there is a constant need to return to Gethsemane and undertake that sharing in the prayer of Christ our Lord.[244]

Jesus Christ in the Eucharistic mystery is not indifferent and insensitive towards the behavior which men show in His regard in this Sacrament of Love. Christ is present in this Sacrament also with His soul, which is hypostatically united with His Divine Person. The Roman theologian Antonio Piolanti presented a sound theological explanation in this regard. Even if the body of Christ in the Eucharist cannot see or sensibly feel what happens or what is said in the place of His sacramental presence, Christ in the Eucharist "hears all and sees with superior knowledge." Piolanti then quotes Cardinal Franzelin:

> The blessed humanity of Christ sees all things in themselves by virtue of the abundant infused knowledge due to the Redeemer of mankind, to the Judge of the living and the dead, to the Firstborn

[243] *Pensées*, n. 553; cf. Krailsheimer translation (Penguin, 1966), 313.

[244] *Sign of Contradiction* (London: Hodder and Stoughton, 1979), chapter 17, "The Prayer in Gethsemane," 151–52.

of every creature, to the Center of all celestial and earthly history. All these treasures of the beatific vision and of the infused knowledge are certainly in the soul of Christ, also in so far as it is present in the Eucharist. In addition to these reasons, by another special title, precisely as the soul of Christ is formally in the Eucharist, for the same purpose of the institution of the mystery, it sees all men's hearts, all thoughts and affections, all virtues and all sins, all the needs of the whole Church and of the individual members, the labors, the anxieties, the persecutions, the triumphs—in a word, all the internal and external life of the Church, His Bride, nourished with His Flesh and with His Precious Blood. So by a threefold title (if we can say so) Christ in the sacramental state sees and in a certain divine way perceives all the thoughts and affections, the worship, the homages and also the insults and sins of all men in general, of all his faithful specifically and his priests in particular; He perceives homages and sins that directly refer to this ineffable mystery of love.[245]

One of the greatest apostles of the Eucharist of modern times, St. Peter Julian Eymard, left us the following profound reflections on the affections of the sacrificial love of Christ in the Eucharist:

> By instituting His Sacrament, Jesus perpetuated the sacrifices of His Passion.... He was acquainted with all the new Judases; He counted them among His own, among His well-beloved children. But nothing of all this could stop Him; He wanted His love to go further than the ingratitude and malice of man; He wanted to outlive man's sacrilegious malice. He knew beforehand the lukewarmness of His followers: He knew mine; He knew what little fruit we would derive from Holy Communion. But He wanted to

---

[245] Johann Baptist Franzelin, *De Eucharistia*, 199–200, cited in Antonio Piolanti, *Il Mistero Eucaristico* (Florence: Libreria editrice fiorentina, 1953), 225–26.

love just the same, to love more than He was loved, more than man could make return for. Is there anything else? But is it nothing to have adopted this state of death when He has the fullness of life, a glorified and supernatural life? Is it nothing to be treated and considered as one dead? In this state of death Jesus is without beauty, motion, or defense; He is wrapped in the Sacred Species as in a shroud and laid in the tabernacle as in a tomb. He is there, however; He sees everything and hears everything. He submits to everything as though He were dead. His love casts a veil over His power, His glory, His hands, His feet, His beautiful face and His sacred lips; it has hidden everything. It has left Him only His Heart to love us and His state of victim to intercede in our behalf.[246]

St. Peter Julian Eymard wrote the following moving and almost mystical profession of the Eucharistic love of Christ, with an ardent appeal for Eucharistic reparation:

The Heart which endured the sufferings with so much love is here in the Blessed Sacrament; it is not dead, but living and active; not insensible, but still more affectionate. Jesus can no longer suffer, it is true; but alas! man can still be guilty towards Him of monstrous ingratitudes.... We see Christians despise Jesus in the Most Blessed Sacrament and show contempt for the Heart which has so loved them and which consumes itself with love for them. To spurn Him freely they take advantage of the veil that hides Him. They insult Him with their irreverences, their sinful thoughts, and their criminal glances in His presence. To express their disdain for Him they avail themselves of His patience, of the kindness that suffers everything in silence as it did with the impious soldiery of Caiphas, Herod, and Pilate. They blaspheme

---

[246] *The Real Presence: Eucharistic Meditations* (Cleveland, OH: Emmanuel Publishing, n.d.), The Most Blessed Sacrament Is Not Loved!, III, 151–53.

sacrilegiously against the God of the Eucharist. They know that His love renders Him speechless. They crucify Him even in their guilty souls. They receive Him. They dare take this living Heart and bind it to a foul corpse. They dare deliver it to the devil who is their lord! No! Never even in the days of His Passion has Jesus received so many humiliations as in His Sacrament! Earth for Him is a Calvary of ignominy. In His agony He sought a consoler; on the Cross He asked for someone to sympathize with His afflictions. Today, more than ever, we must make amends, a reparation of honor, to the adorable Heart of Jesus. Let us lavish our adorations and our love on the Eucharist. To the Heart of Jesus living in the Most Blessed Sacrament be honor, praise, adoration, and kingly power for ever and ever![247]

In his last Encyclical *Ecclesia de Eucharistia*, Pope John Paul II left us luminous exhortations with which he stressed the extraordinary sanctity of the Eucharistic mystery and the duty of the faithful to treat this sacrament with utmost reverence and ardent love. Of all his exhortations, this statement stands out: "There can be no danger of excess in our care for this mystery, for 'in this sacrament is recapitulated the whole mystery of our salvation.'"[248]

It would be a pastorally urgent and spiritually fruitful measure for the Church to establish in all dioceses of the world an annual "Day of Reparation for Crimes Against the Most Holy Eucharist." Such a day could be the octave day of the Feast of Corpus Christi. The Holy Spirit will give special graces of renewal to the Church in our days when, and only when, the Eucharistic Body of Christ will be adored with all Divine honors, will be loved, will be carefully treated and defended as really the Holiest of Holies. Saint Thomas Aquinas says in the hymn *Sacris solemniis*: "O Lord, visit us to the extent that we venerate you in this

---

[247] *The Real Presence*, The Sacred Heart of Jesus, III, 283–85.

[248] *Ecclesia de Eucharistia* §61, citing St. Thomas Aquinas, *Summa theologiae* III, qu. 83, art. 4.

sacrament" (*sic nos Tu visita, sicut Te colimus*). And we can say without doubt: O Lord, you will visit your Church in our days to the extent that the modern practice of Communion in the hand will recede and to the extent that we offer to you acts of reparation and love.

In the current so-called "COVID-19 Pandemic Emergency," horrible abuses of the Most Blessed Sacrament have increased still more. Many dioceses around the world mandated Communion in the hand, and in those places the clergy, in an often humiliating manner, deny the faithful the possibility to receive the Lord kneeling and on the tongue, thus demonstrating a deplorable clericalism and exhibiting the behavior of rigid neo-Pelagians. Furthermore, in some places the adorable Eucharistic Body of Christ is distributed by the clergy and received by the faithful with household or disposable gloves. The treating of the Blessed Sacrament with gloves suitable for treating garbage is an unspeakable Eucharistic abuse.

In view of the horrible maltreatments of Our Eucharistic Lord—He being continuously trampled underfoot because of Communion in the hand, during which almost always little fragments of the Host fall on the floor; He being treated in a minimalistic manner, deprived of sacredness, like a cookie, or treated like garbage by the use of household gloves—no true Catholic bishop, priest, or lay faithful can remain indifferent and simply stand by and watch.

There must be initiated a world-wide crusade of reparation to and consolation of the Eucharistic Lord. As a concrete measure to offer to the Eucharistic Lord urgently needed acts of reparation and consolation, each Catholic could promise to offer monthly at least one full hour of Eucharistic Adoration, either before the Blessed Sacrament in the tabernacle or before the Blessed Sacrament exposed in the monstrance. The Holy Scripture says: "Where sin abounded, grace did more abound" (Rom. 5:20, DR) and we can add analogously: "Where Eucharistic abuses abounded, acts of reparation will more abound."

The day when, in all the churches of the Catholic world, the faithful will receive the Eucharistic Lord, veiled under the species of the little

The Holy Bread of Eternal Life

sacred Host, with true faith and a pure heart, in the biblical gesture of adoration (*proskynesis*), that is, kneeling, and in the attitude of a child, opening the mouth and allowing oneself to be fed by Christ Himself in the spirit of humility, then undoubtedly will the authentic spiritual springtime of the Church come closer. The Church will grow in the purity of the Catholic Faith, in missionary zeal for the salvation of souls, and in the holiness of the clergy and the faithful. In deed, the Lord will visit His Church with His graces to the extent that we venerate Him in His ineffable sacrament of love (*sic nos Tu visita, sicut Te colimus*).

God grant that through the Eucharistic crusade of reparation, there may increase the number of adorers, lovers, defenders, and consolers of the Eucharistic Lord. May the two little Eucharistic apostles of our time, St. Francisco Marto and Blessed Carlo Acutis, and all of the Eucharistic saints, be the protectors of this Eucharistic crusade. For, as St. Peter Julian Eymard reminds us, the irrevocable truth is this: "An age prospers or dwindles in proportion to its devotion to the Eucharist. This is the measure of its spiritual life, faith, charity, and virtue."

Prayer of the Crusade of Reparation to the Eucharistic Heart of Jesus

My God, I believe, I adore, I trust, and I love you! I ask pardon for those who do not believe, do not adore, do not trust and do not love you. (3x)

O Divine Eucharistic Heart of Jesus, behold us prostrate with a contrite and adoring heart before the majesty of your redeeming love in the Most Blessed Sacrament. We declare our readiness to atone by voluntary expiation, not only for our own personal offenses, but in particular for the unspeakable outrages, sacrileges, and indifferences by which you are offended in the Most Blessed Sacrament of your Divine love in this our time, especially through the practice of Communion in the hand and the reception of Holy Communion in a state of unbelief and mortal sin.

The more unbelief attacks your Divinity and your Real Presence in the Eucharist, the more we believe in you and adore you, O Eucharistic Heart of Jesus, in Whom dwells all the fullness of the divinity!

The more your sacraments are outraged, the more firmly we believe in them and the more reverently we want to receive them, O Eucharistic Heart of Jesus, fountain of life and holiness!

The more your Most Blessed Sacrament is denigrated and blasphemed, the more we proclaim solemnly: *"My God, I believe, I adore, I trust, and I love you! I ask pardon for those who do not believe, do not adore, do not trust and do not love you,"* O Eucharistic Heart of Jesus, most worthy of all praise!

The Holy Bread of Eternal Life

The more you are abandoned and forgotten in your churches, the more we want to visit you, who are dwelling amongst us in the tabernacles of our churches, O Eucharistic Heart of Jesus, House of God and Gate of Heaven!

The more the celebration of the Eucharistic Sacrifice is deprived of its sacredness, the more we want to support a reverent celebration of Holy Mass, exteriorly and interiorly oriented towards you, O Eucharistic Heart of Jesus, Tabernacle of the Most High!

The more you are received in the hand of standing communicants, in a manner lacking a sign of humility and adoration, the more we want to receive you kneeling and on the tongue, with the lowliness of the publican and the simplicity of an infant, O Eucharistic Heart of Jesus, of infinite majesty!

The more you are received in Holy Communion by uncleansed hearts in the state of mortal sin, the more we want to do acts of contrition and cleanse our heart with a frequent reception of the Sacrament of Penance, O Eucharistic Heart of Jesus, our Peace and Reconciliation!

The more hell works for the perdition of souls, the more may our zeal for their salvation burn by the fire of your love, O Eucharistic Heart of Jesus, salvation of those who hope in you!

The more the diversity of religions is declared as the positive will of God and as a right based in human nature, and the more doctrinal relativism grows, the more we intrepidly confess that you are the only Savior of mankind and the only way to God the Father, O Eucharistic Heart of Jesus, King and center of all hearts!

The more Church authorities continue to be unrepentant about the display of pagan idols in churches, and even in Rome, the more we will confess the truth: "What agreement has the temple of God with idols?" (2 Cor 6:16), the more we will condemn with you "the abomination of desolation, standing in the holy place" (Mt 24:15), O Eucharistic Heart of Jesus, holy Temple of God!

The more your holy commandments are forgotten and transgressed, the more we want to observe them with the help of your grace, O Eucharistic Heart of Jesus, abyss of all virtues!

The more sensuality, selfishness, and pride reign amongst men, the more we want to dedicate our lives to you in the spirit of sacrifice and self-abnegation, O Eucharistic Heart of Jesus, overwhelmed with reproaches!

The more violently the gates of hell storm against your Church and the rock of Peter in Rome, the more we believe in the indestructibility of your Church, O Eucharistic Heart of Jesus, source of all consolation, who do not abandon your church and the rock of Peter even in the heaviest storms!

The more people separate from each other in hatred, violence, and selfishness, the more intimately we as members of the one family of God in the Church want to love each other in you, O Eucharistic Heart of Jesus, full of goodness and love!

O Divine Eucharistic Heart of Jesus, grant us your grace, that we may be faithful and humble adorers, lovers, defenders, and consolers of your Eucharistic Heart in this life, and come to receive the glories of your love in the beatific vision for all eternity. Amen.

My God, I believe, I adore, I trust, and I love you! I ask pardon for those who do not believe, do not adore, do not trust and do not love you. (3x)

Our Lady of the Blessed Sacrament, pray for us!

St. Thomas Aquinas, St. Peter Julian Eymard, St. Francisco Marto, St. Padre Pio, and all Eucharistic Saints, pray for us!

Select Bibliography

This bibliography does not list all the works cited in this book; its purpose is to recommend some of the best reading of which the author is aware concerning the mystery of the Most Holy Eucharist and, above all, the reverence due to Our Lord. Readers looking for more extensive bibliographies will find them in my other books, listed below in the second category.

The Holy Eucharist

Anonymous (a Benedictine Monk). *In Sinu Jesu: When Heart Speaks to Heart—The Journal of a Priest at Prayer*. Kettering, OH: Angelico Press, 2016.

Bernadot, M.V., O.P. *From Holy Communion to the Blessed Trinity*. Trans. Dom Francis Izard, O.S.B. London: Sands & Co., 1951. [A paperback edition is available from Amazon.]

Eymard, St. Peter Julian. *The Real Presence: Eucharistic Meditations*. Cleveland, OH: Emmanuel Publishing, n.d. [One of many volumes in the *Eymard Library*; all make for excellent reading.]

Groeschel, Benedict J., C.F.R., and James Monti. *In the Presence of Our Lord: The History, Theology, and Psychology of Eucharistic Devotion*. Huntington, IN: Our Sunday Visitor, 1997.

Laise, Most Rev. Juan Rodolfo. *Holy Communion. Communion in the Hand: Documents & History; Some Reflections on Spiritual Communion and the State of Grace.* 5th expanded edition. Boonville, NY: Preserving Christian Publications, 2018.

Manelli, Fr. Stefano M., F.F.I. *Jesus, Our Eucharistic Love: Eucharistic Life Exemplified by the Saints.* New Bedford, MA: Academy of the Immaculate, 1996.

Mectilde de Bar. *Mystery of Incomprehensible Love: The Eucharistic Message of Mother Mectilde of the Blessed Sacrament.* Brooklyn, NY: Angelico Press, 2020.

O'Connor, James T. *The Hidden Manna: A Theology of the Eucharist.* 2nd edition. San Francisco: Ignatius Press, 2005.

Reid, Alcuin, ed. *From Eucharistic Adoration to Evangelization.* London/New York: Burns & Oates, 2012.

Schneider, Bishop Athanasius. *Corpus Christi: Holy Communion and the Renewal of the Church.* Vatican City: Libreria Editrice Vaticana, 2013.

———. *Dominus Est—It Is the Lord!* Translated by Nicholas L. Gregoris. Pine Beach, NJ: Newman House Press, 2008.

Tück, Jan-Heiner. *A Gift of Presence: The Theology and Poetry of the Eucharist in Thomas Aquinas.* Trans. Scott G. Hefelfinger. Washington, DC: Catholic University of America Press, 2018.

The Sacred Liturgy

Bux, Nicola. *No Trifling Matter: Taking the Sacraments Seriously Again.* Brooklyn, NY: Angelico Press, 2018.

Crean, Thomas, O.P. *The Mass and the Saints.* San Francisco: Ignatius Press, 2009.

Fiedrowicz, Michael. *The Traditional Mass: History, Form, and Theology of the Classical Roman Rite.* Trans. Rose Pfeifer. Brooklyn, NY: Angelico Press, 2020.

Jackson, James W., F.S.S.P. *Nothing Superfluous: An Explanation of the Symbolism of the Rite of St. Gregory the Great*. Lincoln, NE: Fraternity Publications, 2016.

Kent, Michael. *The Mass of Brother Michel*. Milwaukee: Bruce, 1942; repr. Kettering, OH: Angelico Press, 2017. [A deeply moving work of historical fiction set in Reformation France.]

Kwasniewski, Peter A., ed. *John Henry Newman on Worship, Reverence, and Ritual: A Selection of Texts*. N.p.: Os Justi Press, 2019.

———. *Noble Beauty, Transcendent Holiness: Why the Modern Age Needs the Mass of Ages*. Kettering, OH: Angelico Press, 2017.

———. *Reclaiming Our Roman Catholic Birthright: The Genius and Timeliness of the Traditional Latin Mass*. Brooklyn, NY: Angelico Press, 2020.

———. *Resurgent in the Midst of Crisis: Sacred Liturgy, the Traditional Latin Mass, and Renewal in the Church*. Kettering, OH: Angelico Press, 2014.

Mosebach, Martin. *The Heresy of Formlessness: The Roman Liturgy and Its Enemy*. Revised and expanded edition. Trans. Graham Harrison. Brooklyn, NY: Angelico Press, 2018.

Ratzinger, Cardinal Joseph. *The Spirit of the Liturgy*. Trans. John Saward. Commemorative edition, with Romano Guardini's work of the same name. San Francisco: Ignatius Press, 2018.

Shaw, Joseph, ed. *The Case for Liturgical Restoration*. Brooklyn, NY: Angelico Press, 2019.

———. *How to Attend the Extraordinary Form*. London: Catholic Truth Society, 2020.

The Crisis in the Church

Amerio, Romano. *Iota Unum: A Study of Changes in the Catholic Church in the Twentieth Century*. Translated by Fr. John P. Parsons. Kansas City, MO: Sarto House, 1996.

De Mattei, Roberto. *Apologia for Tradition*. Translated by Michael J. Miller. Kansas City, MO: Angelus Press, 2019.

————. *Love for the Papacy and Filial Resistance to the Pope in the History of the Church*. Brooklyn, NY: Angelico Press, 2019.

————. *The Second Vatican Council—An Unwritten Story*. Translated by Patrick T. Brannan, S.J., Michael J. Miller, and Kenneth D. Whitehead. Fitzwilliam, NH: Loreto Publications, 2012.

Schneider, Bishop Athanasius, and Diane Montagna. *Christus Vincit: Christ's Triumph over the Darkness of the Age*. Brooklyn, NY: Angelico Press, 2019.

Sire, H.J.A. *Phoenix from the Ashes: The Making, Unmaking and Restoration of Catholic Tradition*. Kettering, OH: Angelico Press, 2015.

Ureta, José Antonio. *Pope Francis's "Paradigm Shift": Continuity or Rupture in the Mission of the Church?* Spring Grove, PA: The American Society for the Defense of Tradition, Family, and Property, 2018.

Index of Names and Subjects

Index of Scripture

Pages that mention a book of the Bible in a general way are listed immediately to the right of the book's title; references to specific chapters and verses follow.

About the Author

Dr. Peter Kwasniewski, Thomistic theologian, liturgical scholar, and choral composer, is a graduate of Thomas Aquinas College in California and The Catholic University of America in Washington, DC. He taught at the International Theological Institute in Austria and the Franciscan University of Steubenville's Austria Program, then helped establish Wyoming Catholic College in 2006. There he taught theology, philosophy, music, and art history and directed the choirs until leaving in 2018 to devote himself full time to writing and lecturing. Today he contributes regularly to many websites and publications, including *New Liturgical Movement, OnePeterFive, LifeSiteNews, Rorate Caeli, The Remnant,* and *Catholic Family News,* and has published ten books, including four previous books on traditional Catholicism: *Resurgent in the Midst of Crisis* (Angelico, 2014), *Noble Beauty, Transcendent Holiness* (Angelico, 2017), *Tradition and Sanity* (Angelico, 2018), and *Reclaiming Our Roman Catholic Birthright* (Angelico, 2020). His work has been translated into at least fourteen languages and Braille. Lectures may be found at YouTube and SoundCloud; his website is www.peterkwasniewski.com.

Sophia Institute

Sophia Institute is a nonprofit institution that seeks to nurture the spiritual, moral, and cultural life of souls and to spread the Gospel of Christ in conformity with the authentic teachings of the Roman Catholic Church.

Sophia Institute Press fulfills this mission by offering translations, reprints, and new publications that afford readers a rich source of the enduring wisdom of mankind.

Sophia Institute also operates the popular online resource CatholicExchange.com. *Catholic Exchange* provides world news from a Catholic perspective as well as daily devotionals and articles that will help readers to grow in holiness and live a life consistent with the teachings of the Church.

In 2013, Sophia Institute launched Sophia Institute for Teachers to renew and rebuild Catholic culture through service to Catholic education. With the goal of nurturing the spiritual, moral, and cultural life of souls, and an abiding respect for the role and work of teachers, we strive to provide materials and programs that are at once enlightening to the mind and ennobling to the heart; faithful and complete, as well as useful and practical.

Sophia Institute gratefully recognizes the Solidarity Association for preserving and encouraging the growth of our apostolate over the course of many years. Without their generous and timely support, this book would not be in your hands.

www.SophiaInstitute.com
www.CatholicExchange.com
www.SophiaInstituteforTeachers.org

Sophia Institute Press® is a registered trademark of Sophia Institute.
Sophia Institute is a tax-exempt institution as defined by the
Internal Revenue Code, Section 501(c)(3). Tax ID 22-2548708.